LOOPERS

LOOPERS

A Caddie's Twenty-Year
Golf Odyssey

JOHN DUNN

CROWN PUBLISHERS

NEW YORK

Published in the United States by Crown Publishers,
an imprint of the Crown Publishing Group,
a division of Random House, Inc., New York.
www.crownpublishing.com

CROWN and the Crown colophon are registered trademarks
of Random House, Inc.

Library of Congress Cataloging-in-Publication Data

Dunn, John.
  Loopers : a caddie's twenty-year golf odyssey / John Dunn.
    p. cm.
1. Dunn, John. 2. Caddies—Biography. I. Title.
  GV964.D85A3 2013
  796.352092—dc23
  [B]
                                    2012044014

ISBN 978-0-7704-3718-3
eISBN 978-0-7704-3719-0

Printed in the United States of America

Book design by Jaclyn Reyes
Jacket design by Oliver Munday
Jacket photography Glyn Kirk/AFP/Getty Images

10 9 8 7 6 5 4 3 2 1

First Edition

Dad, I know my footloose lifestyle led you to believe I never listened when you tried to instill in me the importance of hard work and perseverance. But I was listening more closely than it seemed. I wish you were here to enjoy this with me—it is your accomplishment too.

CONTENTS

Carl Spackler: So I jump ship in Hong Kong and make my way over to Tibet, and I get on as a looper at a course over in the Himalayas.

Angie D'Annunzio: A looper?

Carl Spackler: A looper, you know, a caddy, a looper, a jock. So, I tell them I'm a pro jock, and who do you think they give me? The Dalai Lama, himself. Twelfth son of the Lama. The flowing robes, the grace, bald . . . striking. So, I'm on the first tee with him. I give him the driver. He hauls off and whacks one—big hitter, the Lama—long, into a ten-thousand-foot crevice, right at the base of this glacier. Do you know what the Lama says? "Gunga galunga! Gunga . . . Gunga-lagunga!" So we finish the eighteenth and he's gonna stiff me. And I say, "Hey, Lama, hey, how about a little something, you know, for the effort, you know." And he says, "Oh, uh, there won't be any money, but when you die, on your deathbed, you will receive total consciousness." So I got that goin' for me, which is nice.

—From *Caddyshack*

FOREWORD

I first heard the term *looper* when I saw *Caddyshack* years before my caddie career began, and I wouldn't be surprised if Bill Murray just made it up on the spot, because he ad-libbed many of the funniest lines in the movie. I mean, seriously, do you think the words *gunga galunga, gunga . . . gunga-lagunga* were in the script? I know some older guys who claim they heard the term before the movie, and that's believable too because eighteen holes of golf is called a *round*, and it's not much of a leap to get from *round* to *loop*. But even if the word did exist, Bill Murray is definitely the reason it caught on, because knowing a half dozen quotes from *Caddyshack* is basically a caddie job requirement.

Regardless of its origins, *looper* has become a favorite vernacular title in yards across the country because it speaks more truly to our character and the nature of our job than *caddie*—a word as obscure as the name of the game itself. But in my opinion, just because you've carried someone's bag around a golf course, that doesn't make you a *looper*. The first few times you go around, you are just a *bag toter*. Once you learn the ins and outs of the job—where to stand, when to speak, how to read a green and calculate yardage adjusted for wind and elevation, etc.—then you can call yourself a caddie. But you aren't a bona fide *looper* until you've carried someone else's clubs around a golf course so many times you've lost count, until you've worn holes through a dozen pairs of shoes and collected enough war stories to hold your own in the yard. A looper isn't a caddie who's seen it all; a looper is a caddie who's seen enough to know he never will.

Just like life, the game of golf is constantly full of surprises—if it wasn't, teaching pros and sports psychologists would be out of business. And as loopers, we're a little bit of both. We are masters of the quick fix, wellsprings of optimism, and levelers of hard truth ("With all due respect, sir, you don't hit your eight iron a hundred fifty yards"). But for all the wisdom and experience caddying imparts, having looped one's entire life, it can sometimes be difficult to see the straight line—the measurable gains and personal growth. For every Steve Williams and Fluff Cowan out there making millions on the Tour carrying bags for Tiger Woods and Jim Furyk, there are thousands of regular Joes in resort and country club yards all across the golfing world earning their keep a hundred bucks a strap. There aren't any promotions or milestones or major victories for these local loopers. The caddie fees may vary from course to course and group to group, but there's no such thing as a raise and nobody gets rich.

That doesn't make club caddying *lower* than Tour caddying, any less valuable or interesting, just very different. For one thing, despite all the miles a club caddie may travel commuting from course to course with the changing seasons— from a summer job up north to a winter gig down south or across the country or overseas in search of greener fairways— a club caddie is like a nesting goose compared to the fly-by-night Tour caddie, who lands in a different town every week and lives out of his suitcase and the trunk of his car. And this is one of the things I love most about club caddying—the ability to move to different places around the world, yet *stay there* long enough to really get to know them all.

In twenty years of looping, I've lived and worked in quiet, leafy New England and sandy, windswept Long Island, in the marshy South Carolina Low Country and pine-scented Georgia hills, in the snow-capped Rockies and foggy San Francisco, in sunny, star-studded Los Angeles and the red-rocked California desert, on the dramatic, cliff-lined Oregon coast and blustery North Sea coast. All those places feel like second homes to me now, and I forged many lasting relationships in each of them with the members and guests of the clubs, local residents, and fellow caddies.

Unlike the Tour caddie, who gives his focus and dedication to a single player day in, day out, year after year, the club caddie works for different people all the time. Some become our regular clients—like favorite members of a club or returning guests at a resort—others spend a few days with us during a golf trip or long weekend and others just one round. But even a single round—four hours or more walking side by side, talking and working together to navigate the fairways and greens—can be a very intimate experience, akin to a bartender and patron spending several hours together on a quiet night at the pub. And you never know whose bag will end up on your shoulder, whose ear tuned to your advice. It might be your new best friend or, should he impart some wisdom and advice and share some stories of his own, he might be a great inspiration or someone who offers a unique perspective on life. I've caddied for people from all walks of life, including politicians, businessmen, scientists, doctors, athletes, actors, musicians, firemen, fishermen, plumbers, preachers, and teachers. Golf has exposed me to an incredible variety of life experience.

But great variety includes hard knocks and harsh realities too, and club caddying is no exception. Because of the freedom and anonymity it affords—the ability to move around and reestablish (sometimes even reinvent) oneself in new places and earn quick cash on a daily basis—this vagabond profession has long been the refuge of wayward and troubled souls, heavy drinkers and gamblers and people who've suffered setbacks in their careers and personal lives. It is an easy world to escape into and get swept up in. It provides access to the finest courses and most successful people in the world—people we probably wouldn't have the chance to meet under any other circumstance. On those fairways they give us their undivided attention and respect, and at the end, they pay us for the trouble.

Yes, after the round, after we have shined and put away their clubs or left them out in the valet to be picked up later, we will exit through the back gate, walk past the maintenance shed and compost heap and Dumpsters to where we parked our rusty jalopies and then bump and hiccup over to the dive bar across the tracks while our golfers kick back on the terrace overlooking the course. And odds are, the only way we will ever be invited to play that course is with an employee pass. But just the privilege to temporarily breathe that rarefied air, to walk and play those fairways and rub elbows with the movers and shakers of the world can make the mundane rules and rungs of the everyday ladder outside the gates—the ladder that supposedly leads, somewhere, somehow, to the *front* door of the club—seem like a dubious and exhausting climb. Like a hell of a lot of effort for something we're enjoying the best parts of already. Ironically, the freedom and privileges of caddying can become their own kind of trap.

But this book is not a cautionary tale. Rather, it is a love letter to a ragtag, bohemian subculture populated by characters right out of a Steinbeck or Kerouac novel—mad poets and migrant workers chasing the seasons to pick up work here and there and warm their souls at the end of the day by campfires and in dive bars and gambling halls. Yes, I've caddied for and played with some famous and infamous celebrities, some of whom are mentioned herein, but they are not essential to the tale. The spirit of my journey is easily shared by anyone who has stepped off the beaten path, stayed out on the course and played long after dark, played when the fairways and greens are covered in snow and ice or brought their clubs to an empty beach and pounded shots into the surf. That's how Seve Ballesteros learned to play—barefoot on the beach—and his game had as much imagination and creative spirit as anyone who ever played.

So I invite you to pull up a stool and lend me an ear. Allow me to share with you some stories from my twenty years on the links. I will even buy you a scotch and a pint. Let's raise our glasses and drink a toast to the everyday golfers and loopers whose praises are rarely sung. And if you think you recognize any of the people, places, or experiences I describe, I hope my memory of them matches yours, or if mine be more colorful and positive, I hope it colors yours more positively too. And if we've met before, I hope our first meeting was pleasant. Even experienced caddies misread putts from time to time, so if I misread one of yours, I apologize, and I hope these stories will show me to have a keen mind and kind heart—a love of the big loop of life and all the smaller daily loops that compose it, the ones that are filled with the glorious details.

LOOPERS

1

FIRST TEE

COUNTRY CLUB OF FAIRFIELD,
BROOKLAWN COUNTRY CLUB,
FAIRFIELD, CT,
1986–1988

It's all my dad's fault. He moved our family next to a golf course when I was eleven—a beautiful private course called the Country Club of Fairfield, which he and my mom joined for the beach and the restaurant—but he never took up the game himself. He just released me unsupervised out onto the lightly populated 1980s linksland and left me to develop unrealistic, romantic notions of the game that would make it forever impossible to confine myself to the normal golf reality of Saturday morning tee times, golf carts, and scorecards.

Growing up, I rarely played in foursomes, and because the game was still in the doldrums before the popularity of the Tiger Woods era, most of the other kids were down at the local Y emulating Magic Johnson and Larry Bird on the basketball court or Don Mattingly and Dwight Gooden on the baseball field. The club couldn't even field enough junior golfers to hold a proper tournament. My only reliable playing partner was my beagle, Lumpus, who was more interested in chasing raccoons in the bulrushes.

No offense to the leading Tour players of the day, like Lanny Wadkins, Curtis Strange, and Tom Kite, but they lacked the star power of Tom Watson and Jack Nicklaus, who were now well past their primes—Nicklaus was in his mid-forties and had a paunch on him like my dad's. But paunch or not, he became my hero because of his otherworldly charge on the final nine at Augusta to win the '86 Masters. I'd just turned fifteen and was on the verge of breaking eighty for the first time. I imagined myself to be the Golden Bear and narrated my rounds in hushed TV announcer tones: "Nicklaus with a five-footer to win the Masters . . ."

And if my ball dropped, I raised my putter above my head just as he did and triumphantly pumped my fists and paraded around the green. "Yes, sir! The Bear has come out of hibernation!" It's embarrassing to think what I must've looked like to golfers on other holes. But in the pre-Tiger era, there usually weren't any golfers on other holes. Much of the time I was completely alone out there, so I would play cross-country golf—teeing off on one hole and hitting backward or sideways to the green on another. If I ran out of balls, I just waded out into the ponds, felt for them in the mud with my toes, and tossed them by the hundreds up onto the banks, where I would sit for hours polishing them in the sun. I loved playing so much that not even the setting sun could stop me. Many evenings I was still out on the course long after dark, long after Lumpus had abandoned me and run home to the smell of my mother's cooking. The darkness taught me to feel my swing internally, visualize the shots and guess where the ball flew by the way it felt coming off the club—the score of the round no longer being how many shots I took, but how many holes I survived before I lost the ball.

Those early, informal rounds before I began playing competitive high school golf nurtured in me an appreciation of silence and solitude and gave me an independent streak. The freedom to play alone with my dog, to play cross-country golf and night golf, made the game seem adventurous and romantic and planted the seeds that would eventually blossom into full-blown wanderlust as I later sought to replicate that experience around the country. And it was caddying that made it possible—enabled me to play at the finest golf courses on weekday evenings and off-season days when the members and guests had gone home or back to work. And they paid me well on top of the playing privileges, so I could afford to go on playing those solo rounds forever in an amazing array of environments—seaside, desert, mountain, forest, marsh, prairie. Caddying became my ticket to Neverland.

Had my dad realized I was turning into a golfing Peter Pan and that caddying would allow me to avoid ever growing up and getting a "real job," he might've taken a keener interest in the game. Or maybe he would've just paid for those Hogan Apexes that were gleaming on the shelf in the pro shop when I was sixteen. Because they were the reason I started caddying in the first place.

I couldn't walk past them without picking them up and swinging them or just turning them over in my hands and marveling at the smooth shape of the forged blades and sharpness of the black painted grooves. I winced at the $500 price tag, but my lust didn't go unnoticed. The head pro took pity on me and agreed to sell them to me for zero down and five weekly installments of one hundred dollars. I took them straight to the first tee without a second thought. When he interrupted my newfound bliss a week later with the question, "Have you got that first one hundred?" it dawned on me that my part-time job doing yard work around the neighborhood wasn't going to cut it. He kindly gave me a one-week reprieve and offered to put in a call to the Brooklawn Country Club across town, where, he assured me, I would make more than enough money to pay for the clubs. Thus my caddie career was born.

Back then there was no such thing as caddie training or single-bagging—if you couldn't carry two bags, you didn't work. When the Brooklawn caddie master asked me, "Can you carry two?" I scrunched up my shoulders and took a deep breath. I didn't dare say a word for fear I'd exhale and my chest would shrink and I'd look puny and weak.

He pointed to two bags leaning against a green metal rail. The bags didn't have stands—this was before Ping or Sun Mountain invented the lightweight nylon carry bag, so almost everyone had those big leather Burton bags with the thin straps the caddies called piano wires because they dug so painfully into your shoulders.

These two seemed by the weight of them to be holding about two dozen balls apiece, an extra pair of shoes, a rain suit and umbrella, and about ten pounds of spare change. It wasn't even an option to ask a player to lighten his bag; you just carried it until your shoulders and heels bled and your crotch burned like you'd sat in a pile of poison sumac.

But the owners of these two bags were a nice enough couple, and I was so eager to impress them that I was like a greenhorn Boy Scout on his first patrol—marching ahead with purpose even as the hard plastic bottoms of the bags banged against my ankles, turning them black and blue, and the piano wires dug into my shoulders like hot knives. I was so nervous, so on-point on that first nine that I didn't feel a thing. It wasn't until we got to the halfway house and I put the bags down and sat on the end of one of them that the exhaustion and pain hit me. The husband kindly brought me a Coca-Cola and a plastic cup full of cheddar Goldfish. I devoured them both like I'd just crawled across the Sahara on my hands and knees.

I was next to useless the rest of the round, so tired I couldn't even form consonants with my tongue.

After a wild shot somewhere on the back nine, the woman asked me, "Did you see where that one went?"

I just looked at her stupidly and said, "Wha?" I think I actually drooled.

At the end of the round the caddie master asked them how I'd done. They were very nice. They lied. "He did a wonderful job!"

I was officially hired.

Brooklawn was a beautiful course, with fairways that switched back and forth across the wooded hills of inland Fairfield—a 1920s A. W. Tillinghast design in pristine condition. But it was not a big-deal caddie yard like those closer to the city—Winged Foot, Baltusrol, Stanwich, etc.—where the real pro jocks plied their trade. It was a quiet rural yard filled with mostly local high school kids. There were a couple of older part-time guys, but they kept to themselves and must've felt like the only adults at summer camp.

The members were happy with this arrangement because they didn't have to pay us much. Most of us were still living at home with our parents. I think the rate that first summer was twelve bucks a bag plus tip, which usually came out to a whopping thirty for two. Some of the older golfers regaled us with tales of their own long-lost caddie days—reminded us, every time they paid us, that twelve dollars was a small fortune compared to the nickels they used to make way, way back during the Great Depression, when they carried even heavier bags uphill into the dusty wind and sweltering heat.

When they handed over those precious dollars, they held on to them for an extra second, my fingers on one end, theirs on the other, and gave me a serious fatherly look that was meant to say, *Don't spend this all in one place, remember to save a nickel for a rainy day*, but really said, *God, I hate parting with cash!*

These were the same guys who spent half the round hunting for balls in the bushes and ponds. They loaded their bags full of them until they were so bottom-heavy, they practically dragged on the ground. You'd see them in the evenings, out there alone with their white canvas carry bags, their old, thin frames bent precariously over the water like fishermen with ball retrievers instead of rods.

I always wondered what they did with all those balls, because they never seemed to lose any of them. And then one afternoon, years later, I stopped at a yard sale near Brooklawn. A woman was selling her recently deceased father's golf equipment. Bags of old woods and irons and just about every gimmicky putter every made, most of it junk. I recognized the name on the bag tag, and then I saw the giant barrel full of golf balls—some decent ones, a lot of crappy ones, ones that used to be white but were yellowed with age. I realized this is where all of those balls ended up, and it suddenly made me very sad, knowing they would never be used by the person who spent all those countless hours over the years hunting for them. I picked out a dozen of the best ones and paid the woman a couple of dollars.

I didn't have any expenses that first summer, so even making $30 a loop, I paid off those Hogans quickly, and it wasn't long before the cash was burning a hole in my pocket, screaming, *Spend me!* A feeling that would become very familiar over the years because even though club caddies don't really make a ton of money (even today a great year at the best clubs *might* top $40,000), we feel rich because we get paid in cash every day and always have a stack of bills on hand.

Because it was a quiet country club, especially during the week when most of the members were at work, there was a lot of down time. We played stickball in the parking lot, chipped balls behind the cart barn. We snuck cigarettes and looked at *Playboys*. Normal teenage boy stuff. But because we had all that cash, we gambled a lot, too, on just about everything— arm wrestling, chipping contests, who could hold on to a burning match the longest, you name it. I once bet on whether a cricket would jump or not before I counted to ten.

We gossiped and trash-talked too—who tipped the most, who was notoriously cheap, who was the best golfer, who had the hottest wife. There was one poor girl, a member's daughter who had the misfortune of being the only girl our age who played golf at the club and therefore became the sole object of desire for thirty-plus underworked adolescent boys. It hardly mattered whether Justine was actually good looking or not, because our idle minds held her in such exaggerated esteem. We noted her arrivals and departures. We commented on her clothing choices. We watched her putt and chip with endless critical fascination and peered through the hedge beside the driving range when she hit practice balls.

Let's just say that Justine put "all of herself" into every shot. She was literally on her tippy toes at impact with arms and legs fully extended, other parts of her anatomy clenched and still others "swinging" through the ball. She really could hit the shit out of it. And while we all made fun of her in front of each other, every single one of us would secretly have given our entire summer savings to spend an evening "night-putting" with her. That is, until Tommy, the coolest caddie in the yard, shattered our illusions and broke all of our hearts.

Tommy was a real charmer. All of the hot wives fought over him on Tuesday mornings, and the cool husbands did the same on Saturdays. He was a pretty good golfer, too—the second man on his high school varsity. Tommy sometimes helped pick the range. He'd go out there with a sand wedge and seven iron and hit all the balls out of the deep rough and trees. He didn't actually get paid to do this, but it got him in tight with the pro, who then let Tommy practice on the corner of the range on weekday afternoons. This gave him access to Justine.

I'll never forget the first time I saw him help her with her swing. I'd just come in off a loop, and one of the younger caddies, a fifteen- or sixteen-year-old, was going crazy waving his arms in the air trying to get anyone's attention who would listen. There were a few other caddies milling around and some older kids who worked in the cart barn too, and this kid was so excited and breathless we practically had to smack him in the head just to get him to make sense. He finally managed to blurt out, "Tommy is giving Justine a lesson on the range!"

We all rushed over to the hedge and, sure as shit, there was Tommy with his hands all over her! We went so berserk jumping up and down, cursing and punching each other—one of us even fell into the hedge—that I have no idea how Tommy didn't hear us. The truth is, I think he did, because I swear he looked our way and winked and then really laid it on thick just for our benefit. He stood right behind her, reached around her waist, took her arms in his and guided them up to his shoulders to show her the proper turn.

The next day we marauded him. He played it off like it was nothing. And for him it probably was nothing; I was well aware of Tommy's reputation with the girls. He could date girls way cuter than Justine, but it was summer, and we spent nearly every hour of daylight for three months at that country club, and Tommy was drinking the same water we were. Justine just got better and better looking, to the point where we were all willing to commit suicide for her, and even cool Tommy started to look at her like she was a supermodel.

So it didn't come as that much of a surprise when one day the news broke that Tommy had hooked up with her. We all gathered around him in the cart barn. Guys were sitting in carts and on top of the ball washer, anywhere to get a view of Tommy, who was sitting in the center on an overturned range basket, casually smoking a cigarette and taking his time about getting to the juicy details. We hung on his every word.

One impatient caddie said, "Come on, Tommy, get to the good stuff!" and we all hissed, "*Sssshhhhhh!!!*" and threw tees and ball markers at the kid because we wanted to savor every word.

Tommy had hooked up with her on the golf course, out

on the thirteenth fairway under the full moon. He'd gotten her shirt off and her white skin was as pale as the moonlight; her big breasts were swelling against her bra so that you could actually hear the material stretching. OK, OK. Those probably weren't Tommy's words, but that's the way I heard it, and I know for certain the next crushing sentence came out of his mouth verbatim, because it permanently seared itself onto my adolescent brain.

Everyone was so worked up at this point. Guys were yelling, "Did you take her bra off?" "What were her tits like?" "What were they like?"

And then Tommy said it. "I popped the clasp and those things unwound like I'd just ripped the cover off a balata. They almost hit the ground."

We were devastated. There was moaning and writhing. Someone yelled, "Sick!" and someone else, "No!"

No one needed to explain the metaphor to us. Every single one of us had ripped the cover off a balata and watched the tightly wound rubber band core unwind like silly string. It was a frightening image. I imagined her breasts exploding like the alien's tentacles from that wolf in the movie *The Thing*.

I don't think any of us understood how a woman's breasts could actually do this. I know I didn't. Tommy had only added another dark layer to the already mysterious female anatomy and, in doing so, sullied our puerile, airbrushed visions of Justine.

But this was not an entirely bad thing. We'd goaded each other into such a frenzied peak of collective obsession that if she hadn't been outright aware of the rustling in the hedge and all the furtive glances, her female radar must surely have picked up a massive cloud of overactive male hormones. And whether she was consciously aware of it or not, the sudden dissipation of this cloud had to have felt like a weight being lifted.

I'm not saying we completely lost interest in her. Far from it. Tommy's story just acted like smelling salts. It brought us back to our senses and allowed us to refocus on other important things, like golf. After all, golf was the reason we worked there instead of mowing lawns or flipping burgers at a beach club. Our love for the game was strong and pure, but the sins of the caddie yard followed us onto the course.

The on-course gambling began innocently enough for me. I'd played on my high school golf team the spring before working at Brooklawn, and during practices we played for the cookies they baked in the golf course restaurant— huge, chunky chocolate chip, oatmeal, and walnut beauties that had the power to silence the entire golf team van while covering the seats and floor mats with crumbs. Our coach momentarily objected to our daily cookie consumption and the mess it made until he realized it was the only thing that shut us up—silenced the usual hyperactive banter and heckling that lasted the entire twenty-minute ride home from the course.

The cookies were accumulated like points, and just about anything could win you a cookie: a birdie, sandy, proxy, barky, or lakey—a *proxy* being closest to the pin on a par three, a *barky* when your ball hit a tree and you saved par, and a *lakey* when it touched the water inside a hazard and you saved par (important note: the ball didn't have to remain in the water; it just had to touch it).

The best player on our team, Hans, so mastered the

cookie game that I quickly burned through the meager amount of money left over from doing yard work the previous summer and was forced to go to my parents to settle my debts. Even if Hans couldn't eat all the cookies, he still always demanded payment in full.

"You spent all of your money on cookies?" my dad asked. His incredulity quickly morphed to concern. "Is there something you want to tell us? Do you have a drug problem?"

"No! I swear. I spent it on cookies!"

Hans won those cookies in myriad genius ways. There was this one reachable, downhill par five on the course where we regularly practiced that he flat-out owned. I think 90 percent of my cookie losses came on that one hole. Hans purposely aimed his tee shot toward a thin row of pine trees down the left side of the fairway. He'd hit a high fade into the wispy boughs and beg for it to get a good kick, then smash a three wood into the greenside bunker and, more times than not, get up and down for a barky-sandy-birdie (the birdie being the real killer because it doubled the cookie total for the hole). In the event that he got a bad bounce and ended up under the trees, Hans would sometimes attempt to skip a low, screaming three wood across the lake for a barky-lakey-birdie. And one time he even skipped his three wood across the lake *into* the bunker and got up and down for an astonishing, never-equaled barky-lakey-sandy-birdie—an eight cookie hole.

When I started caddying at Brooklawn the following summer and began playing with Tommy, the gambling became a little less innocent. He had no interest in cookies. Tommy played for marijuana. Or as he called it, nugs, as in nuggets—the little, dry popcorn-shaped buds that constitute a bag of kind bud, as in *really strong pot*. My game was getting pretty good—I would break par for the first time before the summer was out—so I might've beaten Tommy on a regular basis if he hadn't had one distinct advantage over me: I couldn't play stoned.

Payment for a lost hole was immediate in the form of a packed bowl (with the participation of the loser required). So as soon as I lost the first hole it triggered a domino effect of further lost holes and further "participation" . . . a deadly downward spiral.

Monday was Caddie Day—the one day a week we were allowed to play the course and the one day members were prohibited, or at least discouraged, from playing. It was also the day that the grounds crew did any major work that would've disrupted member play on a regular day—drainage, irrigation, resodding, edging, aerating, cross-cutting, hydro-injecting, etc. They ran heavy machinery on the fairways and greens and wore protective ear muffs that made them oblivious to anyone attempting to play through. We some-times had to wait an eternity for them to notice us and get out of the way. A grounds crewman focused on a task could be a complete momentum killer.

When I was playing with Tommy, this might've been a good thing, because I was usually losing and could've used the delay to try to collect my pot-scattered thoughts. But wouldn't you know it, Tommy was the one caddie the grounds crew always noticed immediately and made way for.

There was no secret to his VIP status. The grounds crew were a bunch of stoners and Tommy had the best pot. It was amazing how they were suddenly completely aware of their surroundings when there was a bag of weed in the vicinity.

We stopped here and there to burn a bowl with his friends on the crew—hopped into their carts and zoomed off to hidden alcoves to "partake." And when I say zoom, I mean *zoom*. The grounds crew drove gas carts—very different animals from electric carts. Much faster. They were equipped with speed regulators, but all you had to do was shave down a golf tee and jam it in the spring-loaded governor and they were unleashed. They didn't go fifty, but they probably went thirty, which felt fast as hell in a convertible cart with no windshield or doors.

One night, a son of a member who lived next to Brooklawn threw a big party. His parents were away for the weekend, and word spread through high school like wildfire. I don't know how many people he was expecting, but hundreds showed up. It was a scene straight out of a John Hughes movie like *Pretty in Pink*—kids cannonballing into the pool, raiding his parents' bar, smoking in the kitchen, hooking up all over the house and all over the golf course.

The next day the grounds crew collected everything they found on the course and left it in a big box at the foot of his lawn—wallets, watches, cheap jewelry, lip gloss, beach towels, a boom box with an aqua aerobics tape in it (that must've been a surprise to whoever swiped it), countless bottles of liquor and wine, boxes of condoms, and a huge pile of panties and bras.

Tommy and I didn't take anything from the house that night, but we did sneak onto the course with a couple of girls, burned a joint, and drank a couple of beers over by the maintenance shed. And that's when we saw it.

One of the gas carts was parked beside the shed with the

key in the ignition, gleaming in the moonlight. Tommy and I looked at each other and smiled.

"Come on, girls! We're going for a ride!"

We fired up the cart and raced off into the night. Up and down the hills. Through the huge watery arms of the sprinklers. The girls screamed and cheered. They hugged us for safety and kissed us in nervous excitement. Then Tommy had an even more inspired idea. He pulled into a fairway and stopped.

"You drive."

"Where are you going?"

"Back here." Tommy stood on the wet grass behind the cart and grabbed the tail gate. "Gun it!"

I slammed the accelerator. Tommy held on for dear life. He whooped and hollered, his sneakers hydroplaning across the wet grass. It was like hanging on to the bumper of a car in a snowstorm—what we called skitching. We each took turns, even the girls, who went at the same time and both fell off in less than thirty seconds. We turned around and found them rolling around in the fairway laughing, completely soaked. We jumped out of the cart and rolled around with them. It was a memorable night. And it was not the last. We returned a week later decked head to toe in rain suits and flat-soled sneakers. We brought a water-ski tow rope, hitched the rope to the tailgate, and a new sport was born: cart skiing.

Either the grounds crew never got wind of it, or they looked the other way. Regardless, every single night the cart was parked in the same spot with the key in it. The rain suits and tow rope worked like a dream. We slid forward and backward, on our knees, backs, and stomachs. We did

Superman dives and 360s. Caught air off the bumps. By far the most exhilarating move was the *whip*. The driver turned the cart in a tight circle while the skier crouched real low and got whipped out to the side at incredibly high speeds—over thirty miles an hour in sneakers!

But alas, all good things must come to an end, even cart skiing. One night late in the season, we met as usual. Our friend Elliot, who'd become a regular skier too, was hiding up in a tree when we walked up. He jumped down and scared the bejeezus out of us. An inauspicious beginning.

We all took turns as usual, dragging each other through the sprinklers and over bumps, whipping each other in high-speed circles. Then toward the end of the night, when Tommy was skiing, I decided to play a trick on him—drag him into a patch of knee-deep grass beside one of the fairways. In order to do that, I had to drive the cart through the deep grass too.

I pushed the accelerator to the floor and bombed it straight for the rough. Tommy was back there doing his regular moves. He wouldn't notice until he flew into rough and wiped out. Elliot and I snickered wickedly. We were both looking back to watch Tommy eat it when all of a sudden the front of the cart dipped and there was a deafening *bang!* The cart stopped dead and Elliot and I flew out the front— cartwheeled through the air into the grass. The grass was so deep and soft that we both would've been fine except that my thumb got hooked in the steering wheel when we were thrown and was ripped from its socket. It was literally pointing straight down from the middle of my forearm.

I wish I could say I was brave and didn't cry. But the truth is I yowled like a scalded dog. I crawled over to a puddle and pushed my thumb into the mud. I don't know what I thought that was going to do. It was like some primal reaction.

The guys tried to comfort me, but we had other problems. The front end of the cart was completely smashed, the front axle bent at a thirty degree angle. We had to man up, push the thing out of the ditch, and then drive it like a wounded sled back to the maintenance shed, the front wheels skidding pathetically sideways.

When we saw Tommy again a couple of days later, my arm was wrapped in a heavy plaster cast, and Elliot was completely covered in poison ivy from the tree he'd been sitting in. His eyes were swollen shut, his arms and neck covered in bumps. I politely didn't ask about the rest of his body.

Tommy took one look at the two of us and fell apart laughing. "You guys look pathetic!"

Tommy was, of course, unscathed by the incident, and no one at the course put two and two together or, I should say, two and one—two banged up caddies and one banged up cart. But that was the end of cart skiing, and it was the end of the caddie season, too.

I spent only two short summers at Brooklawn, but it felt a lot longer than that. Caddying there ended up being much more than just a summer job. That golf course and caddie yard and my home course across town were playgrounds and proving grounds. Looking back, it's impossible to separate my experiences on those fairways from my formative high school years overall. They were the backdrop against which I now see that last sweet gasp of my childhood. They were my introduction to the caddie culture and, unbeknownst to me, the launching pad for a long, colorful caddie career.

2

A REAL YARD

The Stanwich Club,
Greenwich, CT,
1993–1995

It was several years before I caddied in Connecticut again. I spent most of those summers in between out west, where I went to college at the University of Colorado. And when I did return to loop again, I decided to head closer to New York City, to one of those professional yards I'd heard about where the cart paths were paved in gold, the fairways woven from the finest silk, and the caddies made $70 a loop! Now that I was in my twenties and beer was a regular part of my diet and dating involved more than ice cream and a movie, it was time to follow the money and join the big leagues.

I'm not sure what I was expecting the first time I drove into the Stanwich Club. After all, it's not as though the clubs in Fairfield where I'd worked and played before were slouches by any measure, but Stanwich was the peerless number-one course in the state, head and shoulders above the rest. And that became apparent the second I turned off of North Street and passed through the stone gate.

I hadn't yet been to Augusta National, but the drive into Stanwich was exactly the way I imagined Magnolia Drive—pink and white flowering dogwoods and apple trees blooming in dappled sunlight beneath towering hardwoods whose shadows scrolled in slow motion across my windshield. It was like driving through a car commercial. My shitty old Volvo felt so transformed, I gave a fraternal wave to the driver of a passing Lexus.

The fairways were crosscut with artistic precision, laid out like argyle scarves over the valleys and hills. Flags fluttered here and there with silken ease, marking greens framed by trees, water, and sand. The road climbed a hill and turned right toward the clubhouse—a stately white stone Georgian overlooking the glimmering sliver of Long Island Sound five miles below. I parked and walked around the edge of the clubhouse, where the members were relaxing on the terrace behind the eighteenth green. A group of golfers were paying their caddies off to the side—signing the little pink cash advance slips that I would come to know so well.

The caddies were a remarkable sight. They stood out against that serene scene like a pair of flannel shirts in a closet full of designer suits. Kent, a young black guy, must've been pushing three hundred pounds. He was wearing a ratty old T-shirt, saggy blue jeans, and Timberland work boots with the laces undone. I've never seen a less golf-appropriate outfit in my life. And when he hoisted the bags onto his shoulders and shuffled off toward the caddie shack, he did it with such tired resignation it was like he was carrying the weight of the world. Guy was basically an older, white version of Kent—a sad buddha of a man who had so perfected frowning it looked like smiling. These guys were as far as you could get from the pimply-faced adolescents I'd caddied with before.

I came to know them by the industry term *lifers*—as in caddies for life. Unlike those who only caddied for the summer months during high school and college, lifers followed the seasons, heading down south to Florida and the Carolinas for the winter. They wore the miles on their bodies and faces—the slump of their shoulders was like a weary shrug, the deep lines around their eyes like maps. Most of them smoked and gambled. They traded stories in gravelly voices, that trademark mischievous caddie twinkle in their eyes. It didn't matter if half of what they said was bullshit (caddies have "caddie tales" like fishermen have "fish tales"), because you wouldn't believe the truth if they told it to you anyway.

Every caddie had his story—guys up from the islands working for cash under the table, guys who'd never gone to college and probably never finished high school making more money than they could doing anything else, gamblers and alcoholics paying their debts and feeding their joneses, guys who'd lost their jobs or their wives or both, guys running away from the past, the law, a broken home. The reasons for being there weren't nearly as important as the fact that you were there. It was a loose brotherhood, but a brotherhood nonetheless. Even the summer kids like me were accepted, because we spent so much time together. And there were so many characters in the yard that instead of bothering with the futile and exhausting exercise of judging everybody, the caddies went by the much saner policy of judging no one.

As if to prove this point the two caddies who were in

tightest with the caddie master, Skip, and acted the most "veteran" were my age—two college kids working for the summer named Matty and Jason. I don't know the secret to their "status," but the lack of grumbling about it from the older caddies suggested that they earned their loops by showing up early every day and staying late whenever Skip asked them to, something that, for example, Buzz (a veteran Tour caddie) and Buddha (I was not surprised to discover that Guy's round belly and quiet, fatalistic demeanor had earned him the very nickname that occurred to me when I first saw him) were loath to do. They didn't want to make the considerable extra effort required to effectively kiss Skip's ass. And big three-hundred-pound Kent literally didn't have the energy. He fell asleep everywhere—on the bench in the yard, in the carts in the cart barn. I even saw him nod off while tending the pin once. (Amazingly, he came to with a snort and pulled the pin just as the ball reached the hole.) The only other caddie I remember walking as hard as Matty and Jason was Chris, who was nicknamed "Robo" because of his meticulous appearance (galoshes over his shoes, zinc oxide on his nose, round sun hat to protect the back of his neck, tee and ball marker pouch attached to his belt) and the tireless, machine-like way he went around the course. And nobody had a problem with Robo either because he was one of the nicest, least confrontational guys I've ever met. In sum, with the hindsight of twenty years now, I realize that Stanwich was one of the friendliest, most low key and welcoming caddie yards in the country. Regardless of individual backgrounds, it was a shared experience—you put in the time, you walked the miles, you pulled your weight, and you were a part of the team.

But that first day, I didn't realize any of this. It was just a whirlwind of first impressions. I hadn't even called ahead and made an official appointment, but Skip, the caddie master, took one look at me with my golf shirt tucked into my pleated Bermuda shorts (at least I *appeared* more professional than half the bedraggled souls he had working for him) and said, "Want to start this afternoon?"

I interpreted Skip's warm welcome as a high appraisal of my professed caddie skills, but would later come to realize that Skip's view of me was somewhat more nuanced, a tad more opportunistic. He saw me as an eager, young newbie he could stick with the cheapest, squarest, least athletic members— the ones the old veteran caddies bitched and moaned about, the ones who played on Saturday afternoons and wore their pants hiked up so high, their belts were cinched around their rib cages, and they needed suspenders to hold up their socks. I kid you not—*sock suspenders*. They were basically clones of my dad. And had just as tight a grip on their wallets.

But I was fine with that, because even the cheapest members at Stanwich paid way more than anybody where I'd come from, and having dealt with my dad on a daily basis since birth, I was immune to awkward silences and meticulous, self-conscious nerdiness. And thanks to my years in the Fairfield caddie yards, I was immune to bad golf, too, because when I'd first started, I was often assigned to total hacks. In other words, I was more than happy to endure what the older Stanwich caddies considered a slow, painful death.

Just walking around Stanwich was a pleasure. The greens, especially, were so severely sloped, it was entertaining to watch anyone putt on them, even hackers with strokes like nervous twitches. The greens looked like reflections in a funhouse mirror and were so hard and fast, the balls rolled across them like raindrops on a Rain-X'd windshield. God forbid your ball ended up on the opposite side of the green from the flag because most of the greens were crowned, or folded like tents, so the front half sloped toward the front and the back half toward the back, forcing you to judge uphill and downhill speeds in the same putt and at least three or four breaks along the way.

I became a master of contradictory statements reading greens for my players. "Just die it right here, sir, you want it to be barely moving, creeping really. But you've got to start it way over here because it's going to swing hard early. And make sure you give it enough to get here. Don't leave it short. That's even worse. Be bold, but delicate."

The greens' severe contours wreaked just as much havoc on approach shots. Back pins were especially hard to get at, even with a wedge, because if you landed back by the hole, it would bounce over, and if you landed it on the front, it would hit the upslope and stop. After two years of playing there, I learned to perfect the only shot that consistently worked: the low spinning knockdown—which is exactly what it sounds like, a shot that is low enough to skip off the upslope in front on the first bounce, but has enough spin to stop on the downslope in back on the second bounce. But for your average Stanwich member (or I should say the average Stanwich member I caddied for), the low spinning knockdown simply wasn't in the bag. It wasn't even in the DNA. And golf is hard enough as it is. This place just added insult to injury. I imagined these guys tossing and turning in their beds, reliving their rounds at Stanwich as night terrors. That's how bad they looked in live action.

The difficulty of the course was even more unnerving because of how beautiful and serene the place was. I mean, it's one thing to play the PGA West Stadium course and face a jagged rock-encircled green or a half-acre bunker with a thirty-foot face. You're expecting to get screwed. You *paid* to get screwed. Half the fun is laughing at all of the ridiculous shots and then telling your friends about them later. But Stanwich is a members' club, a country club. It's where people theoretically go to relax after a long, hard workweek.

Buzz, who'd been on and off the PGA Tour and caddied at clubs all over the country (and developed an extremely macabre sense of humor in those rough-and-tumble ranks), described the Stanwich paradox—the clash between the club's welcoming appearance and its brutal playability—in a creatively crude way that, honestly, could have come only from the mind of a caddie.

One day Buzz, who usually got paired with the low hand-icappers, somehow got stuck with me in the sock-suspender group, and there we were standing next to the third green watching a particularly painful display of ineptitude (made significantly worse by the third green's deadly contours). Balls were skipping and flying back and forth across the green in such rapid succession, it was like watching two doubles teams warm up for a Ping-Pong match. There was no point in intervening or offering advice or consolation. We just had to stand there and wait until everybody either found the green surface or gave up.

Buzz was shaking his head at the absurdity of it. He turned to me and said, "You know what this place is like?"

"I have a feeling you're going to tell me."

"It's like a beautiful, preppy blond girl. She rides horses, goes to private school, plays field hockey, you know the type. And all your life you've wanted to date her. You work your ass off to make enough money to impress her and finally one day she agrees to go out with you. You take her to a nice dinner, and you can't believe your luck when she agrees to go home with you afterward. . . ."

I looked at the sunbeams angling down through the trees, highlighting patches of argyle fairway, and found myself agreeing with Buzz—it wasn't hard to imagine them as golden tresses dangling above a field hockey kilt or girls' school uniform. Nor was it a stretch to think of being accepted into an elite club like Stanwich as winning the heart or hand of a beautiful woman. I smiled at the analogy and was about to compliment Buzz on his metaphorical prowess when I realized he wasn't finished. He was still speaking and the devilish twinkle in his eyes had grown brighter.

". . . and she doesn't stop you when you make your move. When you slide your hand under her skirt, she spreads her legs. You're reaching the height of ecstasy. But when your hand touches her panties something just doesn't feel right. She throws you down on the bed, and when she lifts up her skirt, you see it, you see what didn't feel right: she's got a big, black dick!"

Buzz laughed so hard the entire sock-suspender crew turned and looked at us. I was sure he was going to apologize, smooth things over, but he howled even louder, slapped me on the back and yelled, "That's what this place is, man! It's a preppy blond chick with a big, black dick!"

I could never quite look at Stanwich the same after that. Buzz's words gave her an edge, a silent maliciousness beneath her stately beauty.

But it wasn't all horror stories out there. Stanwich probably had the highest concentration of low handicappers in the state—several of them successful at the national level—and I had one brief, glorious moment that summer of '93 caddying for the best of them: a US Amateur quarterfinalist, US Mid Amateur champion, and Walker Cup team member named George Zahringer.

I'd never met him, but I had on several occasions watched longingly as he and the other single-digit handicappers teed off early on Saturday mornings. I'd marveled at his effortless even-tempoed swing and the powerful crack it produced as the ball exploded off the face of his blonde PowerBilt persimmon driver. Skip probably never would've assigned me to him; that was a cherry loop he reserved for his trusted (and demanding) veterans. But he couldn't prevent fate from bringing George and me together or, more accurately, he couldn't stop the Connecticut State Golf Association from choosing my home course in Fairfield to host that summer's State Amateur Championship.

One day after work I was out playing an evening round with Lumpus at home, and as I walked off the fourth green, I saw a figure in the fairway ahead of me hitting luscious, hundred-yard wedge shots—those very knockdowns that were the key to mastering Stanwich. Something about that swing seemed very comforting and familiar. Something more than the fact that it was simply a gorgeous golf swing that clearly didn't belong to any member of Fairfield that I was aware of. The guy looked like a fisherman effortlessly casting flies onto the calm surface of a lake.

I didn't know immediately that it was George, but when I ran to catch up with him and realized it was, I wasn't at all surprised. I waited patiently while he holed out on the fifth green, then introduced myself. I told him I caddied at Stanwich, but that Fairfield was my home course and I knew it like the back of my hand. I offered my services for the tournament that week, and he accepted. I jumped for joy and immediately ran home to call Skip and tell him I wouldn't be at work the rest of the week because I was caddying for, ahem, *George Zahringer in the State Amateur Championship.* I could hear the surprise in Skip's voice.

Now this tournament golf business was a totally different animal from the sock-suspender crew. I knew all about tournaments because I'd played in many of them myself—high school and amateur stuff —I'd even played in this very tournament: the State Am. What I didn't know is that *playing* in a tournament and *caddying* in one have very little in common. When you are the competitor it is all about you. When you are the caddie it is all about the guy hitting the shots— especially when that guy is someone of Geoge Zahringer's caliber. He may not have been a Tour player, but he was a regional, soon-to-be national champion and one doesn't become a champion golfer without being at least slightly self-absorbed and demanding and, dare I say, borderline *neurotic.* Not the most desirable personality traits in someone you are stuck with all day every day for the better part of a week.

Wanting to put my best foot forward, I showed up for the qualifying rounds all ironed and combed and tucked in. Stood straight and tall (may have even saluted), but it quickly became obvious that caddying for George had nothing to do with appearances and everything to do with the details. I could've showed up in flip-flops and a tank top and he wouldn't have blinked, but when I didn't have at least three yardages calculated by the time he reached his ball in the first fairway, all mirth vanished and his eyes shot out miniaturizing rays that shrank me down to a worthless rodent chewing a hole in his wallet. I scurried off to the nearest sprinkler head and squeaked, "You've got 100 to the front, Mr. Zahringer, and 108 to the pin."

"How far to clear the bunker on the left?"

I blinked my rodent eyes. "Maybe 105?"

He frowned. "Is there a false front?"

"Yes!"

"How many paces deep is it?"

"Two big ones?"

He seemed satisfied with this. He pulled his favorite sand wedge—an old classic PGA R-91 model—and hit one of those luscious skippers I'd seen the first day. The ball caromed off the upslope in front and spun to a dead stop just feet from the pin.

"Good yardage."

The secret to George's laser accuracy was the countless thousands of practice shots he hit from specific distances. He literally memorized the exact swing for, say, 90, 100, and 110 yards with his sand wedge (or, as he'd put it, 80, 90, and 100 percent of a full sand wedge) and he always tried to position himself at those exact yardages so he could draw the corresponding swing out of his muscle memory. There was no guesswork. He could tell if he'd hit it close the second he struck it, like a blindfolded archer releasing an arrow into the bull's-eye. It was a beautiful thing to watch, but I had to be very careful with my math. Even two yards of error was enough to summon forth his wrath.

I also had to be very careful what I said to George.

He didn't mind talking. In fact, he liked to talk, and you didn't have to be particularly tasteful or polite—he probably would've laughed his ass off at Mike's "preppy chick with a dick" metaphor for Stanwich, but he nearly ripped my head off when I said, "You don't want to go long here; there's trouble over the back."

"Don't ever tell me where I *shouldn't* hit it!" he hissed. "That's planting a negative thought in my mind. Only tell me where it's *optimal* to hit it."

My face turned red. I hated being dressed down like that in front of the other golfers and caddies in our group, but I immediately recognized the value of his point.

Of more questionable value was the time he scolded me for talking to one of his opponents.

"We're not here to make friends. We're here to vanquish these fucks!"

(Yes, he actually said "vanquish.")

The first day of the tournament we played thirty-six holes to qualify for match play—eighteen in the morning and eighteen after lunch. On our second hole of the day, George had 150 yards to the pin. He played a seven iron and landed it twenty feet left of the hole. And then on the sixth he hit a five iron from 170 to twenty feet again.

I thought, *He's not a very long hitter for such a good player.*

He played a tidy, if unimpressive, round and coasted to a four-over 74.

When we finished, he said, "Where are we going for lunch?"

I'd had a few drinks the night before and no breakfast. I was in the mood for some grease. I took him to the oldest, down-and-dirtiest local burger joint in Fairfield—Rawley's

Drive-In. We sat in one of the old wooden booths that have been carved with every high school kid's initials from the past forty years, and George and I ordered a disgustingly delicious pile of chili cheese dogs, double cheeseburgers, fries, onion rings, and giant Cokes. When we were finished, we both looked like we needed a nap. I was a little concerned.

"Are you gonna be able to play after that?"

"Are you kidding? That was great!"

On the second hole in the afternoon, we had the exact same yardage as the morning—150—and remembering what he hit the first time, I pulled his seven iron.

The miniaturizing rays flickered. "Don't pull my clubs for me! Just give me the yardage!"

I put the club back in the bag. "It's 150."

"Give me the nine."

George hadn't hit a nine more than 130 yards all morning. But he was the boss. I handed him the nine.

He stepped up and took an entirely different swing at it. Like he'd shifted into another gear. Took the club back at least three inches further and exploded through the shot. The ball landed about thirty feet behind the hole and sucked back like it was on a bungee cord. It almost went in.

George tossed me the club and walked off without a word.

I thought maybe he'd done that to prove a point, but for the rest of the day he was hitting the ball two clubs farther than the morning. When I asked him about it, he said, "I was swinging at eighty percent this morning."

He shot 66.

The next day we played our first match. George was seeded second, so we played the thirty-first seed in the thirty-two-man draw, and the guy was severely overmatched. I wouldn't say George toyed with him. But he didn't go out of his way to vanquish him either. He won four and three.

After the match, George patted me on the back and said, "Let's go to Rawley's."

We ordered the same disgustingly delicious pile of food, and George attacked it with the same abandon and somehow avoided dropping into the food coma that overcame me.

I almost couldn't walk, but George was as chipper as ever, and that afternoon we did our first serious vanquishing. George annihilated the guy.

The next morning he was in the groove from the start. No backing off at all. He was knocking down the pins.

On the sixth hole, a beautiful dogleg right along the lake, George hit a high draw approach with his six iron that started out over the edge of the water and landed on the short side of the green. It took the slope and curled right into the back pin. There were quite a few spectators following us at that point, and a local old-timer who played Fairfield every day of his life hurried over excitedly and said, "That's the secret to this hole! You have to hit a draw to that back pin, but no one's brave enough to try it! Did John tell you to play it like that?"

George humored the guy. "Yes, he did."

But I didn't. George had been hitting fades all week and then out of the blue on six he aimed right and hit a towering draw to five feet and made birdie. His opponent took the safe route up the left side, got a shitty kick and made five. We vanquished him, too.

George patted me on the back and said, "Let's go to Rawley's."

Now, don't get me wrong, I love Rawley's, but after two

days of destroying my gut, just the name Rawley's made me sick.

"You can't be serious, George. Three days of Rawley's is enough to kill an elephant. Let's just get something here on the terrace, something healthier."

George didn't put up much resistance. I think he paused for a second and looked longingly in the direction of Rawley's, but ultimately he followed me up onto the terrace, and we had club sandwiches and salad instead. I felt noticeably better on the tee that afternoon. I even felt a little cocky and whispered to the other caddie, "Get ready to get vanquished."

"What the fuck does that mean?"

"Look it up in the dictionary."

But George wasn't the same. He played well enough (he was still George Zahringer after all) but he just never put his foot on the guy's throat. He let him hang around. When the guy pulled even somewhere late on the back nine, the other caddie sneered, "What was that word again?"

I didn't acknowledge him.

George had a chance to take the lead again with only a few holes to go, but he missed a putt and the guy took advantage of the break. He rallied and beat us on seventeen. We politely shook hands all around. George was very cordial to his opponent and his opponent's caddie, but when he turned to me, he left my hand hanging in the air and said, "We should've gone to fucking Rawley's."

Despite having ruined George's State Amateur by depriving him of chili dogs and double cheeseburgers, that week did build my confidence as a caddie, and I returned to Stanwich with a little bit of a swagger. The other caddies couldn't resist commenting on my new status as "George Zahringer's caddie." Even Skip seemed impressed; I immediately noticed a significant improvement in the loops he gave me. I wasn't exactly vaulted into Buzz territory, but I was no longer relegated purely to the sock-suspender group. And apparently George was quick to let bygones be bygones because the next time I saw him he asked, "What was that drive-in called again?"

"Rawley's."

"That's right." He smiled fondly at the memory.

"That place was great."

He even offered to help me with my game. One day he plucked me out of the caddie yard and gave me a putting lesson on the green in front of the pro shop and then took me up to the driving range to watch me hit some shots, which caused Buddha to comment: "What? Are you a member now?"

As much as I was grateful for the heightened status George's approval conferred on me, my short stint as his tournament caddie (I caddied for him once more in the prestigious Metropolitan Golf Association Open Championship, where we finished in the top five and Low Amateur) made me realize that I wasn't all that interested in being a Tour caddie. Spending every day on the course with a tightly wound perfectionist like George was enough to give someone hypertension. I can't believe I'm saying this, but I actually preferred the sock-suspender group. As bad as they were at golf, they at least *knew* it and were genuinely apologetic that you had to endure their ineptitude. Working for them was very endearing and entertaining in a humble, human way because they enjoyed absolutely anything that took the focus off their god-awful games and we talked about a wide range of subjects, including their professions and personal backgrounds and my studies and interests. It was a veritable love fest compared to the cold, calculated *vanquishing* that took place with George.

And any further curiosity I might have had about caddying for the real pros out on the PGA Tour was dispelled by a caddie who visited the Stanwich yard that summer right before a Tour event in our area called the Westchester Classic. He had a regular gig caddying for a top player and we all listened intently to his stories, even Buzz, who usually talked over everybody. For the few days he worked at Stanwich he seemed like a big fish in a small pond and he made the whole Tour experience, what he called *the Big Show,* sound glamorous and exciting. But when I went to the Westchester Classic on Friday and followed him around, it was nothing like he described it.

His golfer was not playing well and was clearly not going to make the cut. He was whining and pouting and throwing little tantrums like a five-year-old. He threw his arms in the air, tossed his clubs on the ground, and berated his poor caddie every time he felt a read or yardage was wrong. The looper who'd seemed larger than life in our little yard now looked as defeated as a faithful hunting dog that has failed to tree a coon. I felt genuinely sorry for him and relieved I wasn't the one on that emotional train wreck's bag.

My ideal loops couldn't have been more different. They were the Thursday afternoon outings when Stanwich hosted charity and corporate tournaments and we were each given our own foursome in carts. There usually weren't any members in these corporate outings, just guests enjoying an afternoon off from work—most of them at their boss's expense because their company had purchased a foursome to support a favorite cause or get a tax write-off or butter up some important vendor or client. So the players were already predisposed to have a good time and this was helped considerably by the fact that there was free food and beer all over the course.

Few of these guys played at a club like Stanwich or had a caddie on a regular basis, so the whole experience was a luxury, and we were treated as such—more like hosts or tour guides than caddies. We didn't even carry any clubs, just calculated yardages, read the greens, looked for errant shots, told stories, and entertained in general.

Skip had no way of knowing which players were friendliest or paid the best; he just assigned the groups based on the handicaps they submitted, and despite my improved standing in the yard, I still often ended up with the guys who'd listed themselves as 36 (the highest possible handicap)—the guys who pulled their dad's or granddad's rusted old cobweb-covered clubs out of the basement once a year just for this one event. Buzz, who inevitably got one of the rare single-digit groups, would walk over, check the clubs on my cart and laugh.

"Spalding Executives? I haven't seen these in years! And Pinseeker *woods*? I didn't even know they *made* woods."

He'd pull a sad-looking seventies-model club out of one of my bags and swing it with mock seriousness. "Technically I think these things are made of laminated particle board, but they are wood-*like*."

"Fuck off, Buzz."

These once-a-year golfers had one redeeming quality: they didn't give a shit about the golf. It was all about partying on an afternoon when they'd usually be at work, and they were more than happy to have one more drinking buddy, so

I often ended up riding in the cart with my feet up or strolling casually down the middle of the fairway with a cold beer in hand.

Reading the Stanwich greens drunk was my favorite thing about Thursdays because these guys simply couldn't believe how much break they had to play. When I pointed fifteen or twenty feet wide of the hole and told them to die it halfway, they just shook their heads in disbelief. "I *never* would've played it there!"

And if they rolled it where I told them and the ball burned the hole or miraculously went in, we all cheered and high-fived and chest-bumped. It almost didn't matter how anyone played the rest of the game.

Saying good-bye in the parking lot at the end was like saying good-bye to my best buddies outside the bar at closing time. It was all drunken hugs and sincere thanks. We traded phone numbers and promised to meet up again in the future no matter how unlikely this was to happen.

And after the outing, the caddies, all buzzed and flush with cash, traded stories and compared loops as we cleaned and put away the carts. We burned rubber in the cart barn like Mario Andretti and waited for Skip to come down and grace us with the envelopes that contained our base pay which, even back then, was usually at least seventy bucks. I remember driving home once with over $200 and feeling like I'd won the lottery.

But that $200 was a signal fire. The caddies came circling like a team of rescue planes and shuttled me off to the nearest bar where they proceeded to *save me* from being so rich. These weren't late nights because we were all completely hammered before the sun set. I'll never forget the first time

I arrived home tanked right as my dad was coming home from work. He was in his business suit, briefcase in hand. He was tired, sober, serious. I was sunburned, flip-flopped, bar tanned, and completely lacking in tact and judgment. I slapped him on the back. Tried to give him a noogie and a kiss. He pushed me away. Looked me up and down suspiciously. "Are you drunk?"

"Yup!"

"I thought you worked today?"

"I did! I made $230!" I pulled out the crumpled evidence (which was now more like $170 after the bar).

Because he didn't play the game, he had no concept of the booze fest that was a golf outing nor the ragged troupe of misfits I called my coworkers. His only real experience with golf had been watching my high school matches, where we were all serious and competitive. We lined up our shots and studied our putts like Tour players. He'd been so nervous the first time he came out to watch me play, he'd hid behind the trees hoping I wouldn't notice he was there. It was genuinely touching that he wanted to watch me play, but was also totally annoying because I kept seeing a man dashing from tree to tree and strolling nonchalantly way back in the distance. It was like being trailed by a really bad CIA agent. Finally I just yelled, "Dad, I see you!"

He stepped out and apologized.

Now seeing me absolutely hammered after caddying at what he knew to be a reputable club just didn't compute. But I was twenty-two years old and making decent grades in college, so his alarm bells weren't completely ringing—if this had been an isolated incident, I think he would've forgotten it completely. But I caddied at Stanwich for the better part of two more summers and he witnessed the aftermath of many more Thursday outings, not to mention our regular Monday afternoon matches when Buddha and I took on Buzz and the assistant caddie master, Jimmy, whose job came with the privilege of playing in a cart (which we promptly loaded with beer). I began to see in my dad's eyes the first glimmer of concern that this whole caddie thing could someday lead to trouble.

3

COATTAILS

MAROON CREEK CLUB,
ASPEN, CO,
1996–1997

It's not that I intended to keep caddying after I graduated from college, in December 1995. In fact, caddying was the furthest thing from my mind when I moved from Boulder up to Aspen to work in a ski shop for the rest of the winter. But the Golf Gods didn't let the snow stop them. They found me one afternoon as I raced to catch the last gondola up the mountain, as the silver sun kissed the tops of the Maroon Bells and cast the north face of Ajax in shadow. I tucked the catwalk all the way out to the Jackpot glades into the last patch of sunlight hitting the west-facing slope. There was another skier beside me. We raced to the bottom and into the lift line just as the lift op was clipping the rope shut on the maze. We hopped into the final gondola car of the day and smiled. One more run!

Lex managed a local hotel. I told him I'd just moved to Aspen after graduating from University of Colorado.

"Are you going to stay for the summer?" he asked.

"That's the plan."

"Where are you going to work?"

"I have no idea. Do you manage the hotel year round?"

"I do, but I also work at a new golf course in town called the Maroon Creek Club."

"Really? What do you do there?"

"I'm the assistant caddie master."

"Caddie master? They have caddies?"

"Oh yeah. Maroon Creek is a gold mine."

At that moment, back in Connecticut, my father must have felt a chill go up his spine.

Lex wasn't kidding about the gold-mine part. The entire town was a gold mine. It didn't matter whether you were a caddie or ski instructor or waiter or carpenter. The gold flowed downhill from the mansions on Red Mountain and the suites atop the Ritz-Carlton and Little Nell hotels. All you had to do was hold out your pan.

Originally Aspen Mountain was a silver mine. Steep, shadowy Ajax (as the mountain is also called), was nicknamed the Silver Queen because she gave up silver ore like a slot machine in the late 1800s, before the United States switched to the gold standard. Today there's a ski run named Silver Queen that pours down the front of the mountain like a tongue of mine tailings spilling from the mouth of an ore shaft. And many of the runs are just that—old mine dumps. The town of Aspen is a relic of that era, too. Many of the old brick buildings are still as they were—the Hotel Jerome, the Wheeler Opera House, the Ute City Bank (now a restaurant with the old barred teller windows partitioning the dining room).

But the new currency is gold—gold necklaces, gold Rolexes, gold fur, gold lamé, and of course, gold *diggers*. And all those fancy and fabulous people—the jet-setters and playboys, the politicians and moguls, the models and movie stars, and a couple of princes thrown in for good measure, still stay at the Hotel Jerome and still see shows at the Wheeler Opera House and still go to the Ute City Bank (now to fill their bellies instead of their bank accounts). And in the summer they go out to the new Maroon Creek Club on the edge of town to play tennis and golf.

Aspen has a short golf season—a little more than three months, from around the first of June to late September or early October, when, in a seeming reflection of the town's affluence, the aspens turn gold in great swaths among the pines as though Midas reached out and touched the surrounding slopes. This is the signal for the gilded set to jet back to warmer climes until Christmas, when the whole hilarious show the caddies witnessed every day on the Maroon Creek fairways moves over to the ski hill.

It really didn't matter whether the activity was golf or skiing. They were socially interchangeable. And the caddies and ski instructors were interchangeable, too. In fact, several of us, including me, were ski instructors in the winter. Our patrons viewed us the way they viewed their pilots, boat captains, big game trackers, and dude ranch hands. We were a variation on a theme. A specialized breed of the ubiquitous young hunks who act as local point men for their global adventures.

And our wealthy patrons didn't drastically distinguish

between us financially, either. If they paid their ski instructor $500 a day, they paid their caddie $500 a day. If they invited their ski instructor to dinner, they invited their caddie to dinner. If they invited their ski instructor to join them on their yacht in Cabo, they invited their caddie. And so on.

It didn't hurt that most of us were strapping young college graduates in the midst of a two-year blowout before heading home to get a "real job." If you took us out to dinner, we weren't going to take our dentures out and attack the buffet the way, say, Buddha from Stanwich famously attacked plates of all-you-can-eat crab legs at Red Lobster. But on the flip side, we might end up in the hot tub with your wife.

Surprisingly, for some of these wealthy guys, this was actually a plus because it probably made them feel better about the fact that they were doing a lot of hot-tub hopping themselves. And the wives definitely liked the attention. The mores in Aspen were as loose as the purse strings.

I met one such wife on a chairlift on a beautiful spring day in March. The sky was robin's egg blue, and the sun was beginning to ripen and turn gold. It was warm enough to wear just a shirt and sweater, but cool enough in the shade to keep the powder feather light. Birds were flitting from tree to tree, feeling frisky in the burgeoning spring. We were half-way up Bell Mountain, just the two of us, and I could tell that the older woman next to me was feeling frisky, too, because she kept sighing and cooing and commenting in that leading way that is meant to open the door to conversation. "I can't believe how warm it is! I'm *sooo* overdressed!"

She took her headband off and shook out her long blond hair, her dark roots barely visible in the bright sunshine. She unzipped the top of her down vest, revealing her professionally sculpted breasts. Took off her mittens and examined her garnet nails.

All this was fine. I was used to it. Aspen was filled with aggressive older women on the prowl, and it was such a beautiful day, I even humored her with a few leading comments of my own, safe in the knowledge that as soon as we reached the top, I would ski away and disappear in a puff of powder, never to be seen again. But my escape plan was foiled when the lift suddenly shuddered and conked out and left us swinging silently above a cozy little patch of trees. She looked over at me, smiled, and batted her long black lashes. In a sultry Texas drawl, she said, "Oh my! Looks like we're stuck."

She inched her stretch-pants-clad bum a little closer. I inched an equal distance away.

"Are you from around here, honey?"

"I live here now, yes."

"Well, you must be a *very* good skier. Are you a ski instructor?"

"I am."

She inched a little closer.

"Oh I just *love* being taught. I respond *very well* to instructions."

I'd slid all the way to the edge of the chair. There was nowhere else to go. With all the weight now on one side, we were tilted at a precarious angle. I was afraid she was going to slide right down into my lap. By the look on her face, I'm pretty sure she was thinking the exact same thing.

"My husband went back to Texas on business and left me all by my lonesome. And he expects me to just take care of everything while he's gone! I had to wait around all morning for the pool boy to fix the hot tub. There's nothing like a hot tub to loosen up the muscles after a long day of skiing. Don't you think?"

I peered down at the snowy slope beneath me and wondered how soft the landing would be if I jumped.

I can't say exactly how long we were trapped up there, but it was long enough that the Aspen Skiing Company offered us complimentary lift tickets. And, believe me, that's a long time. But it was nowhere near the four hours it takes to play a round of golf. Six months later, I found myself alone with the same woman again, only this time we were riding side by side in a golf cart, and I was inching just as uncomfortably toward the edge of the seat as her hand nonchalantly strayed to my bare knee below the hem of my shorts. This time I was working for her, so there was no escape, at least not until we walked off the eighteenth green.

She had me running around with my white polo shirt tucked into my khaki shorts—the Maroon Creek Club caddie uniform made us look like dockhands at a yacht club. I bent over to seed her divots and mark her ball on the greens; I even teed her ball up for her because she'd conveniently developed a sore back that she then asked me to massage when we reached the secluded holes behind the mountain. I felt more like a golfing Chippendales dancer than a caddie.

Maroon Creek is a steep mountain course so almost no one walked—a few of the early morning fitness types did, and some of the hardcore men from traditional clubs back east, but the booze cruisers and the girls we called the midday hit-and-gigglers rode in carts—so the most accurate description of our job was really golf *butler*. We held their drinks and shined their clubs and pulled their carts around behind the green when they decided to stretch their legs and stroll the last thirty yards to the green with putter in hand.

I had to develop a whole new skill set: appearing to be busy when there was actually very little to do. It was all about body language—the way you draped the towel over your arm, the way you offered and accepted the clubs, the way you bent down to seed the divot. It was all about making yourself seem experienced and indispensable, performing simple tasks that golfers could easily, effortlessly perform themselves.

But these people were used to existing in a state of suspended disbelief, their lives so far removed from normal existence, they were like characters in a James Bond or *Mission: Impossible* movie. They jetted in for the afternoon to play a round of golf. They arrived at the course in stretch Range Rovers, feasted on foie gras and caviar from the martini cart (Maroon Creek's take on the traditional beer cart), and then jetted off again to attend a party in L.A. that evening.

And the caddies kept a straight face the entire time as if all this was completely normal. We seeded divots with elegant purpose and read greens with polite grace. We watched the tee shots fly like good hunting dogs on-point, ready to run off down the fairway as soon as the last ball was in the air, and chase it like it was a duck that had just been shot out of the sky.

It's not as though I hadn't caddied for wealthy people before. Most of the Stanwich members were extremely wealthy. But Greenwich, for all its wealth, is a real town, and the Stanwich members are part of a real community. They live locally and work proper nine-to-five jobs. They attend Little League games and ballet recitals together and frequent the same restaurants, dinner parties, and charitable functions. All of this necessitates a certain level of accountability and decorum. For example, it was considered bad taste to drink too much at Stanwich (or more accurately, to *appear* to have drunk too much) and to throw money around (by overtipping the caddies and staff, for example) because that makes the other (read: cheaper) members look bad.

And since the Stanwich members play their course day in and day out, year after year, most of them know the course as well as we do—the layout and yardages and the breaks on the greens (as much as it is possible to ever know those greens)—so they really need us only to carry the bag, a task I had always understood to be the main function of a caddie.

At Maroon Creek Club, on the other hand, making the caddie carry the bag was considered cruel, almost a human-rights violation. And it was amazing how unfamiliar many of the members were with their own course. In their defense, the course was only two years old, so nobody had been a member for very long. Still, it took a lot to keep a straight face when the first tee was backed up on a crowded August afternoon and the caddie master sent us out to an open hole, say, the twelfth, and the member asked, "How do you get to twelve again?"

And when we dutifully gave them instructions, they thanked us profusely. And if they had a guest with them they might even add, "The caddies here are excellent!"

To the casual observer this would appear to be an inno-cent, straightforward exchange. But that first dumb question and our sincere response acted like a password whispered through the door of a speakeasy. The member's gushing *thank-you*, the firm handshake, and the complimentary comment to the guest were loaded with subtext.

It could roughly be translated as: *Very nice to meet you, John. Glad you're a team player and totally on board with the fact that I'm going to play dumb and ask ridiculously self-evident questions like "How do I get to the twelfth hole on my own course?" and "Is this putt uphill?" when we are obviously putting straight up into the mountain. And you are going to answer gravely and earnestly as if you have never received a more valid inquiry, one that you are uniquely qualified to answer. And at the end I am going to ridiculously overpay you for playing along, for pretending it's perfectly normal that my spending habits between noon and midnight could feed a hundred starving children for a year.*

It was an agreement to honor and abide by the pact that exists between those who live at the pinnacle of existence and those who ride on their coattails. And believe me, blowing a little hot air was a small price to pay for a ride on those coattails.

It was such a good ride that I could tell the lonely Texas housewife that I couldn't massage her back, because I suffered from arthritis. And then not give half a shit when that comment cost me at least fifty bucks that first day and who knows how much more later because she never asked for me again.

She wasn't the only good loop, not by a long shot. I had options and I had cash. Not enough cash to buy a house or even a car, but we were making somewhere between two and five hundred every day, and that was plenty to buy dinner and drinks all night in the finest restaurants and clubs. Enough to hang around to the bitter end when the after-party invites began to the mansions up on Red Mountain. And if I went deep and did some real damage to my wallet and woke up the next morning with only a few crumpled fives and tens in my pocket and maybe an illegible phone number or two scrawled on cocktail napkins, I just peeled myself out of bed, draped my polo shirt and khaki shorts over the shower curtain rod to steam the wrinkles out, and did it all over again. It was some ride.

But it wasn't always pretty. The mornings came hard, and our caddie master, Dick Millweed, had a temper that could make a hangover seem like a seismic fracture. He was a small man with a soft, friendly voice. He was not intimidating at all, until he lost it. In his defense, he took shit from all sides—from the members who wanted their favorite caddie and their preferred tee time, from the golf staff who wanted him to perform a million menial duties, and from us when we showed up bleary eyed and incoherent and sometimes didn't show up at all. And God forbid a caddie should stumble in late, because then Millweed's lips would begin to tremble and his blue eyes would explode from his head. They grew as large as saucers and shook as though his skull was suffering an earthquake. And he appeared to grow with them. It was like some shaman or yogi trick. Pound for pound, I've never met anyone else who could so effectively deliver anger. He would yell, "You like fucking with me, don't you? You like making me look bad! You wake up and say, 'Today I'm gonna fuck with Millweed!' and it makes you happy, doesn't it!"

And we had no choice but to stand there and take it— hang our heads and blubber apologies and promise never to be hung over again, never to show up late again, because he held the ultimate trump card—he could fire us and cut us off from the golden tit. But once we were out on the course walking it off, the hangover and any cares associated with it (including Millweed) evaporated into the light mountain air. And after the round, with our pockets replenished and our spirits restored by the carefree, self-congratulatory ebullience of the überrich, we were powerless to resist the siren song of clinking glasses, the inviting golden light of the streetlamps and tavern windows in town, and the slopeside hot tubs steaming under the stars. We all jumped ship and dined, danced, and romanced the night away and then were dashed against the rocks of Millweed's wrath all over again the next morning.

This was such a different scene from a traditional East Coast yard like Stanwich, where caddies parked in the employee parking lot and came and went through the back entrance. There our worlds were separate, and we never pretended they weren't. At Maroon Creek, our worlds began separately, but the lines could become so blurred that it was possible to cross over—usually just for a night, a conversation at a bar or an invite to dinner; sometimes for longer, a trip to Vegas on the private jet, deep-sea fishing on the yacht in Cabo. But there were those rare occasions when the crossover was permanent, like when our fellow caddie Jerry married a Maroon Creek member's daughter.

When they first started dating, they both tried to keep the whole thing hush-hush, but we all knew about it; it was impossible to keep anything hidden from each other in that frat house. When Jerry wanted to borrow my sleeping bag to go camping one night, I asked knowingly, "Who you going camping with?"

He said, "Nobody."

I frowned. "Make sure you wash that fucking thing before you return it."

But whatever cover they thought they had blew off completely one morning when Jerry got requested by the girl's mother, whom he'd never met.

Millweed knew the story, too, and was visibly pleased to deliver the request as we all hissed and jeered at poor Jerry, who displayed his usual good humor but was clearly shitting a brick. And when he got back in from the loop, we all mobbed him and asked how it went.

Apparently her mom hadn't said anything for the first five holes. Just iced him. Acted as if she was just out for a leisurely round and had requested Jerry purely for his fine caddie skills (which was laughable if you knew Jerry). And he gamely played along. Paced off the yardages. Read each one of her putts like they were in the US Open. Addressed her deferentially: "Yes, ma'am." "No, ma'am." "It's a five-iron, ma'am." And while Jerry might not have been much of a caddie or a golfer, there was no denying his genuine affability, so after five holes of being studied like a horse at a livestock auction, she finally broke the ice and said, "So, Jerry. I think both you and I know why I requested you this morning."

And when she patted him on the shoulder and smiled reassuringly, he exhaled so thoroughly, he deflated into a heap on the fairway.

Now Jerry is probably a member of the Maroon Creek Club, too. It's rare to cross over permanently, but it happens.

A lot of us got offered jobs, and some of the guys took them—working for Aspen Airlines and the Aspen Skiing Company, even trading stocks for the local Merrill Lynch branch. I got offered a position in the Clinton White House by a woman who was a Democratic fund-raiser and Washington socialite. I probably would've been just a glamorized coffee boy, but I was only twenty-five, and that was right at the beginning of the tech bubble and the Kenneth Starr–Monica Lewinsky mayhem, and it sure as hell would've been interesting. I still wonder sometimes what my life would be like if I had accepted that offer. But I wasn't trying to cross over; I was enjoying the freedom of being a caddie and so were most of the other guys I worked with.

The caddies lived in an old converted hotel overlooking the sixth fairway and Buttermilk Mountain. I roomed with my friend Eric, who was in grad school down in Boulder, getting his education degree, and was very serious about saving his money and making something of his life—"contributing," as he put it. Eric and I got along very well, and he was a fun, fun-loving guy despite being such a hard worker, but he was exasperated by my laissez-faire ways, by the fact that I didn't jump at the White House job (didn't even blink, really) and that I seemed more concerned with golfing and partying than pursuing something meaningful. It was as though my dad had planted a mole in the Maroon Creek caddie yard. But no matter how passionate or persuasive, Eric's voice of reason didn't stand a chance against the hedonistic din.

The hotel wasn't populated only by caddies, but it seemed that way because we were so loud and unruly. I genuinely felt sorry for the woman who managed the place. She'd never experienced anything like us before; it was like trying to control a three-month keg party. Most of the caddies were there only for the short golf season, but I stayed in the hotel for the winter, too, and let me tell you, the transformation of the place after Labor Day was incredible. It went from *Animal*

House to a retirement home. And even though I was very much a willing participant in the summer mayhem, it was nice to be able to get a soda from the vending machine without worrying about finding a caddie screwing a girl in there because his roommate had kicked him out or to be woken by a drunk caddie screaming from the rooftop because he'd mixed too much whiskey with his anxiety medication.

And there was one woman living there with her two daughters—a twelve- and a fifteen-year-old—who felt like a hen with two chicks who had survived three months in a fox den. Things had gotten so bad at one point, she'd resorted to sleeping with a caddie who was chasing her fifteen-year-old because that was the only way she could be certain her impressionable daughter wouldn't fall prey to his considerable (and questionable) charms. She got him wasted one night, bedded him, and then called her daughter into the room when they were both lying there naked. The sight of him in bed with her mom nipped that problem in the bud.

The frat-house atmosphere wasn't limited to the hotel. It was just as prevalent on the course, where some of the members behaved like superrich caddies. One of my regular guys, Bill, had two full-time prostitutes he golfed with. He called them his girlfriends, but the rumor mill was buzzing with gossip that they were actually on his payroll. The difference between this arrangement and the arrangements many of the other men at the club had with their trophy wives wasn't crystal clear in my mind, but it was perceived to be more scandalous because it wasn't veiled under the guise of legitimacy. Plus, Bill had *two* girls.

It was a favorite topic of conversation among the caddies, and once I started caddying for him regularly, the guys hounded me to find out if it was true. Honestly, I was dying to know myself, so after caddying for him a half dozen times or so, I finally mustered up the courage to ask. We were on the fourth green. I was standing behind him, reading his putt. The girls were prancing around up by the hole in their short shorts and tank tops, clearly enjoying themselves even though they were terrible at golf. They were putting out of turn with their golf gloves on, tromping all over our line. They squealed for joy when they finally tapped in for like a fourteen.

Bill waited patiently, a huge smile on his face.

"Um, Bill . . . uh . . . rumor has it that your 'girlfriends' are . . . um . . . *on the payroll*."

I think I actually closed my eyes, expecting him to be offended, maybe even clock me for my audacity. But I just heard his voice say, "Girls, give each other a kiss."

And when I opened my eyes, the girls were on their tippy toes with their lips locked and their hands all over each other. Bill winked at me and said, "Now, John, which way did you say this putt breaks?"

Bill was famous for his generosity. I was often the beneficiary, but I missed out on his most munificent moment, when, after a round one day, he invited the two caddies in the group, Mike and Sam, to join his entourage in Vegas for the weekend. They begged Millweed to give them the weekend off and as much as he probably needed them to work, Millweed had a soft spot and couldn't deprive them of an invitation like that. With his endorsement they ran back to the hotel to grab some things and were flying to Vegas in

Bill's private jet within the hour. He even got them a room at the Bellagio.

I was a little hurt for not being included, but as Bill casually put it when I saw him next, "You weren't in the right place at the right time."

Mike and I caddied for Bill the day they got back. He was playing with another member who'd been on the trip and had lost his shirt trying to keep up with Bill on the tables. Now this guy, Adam, was trying to win a small fraction of his money back on the golf course, and he was really sweating it because he was nowhere near as wealthy as Bill and his weekend losses had genuinely hurt.

Adam was notoriously cheap with the caddies and, under duress, he was riding Mike and me pretty hard—second-guessing every read and yardage we gave him.

"Are you sure it's one fifty? This is a *really* important shot!"

And then not trusting us no matter how emphatic we were, he paced every yardage off himself after we already had.

We were both rooting for Bill the entire time, even though we were supposed to be distributing our services evenly. When the entire match came down to Bill's final putt—a ten-footer to win—our allegiance was ridiculously obvious. Mike was crouched on one side of the hole and I was on the other. We were studying Bill's line and conferring with each other as if preparing for the bar exam. Bill just stood there, leaning on his putter while casually admiring the puffy white clouds drifting in over the Buttermilk Mountain. When we reached our verdict, he stepped up, took one practice stroke, and rolled it right into the back of the cup.

Adam crumbled to the ground. "You've got to fucking be kidding me!"

It was a $700 putt. Adam started peeling off the hundreds, but Bill just raised his hand, said, "Give it to the caddies," and walked away.

I could see the mischievous grin right through the back of his head. He knew handing seven Ben Franklins to a caddie was going to kill Adam, and he loved it.

I might've missed the trip to Vegas, but I was the recipient of Bill's generosity on many occasions. For example, he paid me the most money I've ever made *per shot*. I know that's an odd category, but I really don't know how else to classify it, because it wasn't anywhere near the most money I've made for a complete round. It happened one afternoon when I came in from my morning loop and there were no caddies left in the yard.

Millweed said, "Bill wants you. He's out on the course already."

One of the guys shuttled me out to the seventh, where Bill's group was playing caddieless, because it was August and the club was swamped and we didn't have enough guys to cover all of the groups. It's not like Bill and his playing partners were fumbling around cluelessly out there, lost and adrift without a caddie. They were fine. As I said, our job was completely gratuitous. We were far from needed. We were a luxury.

But Bill reacted to my arrival as if I was Superman flying up just as the plane is about to hit the ground. "Where have you been? I'm dying out here!"

He handed me his driver to perform some completely unnecessary task like wipe the grip off. I handed it back, and all was right with the world . . . *the pact.*

He teed his ball up and gave it his trademark not-a-care-in-the-world swing, and as the ball sailed through the air, a dark cloud emerged over the shoulder of Buttermilk Mountain and gave an ominous rumble. Before the next guy could hit, a lightning bolt flashed and the warning siren sounded, instructing us all to immediately find shelter.

This was clearly no passing storm. Hailstones were already pelting the ski slopes and speeding toward us in a wall. Bill gave the storm a split second of consideration and said, "To the bar, gentlemen."

We raced back to the clubhouse in the carts. Bill insisted I ride on the seat next to him even though I usually hung on the back, and when we got in, he peeled off two Ben Franklins and said, "Thanks for the trouble, kid. Sorry we quit on you."

Two hundred for one shot.

The only time I ever heard of Bill getting upset was the day the martini cart went missing. I wasn't out with him, but I was aware of his displeasure because the martini cart was with me—or more accurately, it was with my group, which included Kevin Costner, whom the martini-cart girl, Dawn, was in love with. She never left our side for the entire round.

Kevin had just finished shooting the movie *Tin Cup*, and he was there celebrating with his manager, his body double (yes, even for *Tin Cup* he had a body double), and another close friend. Kevin hadn't really been a golfer prior to the movie, nor had his double, so the ex–Tour pro–turned–TV commentator Gary McCord had been hired to *shape* their swings and make them look authentic for the movie. For Kevin, the results were quite impressive—the legitimate-looking swing he had crafted for the film actually produced results. He shot in the eighties that day.

McCord's guidance proved less effective for Kevin's double. His swing *looked* pretty good, but the resulting ball flight wasn't nearly as elegant. Gary had encouraged him to focus on the trademark *high finish* of a Tour player's swing—to stand tall, hold the club high in that perfect follow-through position and watch the flight of the ball as if it was soaring toward the pin. This led to quite a few hilarious moments when Kevin's double either completely whiffed or topped the ball about ten feet, but he still held his finish and stared the flag down as if his ball was actually in the air and about to go in the hole.

Kevin yelled, "Hold that finish! Hold that finish!"

And the other guys shouted, "Get in the hole!"

His double gamely held that picture-perfect finish until Kevin yelled, "Cut!" like a director.

Kevin opened a package of Cuban cigars on the sixth hole and offered me one. I'd never smoked a genuine Cuban cigar, but not one to turn down any fine tobacco or liquor products, I gratefully accepted. I was forecaddying for the group so my arms were full of clubs—putters, wedges, drivers (basically any clubs they'd just hit that I hadn't cleaned and returned to the bags yet). As a result, I was pretty much smoking the Cuban hands free and inhaling more smoke than is advised.

Two holes after I lit it, I was tending the pin for Kevin, who was some forty feet away, and I was starting to feel a little green. A cold sweat was forming on my brow. I couldn't be certain I'd read his putt correctly because the contours of the green were moving like waves. I felt I was getting seasick. Kevin looked up one final time to double-check his line and then did a double take when he saw me. Instead of putting, he walked over to me and took the clubs from my arms and the cigar from my mouth. He gently removed the pin from my grasp and put his arm around my shoulders, which was a good thing, because the second I let go of the pin I began to fall over. He helped me over to the martini cart and sat me next to Dawn. He pulled three cans of Budweiser from the ice chest and laid them in my lap.

Very kindly and reassuringly, he said, "Drink these and you'll feel much better."

His voice sounded very far away.

Apparently I'd been so off balance tending the pin that it was bent halfway to the ground like a drawn bow. Now, completely useless, I had to ride with Dawn for two holes and try to clear my head with cold beer. I pounded two cans of Bud while I held the third to the back of my neck. By the time we reached the par-three ninth, I'd recovered enough to rejoin the group.

"What club would you hit here?" Kevin asked.

"You should hit a seven iron," I said.

"What club would you hit?" he repeated.

"Eight iron."

Kevin pulled the eight iron from the bag and handed it to me. "Let's see it."

I somehow managed to hit the green. Kevin gave me a big bear hug and yelled, "Our caddie is back!"

Two hours and a dozen beers later, all five of us were

walking up the eighteenth fairway arm in arm, singing Queen's "We Are the Champions" at the top of our lungs. Dawn still trailed us faithfully. I got an earful from Millweed after the round, because Bill had complained to him about the missing martini cart. I just shrugged. What was I supposed to do about it? Bill's financial generosity (he tipped the martini girls extremely well, too) had finally met a force more powerful—Kevin Costner's sex appeal.

At the end of the summer, one of the assistant pros who lived across the hall moved out and gave me his second-floor room overlooking the sixth fairway and the mountains. I could throw a golf ball down on my carpet and fire a five iron right through the open sliding glass door into the sixth fairway. The caddies had seven-day-a-week playing privileges, but during the height of the season, we were often too busy to take advantage of them. Now that it was September and most of the members had gone home, we played almost every afternoon. We started our matches by placing two cans of beer on my carpet and teeing off between them. We called them the Miller tees, and that became code for those late-season rounds. When I was working in the morning and saw another caddie out on the course I'd yell, "Miller tees?"

And he'd yell back, "Miller tees!"

And then he'd yell to another caddie, "Miller tees?"

And so on. And we'd all meet up in my room after work, load our bags with cold beers, tee off my carpet, and walk right down the stairs and out onto the course.

The last of the caddies left when the first snow came in late September, and a restful peace finally descended on the hotel. I started waiting tables at the Chart House restaurant, but we barely had any customers because the off-season was upon us and the crowds wouldn't return in force till Christmas. And that was fine. I caught up on months of lost sleep, hiked up the backside of Aspen Mountain with my skis on my back to catch the year's first untouched powder stashes, saw movies at the little theater in town, and spent quiet evenings with friends at the local bars. The Miller tees were returned to the fridge, and my golf bag placed in the back of the closet, not to be touched again until spring and the arrival of the next season at Maroon Creek.

4

SHOULDER SEASONS

Olympic Club,
San Francisco, CA,
1996–1997

The gilding of the aspens was an apt metaphor for the real wealth of the Colorado or "Western" experience—diamonds of powder adorning the crowns and necklines of the highest peaks, golden brooches of aspen pinned to their shoulders. Springtime dressed the mountains and canyons equally lavishly in waterfall sashes and wildflower brocades.

These were the shoulder seasons —or in caddie parlance, the "off-the-shoulder" seasons, when we finally put the bags down, trading martinis for microbrews and the fairways for the freedom of the West's vast open spaces—mountains, canyons, and rivers that opened up equally vast spaces within, unexplored territories of the soul, as the distractions of hard work and hard play gave way to silence and self-reflection.

My time on the mountain in winter was filled with pockets of solitude, too—runs through secret powder stashes in the woods and hikes out to backcountry bowls and chutes. And in the summer there were the solo rounds of golf in the evening when everyone was already in town, and the long afternoon mountain-bike rides up the fire roads and single tracks. But when I returned from the woods or golf course or backcountry, I was again in the thick of the extended holiday seasons of summer and winter and the demands of clients on the golf course and ski hill.

It is true that you live in a ski town to ski and work at a golf course to golf, but the shoulder seasons were every bit as much of a reward for living the golf- and ski-bum life—and while I may not have known it then, every bit as much of the reason I kept living it. It's a part of the caddie life people don't really know about—the time spent traveling between jobs when one season has ended and the other has yet to begin.

There are as many different ways to spend this time as there are caddies. The young adventurers with no golf aspirations and no responsibilities spend their hard-earned cash on travel—on surfing and backpacking trips through South America, Europe, Asia, Australia, etc. The aspiring Tour players cash in on the sponsorships they've worked hard to drum up from their wealthy patrons and head out on the mini-tours. The old, achy lifers rest their backs and feet in sports bars and at the track.

One of the young ones with no responsibilities, I decided to head out to San Francisco from Aspen the next spring, before the season at Maroon Creek began, to visit friends and loop for a couple of months at the Olympic Club. I didn't own a car and didn't want to just fly over all the beautiful country between Colorado and California, so I decided to hitchhike through Utah, Arizona, and Nevada and hike the trails and canyons between the roads. And because I hadn't played golf since September and didn't want to show up in San Francisco with zero game, I decided to strap a sand wedge to my backpack, bring a half dozen balls and play some backcountry golf along the way.

What is backcountry golf? you ask. Well, I don't know how many outdoor-enthusiast, hitchhiking golf fanatics there are out there, so I may very well have invented this sport. It is basically a wilder version of the impromptu backyard rounds I played as a kid, chipping over stone walls and fences and driveways (and even over my parents' house, much to their consternation), and the rounds my college roommate Carlo and I played on the eighteen-hole wedge course we designed around the Norlin Library Quad at the University of Colorado. We lofted shots over the corners of buildings and parked cars and unsuspecting students' heads. It was not a game for the faint of heart or unsteady of hand.

In the backcountry, you didn't have to worry about injuring anyone or breaking any windows. The great challenge was simply finding the ball. I'd played backcountry golf down Aspen Mountain in the summer, and that was hard enough, with the patches of melting snow and deep grass and the great distance the ball flew and bounced down the ski slope, but the ski hill was nothing compared to the golf-ball-devouring beast that was the Utah desert.

This is not the desert in the wide-open Saharan sense. It is a slotted, cliffed, cracked landscape pocked with caves and sinkholes and impenetrable nests of cactus, cottonwood, sage, and saltbush. The sandstone spires and canyon walls act like bumpers in a pinball machine. A shot that looks perfect in the air—one that is headed right toward the open patch of sand acting as the fairway or green—can get caught up in one of those fickle little canyon breezes that swirl up off the river, be nudged ever so slightly off-line, hit an imposing fin or reef of sandstone, and carom off wildly in any direction.

There were many times when I played it off the sandstone on purpose—punched shots off the walls and spires if I got stymied behind a sage bush or cottonwood tree. But when it was accidental, the result was rarely good. The ball rarely went *toward* the target. It was more likely to end up in a nest of thorns or a shadowy slot or up on some inaccessible ledge. Which is exactly what happened to my sixth and final ball about halfway through my trip. I was so distraught, I seriously considered climbing up after it, but when I found myself ten feet off the ground clinging to a handhold the size of a thimble and still well below the ledge, I realized the foolishness of it and tearfully resigned myself to a golfless hike the rest of the way (what most people simply call a hike).

My sand wedge was demoted to walking stick and fire poker—the plastic hosel melted off in the flames and the bottom of the shaft scorched black. I dinged the hell out of the club face taking swipes at stones on the riverbank. I'd pretty much given up on it ever being a functional golf club again, but a couple of days later, the Golf Gods smiled on me once more.

The canyon where I lost my final ball emptied into the Colorado River at a popular put-in for rafters and kayakers. It was quite a sight after all of those days alone—five since an old fellow and his dog dropped me off at the top—trucks backing boats into the water, people loading and unloading gear, others swimming and picnicking.

One guy in particular caught my attention. He was tossing a ball for his dog—a little pointy-eared coyote-looking thing. There was nothing unusual about this except that the ball he was throwing was small and white. I walked over to take a closer look. I was standing right next to the guy when the dog came bounding back from the water's edge and deposited the slobber-covered sphere right next to his Teva-sandaled foot. I could clearly make out the word TITLEIST printed on its cover.

I was so dumbfounded, I asked what could possibly be the stupidest question in the history of man: "Is that a golf ball?"

"Yeah. Funny, huh? I throw her a tennis ball and she won't even pick it up. Just loves golf balls!"

"Got any more of those?"

"A bunch."

My scorched, sorry-looking sand wedge rose like a phoenix from the flames!

The guy gave me three balls. A veritable treasure trove. And he gave me a lift to a gas station/restaurant up on the highway (the highway being a scenic two-lane road that traversed slot canyons and crumbling mesas). I quickly caught a couple of rides out toward the forested Kaibab Plateau on the North Rim of the Grand Canyon and got picked up by a logger there who nodded at my pack and asked, "Camping?"

"Yes. Do you know of any good spots around here?"

"In these parts?"

I nodded.

He shook his head and whistled. "You're a braver man than me."

"Why's that?"

"This is vinegarroon country."

"Vinega*what*?"

"Vinegarroon. Little scorpion about yay big." He pinched his thumb and index finger together indicating something very small. "Most poisonous scorpion in North America. Has a clear shell. You can actually see the venom coursing through its tail. Attracted to heat. Loves sleeping bags."

I was speechless.

"Know how it got its name?"

"Do tell."

"When the poison really takes hold, about three hours after the sting, you get a vinegar taste in your mouth. That's when you're really in trouble. Best to make your peace with God at that point."

Just at that moment we reached the junction where he was turning south and I was heading north.

"Well, here we are. Take care now."

He tapped the horn and drove off trailing dust. I stood there on the dirt shoulder in shock. The sun was alarmingly low in the sky. My only thought was *Please, God, I need a ride all the way to California right now! I will even give up my golf balls! I'll bury them right here in ritual sacrifice to the Scorpion Gods!*

Not a single car passed. The sun set.

I'd packed a bivouac sack—a waterproof shell that wraps around your sleeping bag—in case it rained. There wasn't a cloud in the sky. The stars were so plentiful, it was difficult to even make out the constellations. I zipped the bivouac sack completely shut. Didn't even leave an air hole. I'd foolishly drunk like a gallon of water in the truck and had forgotten to piss before crawling into my sleeping bag. I held it all night and woke about five times in what I thought was a pool of sweat but couldn't be sure because my nightmares about vinegarroons were so vivid that I could hardly be blamed for pissing myself. They hunted me with heat-seeking X-ray vision; they gathered under my bag, their ghostlike bodies translucent in the moonlight, luminescent venom coursing through their tails. I literally didn't even roll over till dawn for fear their stingers would penetrate right through the layers of GORE-TEX, nylon, and down.

In the morning, I carefully extracted myself from my sleeping bag. I'd slept with my shoes in the bag but shook them out anyway. Can't be too careful! I lifted the bag and jumped back. Searched the ground for any sign of a scorpion. Nothing.

I drowned a yucca in pee and stumbled out onto the roadway. Within an hour, I was cruising north in a VW camper van with a couple of climbers on their way back from Zion.

"You look tired, man," one of them said.

"I am. Had nightmares all night about vinegarroons."

"Vinegarroons? Why?"

"Because they are little translucent heat-seeking death machines that hunt this desert for human victims. That's why!"

The two guys burst out laughing so hard that I momentarily forgot about vinegarroons and feared a high-speed impact instead. Finally they collected themselves and returned to the proper lane.

"I don't know who told you that, dude, but I used to have a vinegarroon named Mojo. Big black sucker. Nasty smelling vinegar spray when he got pissed. But other than that, great pet. Used to hide under my textbooks when I did my homework."

Big? Black? Harmless? Vinegar *spray*?

I imagined that logger proudly regaling an entire bar full of fellow loggers, reducing them to stitches as he described the look on the pretty boy hitcher's face when he dropped me off at sunset in "vinegarroon country."

I was pissed, but at least I hadn't buried my golf balls in ritual sacrifice to the Scorpion Gods. Two hours later, I found myself stranded on the side of one of the sorriest, most desolate stretches of roadway in the lower forty-eight—the I-50 (officially dubbed the Loneliest Road in America by some impressive publication like *Western Driver* magazine). I hit about a thousand golf shots that afternoon—pelted the hell out of the WELCOME TO NEVADA sign while trying to flag down the big rigs running back and forth between Salt Lake City and the gold mine in Austin, Nevada. I didn't even bother with the terrified old folks who risked life and limb to climb down out of their RVs and take a picture of the state line next to "the crazy man with the golf club."

I could imagine them showing their grandkids the photo album of their trip. "And here's your grandmother at the New Mexico state line and at the Arizona state line and the Utah state line, and here she is at the Nevada state line. . . ."

"Grandma, why is there a man with a golf club standing behind you at the Nevada state line?"

One of the truckers finally took pity on me because he'd passed me three times already and was on his final gold run of the day. It was so late when he dropped me in "downtown" Austin—consisting of a single gas station and a diner—that the sun was already dropping behind the arid peaks across the valley to the west and I'd resigned myself to spending another night with the vinegarroons.

I bought a stick of beef jerky and a bottle of water and began walking down the hill. It was so dark now that the only car to come up behind me had its headlights on. I hadn't gotten any love from anyone all day, so I didn't expect much from this one, either. I stuck out my thumb but didn't even bother turning around. I was amazed when he pulled over.

He was a late-forties, maybe fiftyish guy in a minivan—a salesman for a small publishing company in Missoula, Montana, called Falcon Press. He was doing his rounds to independent booksellers throughout the Southwest—Grand Junction, Moab, and Flagstaff—all towns I'd just been through. The back of his minivan was filled with so many books I could barely squeeze my pack in beside them. But we made it fit and sped off toward Reno in the gathering darkness.

He was curious what I was doing out there in the middle of nowhere, so for the entirety of the ride from Austin to Reno, I told him stories from my past month on the road. Some are recounted here—the golf-ball-fetching dog by the river, the wiseass logger and his tales of vinegarroons, the old RVers, and the gold truckers. Some are not—falling in and escaping from quicksand in a remote canyon, getting stranded in a Branch Davidian–like polygamist colony in southern Utah. He was riveted, so much so that he bought me a steak dinner in Reno and begged me to keep talking. He interrupted here and there to ask a question or laugh out loud or express his disbelief, and when he finally dropped me at a campground on the Truckee River just north of Tahoe

City around midnight, he shook my hand warmly, handed me one of his cards, and made me promise I'd write a book someday and send it to him at Falcon Press.

I slept on the soft sand by the riverbank serenaded by the roar of the swift springtime water, then hitched into Tahoe City first thing in the morning. I walked out to the end of a wooden dock, took off my dusty shirt and socks and boots, and dived into arctic Lake Tahoe. It was so cold, it felt searing hot. I immediately scrambled back up onto the dock and lay there breathless in the sun, my back against the weathered gray planks, glad to be free of a month of desert grime.

I had breakfast in a little café across the street and wrote in my journal for a good two hours—an inspired piece of writing about hitchhiking the I-50, a piece that was never published but that I was very proud of and read to anyone who would listen. It was in my mind the unofficial beginning of my writing career, and when I walked back out onto the road, the world was filled with promise and inspiration. I was radiating goodwill, and if there is one secret to successful hitchhiking, it is radiating goodwill. I quickly caught two more rides right to my college roommates Carlo and Dave's doorstep on Nob Hill in San Francisco.

It was an amazing place—a three-bedroom apartment with a garage and a rooftop deck overlooking both the Oakland Bay and Golden Gate bridges. My friends were standing on the roof, and when they heard the car door slam and my voice echo up off the buildings, they leaned over the edge and smiled ear to ear. Dave hollered, "I told you he'd be here!"

I'd called Dave weeks earlier and said I was going to arrive on Saturday, May 10. Carlo and Sven, a friend visiting from Sweden, had been rightly skeptical about this and lobbied Dave all morning to forget about me and drive up to Marin County to play some golf, but Dave owned the car and wouldn't budge. "John'll be here," he said.

I had no idea it was Saturday and might've even balked if you'd asked me real quick what month it was, but unbeknownst to me, I did indeed arrive the afternoon I said I would, and we all piled into Dave's grandma's Corolla and drove up to Marin County for what would become our ritual weekend golf trip for the month I was there.

We crossed the Golden Gate Bridge and drove up through dark, wooded Mill Valley—home to our hippie heroes: the Grateful Dead. We passed through San Anselmo and bright sunny Fairfax (where we sometimes parked on the side of the Bolinas–Fairfax Road and snuck onto the back nine of the private Alister MacKenzie–designed Meadow Club for a few barefoot, whiskey-lit holes) and continued up to San Geronimo and the ridiculously renamed San Geronimo National golf course. I think a golf marketing executive somewhere decided that putting National on the end of a course's name immediately justifies doubling the greens fees. But despite having the worst front nine in the continental United States (I think Guam has one that's slightly worse), San Geronimo was in our mind the poor man's Meadow Club, because the back nine was routed through the sublime golden-grassed, oak-shaded California hills. And even though the greens and bunkers back there were shaped like those nonslip flower cutouts you stick to the bottom of your bathtub or shower, those hills were so beautiful that no amount of bad architecture could ruin them. We played the five prettiest holes back there over and over again until dark and then fired up glow-in-the-dark balls and played hockey in the fairway with five irons for sticks and our shoes for goals. Dave pretended to be Rangers goalie Mike Richter. His kick saves looked like shooting stars.

Dave had a proper job at a bank and Carlo was a bike messenger, so that left me to fend for myself during the week. I'd mailed my golf clubs out from Colorado and on Monday morning I shouldered my clubs and walked down the hill to the Market Street BART station and took the train south to Daly City, where the Olympic Club sits on the shores of Lake Merced.

I walked down the hill from the Daly City station, past the gas stations, mini-malls, and office complexes, and snuck onto the edge of the club's huge wooded property through a hole in the fence.

Amazingly, the Olympic Club—host to two US Amateurs and two US Opens, including Hogan's famous, unsuccessful attempt to win his fifth title in 1955—didn't really have a caddie yard, just a bunch of bedraggled cast-offs who couldn't get work at the more lucrative clubs in the area, like San Francisco Golf Club. They were more than happy to include me.

I showed up almost every day for a month and came to know them well. There was old hunchbacked, square-headed Reese, who went through half a dozen cigars a day without even lighting one—just chewed them all the way down to the stump like sticks of Skoal, his chin a trail of leaf and spittle, his teeth and tongue stained black. And skinny old Allen with his old-school dial radio always tuned to the Giants game—he even had headphones so he could listen to the game on the course, the silver antenna sticking out of his apron pocket. There was hyperactive (possibly cracked out) Bobby, who supplemented his caddie income by driving a little old lady around in her giant seventies model Oldsmobile. He took her to the grocery store and the Elks Club and the bingo parlor. Bobby was the caddies' spiritual ringleader. He made us feel better about the fact that we barely ever got work, by making fun of Olympic's notoriously cheap members.

Every time he got off the course, he yelled, "I'm a mule for forty!"

That became our mantra. "We're mules for forty!"

And most surprising of all, there was saxophone-playing Danny, whom I'd caddied with at the Stanwich Club. Back east he and I had become kindred spirits of a sort, because we always showed up late. Danny's excuse was that he played sax all night in the jazz clubs in New York. Mine was that I couldn't bear to watch all those great early loops go out, the ones Skip never assigned me to. Now our bond was redoubled because we'd both traveled across the country on a whim, Danny playing his sax on the streets in the Haight and I golfing my way clear across the southwest desert. Two crazy journeymen reunited.

At Stanwich we'd nicknamed Danny "Spalding" (from *Caddyshack*) because of his complete lack of golf decorum and tact. He was actually nothing like Spalding, but his antics elicited the same scolding disapproval from our caddie master, Skip, that Spalding got from his grandfather, Judge Smails: "Spaaalding! You're going to play golf and you're going to like it!"

But Danny didn't lack enthusiasm for golf. Or anything for that matter. He had a ponytail halfway down his back, a head as big as a basketball, and a personality like a John

Coltrane solo. I would like to say his enthusiasm made up for what he lacked in golf knowledge (and skill), but it often made things worse. My very first loop at the Olympic Club was case in point.

Danny and I were somewhere on the front nine, still ingratiating ourselves with our players. We were in the midst of that initial, delicate introductory period, four or five holes, say, when you have to feel out their personalities and earn their trust. This is not the time you want to boldly misread a putt or be too pushy with the club or shot selection. Best to be soft-spoken and quietly supportive, make suggestions rather than emphatic statements. But Danny just poured it on strong right from the start like a carnival barker: "Step right up! It's a seven iron! Don't be shy! Play it on the left edge!"

There were a lot of guys who did this—like cigar-chomping Reese. He was just as forward. But he could pull it off because he'd mastered the whole salty, seen-it-all-before routine. He persuasively purveyed the "This is my turf and I take shit from no one" attitude. He barked out orders in that authoritative pitch somewhere between a knowledgeable bass and impatient tenor with just the right amount of sharpness to trigger the obedient schoolboy inside even the most self-important millionaire.

But Danny's forwardness was more "improvisational." Maybe it came from the whole jazz thing, the fact that he made at least part of his living engaging strangers on the street corner, playing his horn lively and colorfully enough to keep their attention. He probably even heckled them when they didn't stop to listen or pay him a tip. And just when we were beginning to ingratiate ourselves with that first foursome at Olympic, Danny totally overwhelmed one of his players with too much information. The guy had a simple wedge shot into a par four and all he needed was an accurate yardage. As Danny went on and on about the grass density, wind speed, barometric pressure, and God knows what else, I could see the guy getting more and more rattled with every word. I wasn't surprised when he rushed the shot and chunked it into the bunker. But he was a gentleman, and he was about to take a deep breath and let it go. But Danny wouldn't let it go.

He grabbed the guy's wedge out of his hand and said, "Now, what you did wrong there was, you lifted your head. What you *want* to do is focus on a specific spot on the ball, a dimple, say . . ."

Danny reached into his apron pocket and threw a ball down on the fairway. His player was too stunned to object, and we were already walking ahead, never suspecting in a million years that a caddie, even one with Danny's audacity, would actually attempt to hit a demonstration shot. But that's exactly what Danny did.

"You see that dimple right there? The one shining on the back of the ball? You just keep your eyes focused right on that! And swing away!"

And Danny swung. But apparently he didn't keep his eye on the ball either, because he skulled it. Badly. A head-high screamer that whistled past our ears at skull-crushing speed and crashed into the trees behind the green. The entire group ducked as though we'd just received incoming rocket fire, and my guy gasped, "Holy shit! Does he do that regularly?"

Danny's guy was so stunned—perhaps even worried the

situation could escalate—that he gently extracted the club from Danny's hand and said, "Thank you, Danny. I totally see what you were trying to say."

And we all carried on like nothing had happened.

Fortunately, even Danny was rattled by the involuntary manslaughter attempt he called a golf shot, and he decided to tone it down for the rest of the round. At the end, the guys paid us the regular rate and thanked us politely. Even smiled and patted Danny on the back. But I guarantee you they went straight to the caddie master and asked him never to put them out with that psycho caddie again.

I could hear Skip's voice clear across the continent. "Spaaaaalding!"

I might've felt sorry for the Olympic Club members for not having a better caddie yard, but it was their own damn fault. I mean, seriously, can you think of a more appropriate place to have a professional caddie yard than a club that has hosted four US Opens and three US Amateurs, a club that is consistently ranked among the top twenty courses in the country and is on the "must play" list of every avid golfer in the world? Wouldn't it be nice to have a polished veteran caddie read the greens properly and regale the group with historic anecdotes right there in the places where they happened?— where Jack Fleck made his birdie putt to tie Hogan in 1955, where Billy Casper hit any number of amazing shots in 1966 to erase a six-shot deficit to tie Arnold Palmer, and where Scott Simpson and Tom Watson went back and forth in '87. All three of those huge names—Hogan, Palmer, Watson— ended up losing (two of them in playoffs) and never won another major again. Now, that is some history! It's certainly worth having a caddie crew knowledgeable enough to share some of it.

But for us it was nice that the Olympic yard was the *Bad News Bears* of caddying, because that meant drifters like me and saxophone-playing Danny and Swedish Sven traveling around the States for the summer could just roll in and work there for a few weeks. We could play there on Mondays, too, on the famous Lake Course. It's not always easy to pick up short-term work, because caddie masters who run fully functional caddie programs like to keep their yards stocked with just the right number of guys so there is always a caddie available when a member wants one but not so many that there isn't enough work to go around. This is a delicate balance, and there isn't always room for one more.

Olympic's low and fluctuating demand was a frustrating situation for the caddies trying to make a steady living but great for a wanderer like me, because if I didn't get work, I was just as happy to take the day off. I'd walk out the front gate to the Pacific Coast Highway and hitch a ride around Lake Merced to Harding Park, an amazing old public course on the opposite shore that was designed in the twenties by Willie Watson and Sam Whiting, the same pair who designed the Lake Course.

The greens were a little slower, the bunkers a little rough around the edges, the sand a little inconsistent, but the holes were excellent and the layout beautiful. Unlike Olympic, which really has only one hole on the lake (and even that one, a tight little par three, sits down so low among the trees, there's no real sense of being on the water), at Harding the dramatic finishing holes are up high on a bluff overlooking the lake. Some afternoons the sunlight slanted through the towering pines and turned the surface of the lake gold, and some afternoons the fog rolled in with wispy arms that wrapped around the trunks and coiled above the water. It's a magical place, and I spent many weekday afternoons walking those fairways alone—teeing off after three and still getting in eighteen for only $14.

My most memorable afternoon was during the member-guest tournament when Carlo took the day off and we caddied together in a group with Jim Plunkett, the famous Oakland Raiders quarterback. There was nothing particularly special about Plunkett (his skills were clearly limited to the football field), but it was a beautiful day, in the high eighties, not a breath of wind. We were off the course by one and walked out the front gate across the PCH to Fort Funston—the state park where the hang gliders launch off the cliffs and fly out over the Pacific. There are miles of horseback and hiking trails that switchback down the bluffs to a beautiful secluded beach studded with rock stacks and protected coves. We hiked down next to the horses with our beach towels over our shoulders and dived into the glassy chest-high waves.

The water in San Fran is as cold as it is in Alaska—the current flows north-south along the West Coast, so it is basically melted icebergs. But the surface temperature near the beach can fluctuate massively from day to day, depending on the wind and alongshore currents, and that day the water was up in the high sixties. I know, I know, that sounds freezing to most sane summer beachgoers, but believe me, that's like the Caribbean for San Francisco, and it was almost ninety degrees out. We frolicked, floated, body-surfed, spouted water like whales. We swam for hours and then sat on the beach for a bit before jumping back in and swimming some more. And then when the sun began to arc out over the watery horizon, we climbed back up the cliffs to the Olympic Club, hopped in Carlo's car and drove over to Harding for a sunset nine. That's as good as caddying gets, and it never would've been possible if the Olympic Club had been all buttoned up and serious about the caddie program.

On my last Monday in town, Carlo and I headed out to play the Lake Course in midafternoon. It was a gray, foggy day. The Lake's cypress trees were cloaked in ghostly robes. The shots seemed to ring out louder in the stillness, like firecrackers. The ball would disappear into passing tufts of mist and then reappear like a falling hailstone. It was an eerie day, and there was no one out there because the Lake was technically closed. But Carlo and I were never ones to let a technicality get in the way of anything, least of all golf.

We played until dark, and when we hit our tee shots off eighteen, Carlo said, "I've got a surprise for your last round at Olympic."

He dug into his golf bag, pulled out a little rolled-up zip-lock sandwich bag, and handed it to me. Then he pulled out a pair of glow-in-the-dark golf balls and four fresh light sticks. I opened the ziplock bag and peered inside. It contained two big, perfectly formed magic mushrooms—powdery white with purple veins running down the stems. Carlo smiled. "Psychedelic night golf!"

We sat Indian style on the eighteenth tee box and ate the mushrooms with some snacks we'd brought and a couple more beers. We waited until darkness fell completely before firing up the balls. We played the short eighteenth up the hill and then snuck around the side of the clubhouse and teed off the first hole. The mushrooms were starting to kick in.

Glow-in-the-dark balls leave tracers under the soberest circumstances, but now they were beginning to leave trails that hung in the air like swooshes of a highlighter pen. And when the ball was sitting on the tee, it illuminated the mist around it like one of those Hubble Space Telescope pictures of a spiral galaxy—the ball the bright nucleus surrounded by clouds of gas and stars. I felt like a giant god swatting entire galaxies around for my entertainment.

When we reached the second hole, the trip was in full swing and everything had shifted. I was tiny now. The cypress trees had become giant heads of broccoli and the ball a little firefly surrounded by fairy dust. It was my little magical companion who flew at my command. And rather than render me useless, the mushrooms had imbued me with a ninja-like command of my faculties. I was able to shape the flight of the ball at will. Right to left. Left to right. High. Low. And the little hole through the middle of the ball where the light stick slides in emitted a high-pitched whistle in flight. This whistle became the voice of my firefly squealing with joy as she zipped through the air.

Glow-in-the-dark balls fly only about 75 percent as far as regular balls, and we usually played with a single club, a five or six iron; it was never about the score. We played a match, the wager being that the loser of each hole had to carry the cooler of beer. I have no idea how many holes we played or what I shot. That hardly mattered. Even when you're keeping score, golf is all about focusing on the shot at hand, the total score being a sum of those shots. On magic mushrooms, each shot was an act of self-expression—a karate kick, a pirouette, a paintbrush stroke. The course was an arena, a stage, and a canvas.

That's the way it felt playing in the backcountry, too. Going beyond the simple visual appreciation of a landscape and interacting with it beyond the reach of the physical body. Launching shots across canyons and rivers and down mountainsides and beaches. The motion of the body determining the motion of the ball—its flight an extension of the body like a spider riding the wind on a silken thread or a perfectly cast fly arcing down onto the surface of the water.

This is the part of the game that is hard for nongolfers to see. You have to play to feel it. It isn't visible through the TV screen or from outside the picket fences and privet hedges. The forest gets lost in trees of tartan and argyle, visors, and V-necks. Golf *seems* to be one thing but is very much another, and backcountry golf and mushroom night golf are as true to the nature of the game as any stuffy country club championship or Saturday Nassau or fourball.

And no matter how contrasting hitchhiking and golf may seem, the game has a long, rich vagabond history. Even the game's best players—Hogan, Nelson, Snead—used to carpool to tournaments back before the purses got big enough to fly first class or even fly at all. And I've heard stories of them hitchhiking to tournaments when the big old American boat they were driving broke down on some lonely Texas highway. Hell, John Daly slept in the parking lot at Crooked Stick in 1991 the night before he won the PGA Championship when he got in at the last minute as the ninth and final alternate and drove straight up from Arkansas. And on highways and in parking lots all over the country, you will find mini-tour players and caddies chasing their dreams out of the trunk of their car.

The game is a journey, both literally and metaphorically. It traverses landscapes. It fosters relationships. It offers up life lessons and moments of insight and inspiration, and we play forever in search of that elusive, unattainable perfection that recedes before us into the horizon. It is a trip—not always magical but never mundane.

5

SOUTHERN BELL

SECESSION GOLF CLUB,
BEAUFORT, SC,
1998–1999

I took the train from San Francisco back to Aspen—the Amtrak with the huge glass viewing car. As much as I'd loved hitchhiking, it was a pleasure to just sit back and watch the scenery roll past as I drifted in and out of sleep. A couple of friends picked me up at the station in Glenwood Springs, and the next morning I was back on the fairways of Maroon Creek. I spent the rest of that year in Aspen and then finally succumbed to my dad's pressure to return to the East Coast and get a "real job."

I couldn't stop thinking about the one hitchhiking piece I'd written in my journal and the encouraging words of the salesman who'd picked me up in Austin, Nevada: "Write a book about your adventure and send it to me at Falcon Press." I sent a copy of the story to my dad, and although I wouldn't describe his reaction as *enthusiastic*, he wasn't entirely opposed to the idea of my becoming a writer—a possibility that caused me to question the necessity of my leaving Aspen. After all, the town had a local newspaper, and a magazine, too. But my dad's concerns about my focus and discipline aside, even I feared there were too many distractions in Aspen with skiing, golfing, mountain biking, hiking, camping, and of course, partying. I agreed with him that Connecticut would be an easier place to get off to a good start. So I headed home.

I took up my old job caddying at Stanwich while I looked for a writing position. I interviewed to be a junior reporter at the *Norwalk Hour* in Norwalk, Connecticut, but they didn't find my hitchhiking story to be very "journalistic." On a lead from a friend, I sent a letter to *The Golfer* magazine to inquire about an assistant editor position. My cousin Amy got me an interview to be an editorial assistant at *Travel + Leisure Golf*, but a friend told me that was a "girl's job." And even without this insult to my masculinity, I wasn't completely sold on the idea of becoming a writer by sitting in an office editing other people's writing. That seemed to defeat the purpose.

My pursuit of these jobs was tepid at best, and I could feel my dad's growing impatience. This was the height of the late-nineties economic boom, and unemployment was almost nonexistent. You had to *try* to not get a job. But in a fateful twist, my indecisiveness ultimately ended up securing me a freelance writing gig at both of those magazines because my more career-oriented and persistent friend Colin got the assistant editor job at *The Golfer* and another friend, Tom, became an assistant and eventually senior editor at *Travel + Leisure Golf*. My dad's favorite mantra was "The early bird gets the worm." Mine became "Good things come to those who wait."

That summer Colin accepted my first piece, a silly caddie story about the Maroon Creek Club. This minor success inspired me to begin writing my caddie memoirs, which I'd given the ingenious title "Loopers." The only problem was that the content itself wasn't nearly as brilliant as the title. I didn't yet have enough caddie experience for it to qualify as a memoir, and whatever latent writing skill I possessed, my muse was very fickle and came and went of its own unnerving free will. But I was determined to persevere, so I continued caddying in the name of research. Whenever anyone asked what I was doing with my life, that's what I told them. I wasn't caddying; I was *researching a book about caddying.*

My dad rolled his eyes at this artful bit of denial, especially when I told him this "research" required me to follow my old friends Buzz and Buddha down south for the winter to caddie at the Secession Golf Club in Beaufort, South Carolina. Now that I was twenty-seven, I know he feared that my wanderlust might be an incurable condition and this latest misadventure a permanent detour. I could see it in his eyes when I pulled out of the driveway in late September. I tapped the horn and waved enthusiastically. He just smiled weakly and nodded his head.

I'd like to say that I had a "grand plan," but the truth is, I was far from confident in my writing abilities, and I knew the book was a bit of a smoke screen. My decision was driven by two simple, compatible factors: I did *not* want to work in an office, and I was superexcited about the prospect of another adventure.

The next afternoon, after a twelve-hour drive south down

Interstate 95, I rolled into Beaufort—a historic small town on the Intracoastal Waterway halfway between Savannah and Charleston. This area, known as the Low Country, is South Carolina's version of the Bayou—a massive expanse of tidal marshes and inland waterways that flow in from the Atlantic and wrap around peninsulas and sandy islands dense with mossy oak.

The course took its name from the Articles of Secession, which officially began the War Between the States (known north of the Mason-Dixon Line as the Civil War). They were signed in Beaufort, which is also famous for being one of the very few towns that Sherman spared from the torch on his victorious march south and is therefore blessed with an abundance of pre–Civil War homes, many of them lining the streets on the waterfront next to downtown.

Beaufort is defined by water or, more precisely, by the presence and *absence* of water. There are two Beauforts: the one at high tide and the one at low tide. I arrived at low tide, and it was a frightening sight. The gigantic marsh along Boundary Road looked the way I imagine the seabed looks right before a tsunami—it had suffered an unnatural draining that revealed to the air parts of the world meant to remain submerged. The mud gurgled and popped like a dying person, the last little rivulets of greasy water draining out like pools of blood. Great gray oyster reefs covered the muddy humps amidst fields of razor grass with blades as menacing as Spanish bayonets. Even the oak trees looked drained, bent toward the muddy basin, their mossy beards dangling in the midday heat. This was indeed the Low Country, the bottom of the earth, the *Too Low* Country.

Buzz and Buddha had driven down before me, and I

found them staying on the edge of town at the single rattiest motel I've ever seen in my life, and that is saying something, because I've stayed in some places rats would think twice about. When I looked inside the room and saw at least six cockroaches perched on the walls, I asked Buddha why the hell they were staying in such a shithole.

He shrugged. "They're palmetto bugs."

"Call them what you want. They're disgusting!"

The two of them were sitting out front in the dirt parking lot. They'd set up folding chairs and a little charcoal grill beside their door. They were cooking hot dogs and drinking beer, as was everyone else at the motel. It looked like a tailgating party for people without a sport.

There is no secret about Southerners' propensity for drinking. The languid air breeds it. We sat there for hours, cracking one cold sweating can of Bud after another, contemplating the marsh and moss-draped oaks. Occasionally we grunted indecipherable and inconsequential comments to one another, like "Egret."

"No regrets."

"Some."

"More herons."

"Exactly."

"Bud?"

"Forever."

"True dat."

The sun set. The moon rose. The heat clung.

Sometime after dark, a big black woman sauntered over, her hips swinging like two giant flour sacks. "Can one of you nice boys help me get some Pampers for my baby?"

Without blinking, Buzz said, "John here will help you."

I looked over my shoulder to see if there was another guy I hadn't noticed, named John. There wasn't. I didn't appreciate being volunteered without my consent, but not wanting to be a man who refused to help a woman get diapers for her baby, I agreed to drive her to the store.

She was so big that it was nearly impossible to shift the gears with her sitting in the passenger seat. As soon as we pulled out onto the road and I'd pushed the stick halfway into her thigh to get it in third, her giant hand slithered over my leg and onto my crotch. I was so shocked, I almost lost control of the car. I swerved across the center line and then all the way back across the shoulder onto the grass as I tried to dig her groping paw out from between my legs. She leaned close and breathed in my ear. "You want me to suck your cock?"

"No!"

"Come on. Twenty dollars."

Then she tried to go down on me. She tugged at my belt and wedged her huge shoulders between my chest and the steering wheel. The tires were now squealing as my car zigzagged back and forth across the road. We were going to die if I didn't get her off of me. I grabbed her by the hair and ripped her head out of my lap. She let out a bloodcurdling scream and smacked me on the side of the face. I slammed on the brakes and we skidded to a halt in the dirt shoulder.

"I thought you needed Pampers for your baby!"

"I ain't even got no baby."

"Then get out!"

"Take me to the next road."

I looked closely at the woman, sized her up. I wasn't sure

I could win a fight with her if she *really* tried to have her way with me.

"I'll take you to the next road if you keep your hands off me."

"Fine."

I turned onto the next road, a dark, wooded dead end with dilapidated trailers scattered among the trees. My car was immediately surrounded by a dozen men. They weren't smiling. The big woman got out and slammed the door. Barked something at them. I didn't wait around to see what would happen next. I threw it in reverse and pressed the accelerator to the floor.

When I got back to the motel, Buzz and Buddha were sitting right where I'd left them. Totally relaxed. Beers in hand. Two more dogs on the grill. I was covered in sweat, my hair disheveled, my fly unzipped.

"Did you get her Pampers?" Buzz asked with a wicked grin. They both chuckled.

"You jerks! You knew she didn't have a baby!"

I sat down. Cracked a Bud. Threw a third dog on the grill. An owl hooted somewhere in the dark.

• • •

The golf course was built right through the marsh— surrounded by water at high tide and mudflats at low. Great blue herons and snowy egrets stalked the flats for crabs, and giant alligators slumbered next to the freshwater ponds on the course's interior. There were a few big, beautiful oaks scattered about the property, all gnarled and twisted like tortured souls, and a few dead ones sticking out of the marsh like bleached skeletons. But most of the course was wide open and flat, hemmed in on three sides by water and the other by pines that grew in prim, orderly abundance toward the center of the island.

When the tide was in, the fairways and greens were islands, only the tips of the razor grass swaying above the surface of the water. When it was out, the highest parts of the marsh, near the shore, dried in the sun and became white and sandy, like firm bunkers. The mud dried on the blades of razor grass, turning them purplish gray, and they blended together like rumpled velvet in the soft afternoon light.

But their velvet appearance belied their ability to administer vicious little slices to the legs and arms of any golfer foolish enough to pursue his ball into the deeper, danker sections of marsh where the mud grew soft and slick and could suck a shoe right off your foot and a golfer right off his feet. This happened more than a couple of times, forcing poor fellows to finish their rounds with their clothes covered with mud. And it happened to the occasional caddie, too, myself included, when I got a little too brave in pursuit of balls one day and went down in my white jumpsuit (our Secession caddie uniform) and came up looking like a house painter who'd just had a can of black paint thrown on him. I'd even heard of a caddie getting swallowed up to his waist, so thoroughly stuck, it took all four of his golfers to pull him loose.

I began to view the marshes warily after that—like quicksand or tar pits waiting to claim the careless mammal (me) that strayed from the safety of solid ground. In fact, I viewed the entire Low Country that way—a primordial swamp from which we'd emerged and evolved and were no longer equipped to survive, our soft, unscaled, unfeathered skin vulnerable to all the sharp, scratchy, biting, sucking things that teemed and swooped and rustled and splashed everywhere. Even up on the fairways, it took a gallon of DEET (insect repellent that is also a solvent powerful enough to melt a golf glove) to fend off the clouds of aptly named no-see-ums—invisible flies that attack with the ferocity of nanohornets. And I was careful not to stumble blindly around the edge of the ponds, because there were gigantic alligators everywhere, some-times sunning themselves on the banks, sometimes floating with only their eyeballs above the water like periscopes on an attack submarine. Maybe I'd watched too much *Mutual of Omaha's Wild Kingdom* as a kid, but I was sure they were waiting for an opportunity to lunge out of the water and take me down like a wounded zebra. It probably didn't help when another caddie told me they could run thirty miles an hour and that I should "run in zigzags if one of them chased me, because they can't make sharp turns."

If one of them chased me?

Their rumored speed made their inertness even more dis-turbing. Their constant, quiet presence—just floating, lying, looking—drove me nuts. Like they were trying to lull me into complacency. Hypnotize me with their languid, lidless death-ray eyes. I was determined to call their bluff some-how—make one of the things jump and expose its true man-eating nature—but when I finally succeeded in doing this, it was far more bizarre and frightening than anything I'd imag-ined, anything I'd seen on *Wild Kingdom*. The image haunts me to this day.

I was caddying for a dentist from Cleveland. We were on the fourth hole, and a big sucker was sunning himself next to a little water hole in front of the tee. I gave the gator a wide berth, paused and stared at it. Marveled at its size, at it's whole *prehistoricness*. It was lying diagonally with its tail toward me, its left eye locked on me. I reached into my pocket and dug out a ball I'd found in the marsh on the previous hole. I inched a little closer and tossed the ball underhand at its head.

I don't know what I thought was going to happen or why I thought it was a good idea to provoke the thing, but let me tell you, an alligator's rumored speed is not just a rumor. That reptile whipped its head around and snapped its jaws as fast as an angry wolf.

I stumbled backward and fell. I was about to jump up and run in zigzags when I froze because I saw something white gleaming in its teeth—and I'm not talking about the teeth themselves (the row upon row of flesh shredders). The gator had caught my golf ball in its mouth and was holding it up and hissing like a pissed-off, butt-ugly circus seal who's finally had it with the beach-ball routine.

Now I turned and ran. When I reached the dentist I breathlessly told him what had happened, but it was clear he didn't believe me because he just frowned and said, "Please focus on caddying."

I was determined to prove to him I wasn't lying. Several holes later, as we were walking along the edge of another pond, I tapped him on the shoulder and nodded toward a fat gator sunning on the bank. I inched toward the scaled behemoth and tossed a ball at its head, but the thing didn't even budge.

I quickly dug another ball from his bag and tried again. Still nothing. Now the dentist was convinced his caddie was crazy.

"Please stop throwing my balls to the alligator!" he scolded and stormed off.

"I'd love to throw your balls to the alligator," I mumbled as I followed him.

When I arrived for my loop the next day, the caddie master, Joe, told me I was no longer caddying for the dentist, which was fine with me. But he didn't say it like it was good news. He said it real quiet, then stood there tapping his pencil against his clipboard with his eyebrows raised as if to ask, *Do you want to know why you're not caddying for the dentist?*

I stared blankly. *Not really.*

His eyes narrowed. "I hear you've been abusing our alligators."

He said "our alligators" as though he didn't mean the Secession Club's alligators, but the whole damn *South's* alligators. Which was completely laughable, because Southern boys don't throw golf balls at alligators. They shoot them in the head and turn them into boots and burgers.

But I took it on the chin and did my best impression of contrition. I promised never to bother *his* alligators again. Joe gave me the rest of the day off, told me to go home and think about it. When I walked down the long road to the caddie parking lot, I passed by the pond on eleven. That same fat gator was sunning himself on the bank. I flipped him the bird.

• • •

After the gator episode, Joe's temper always simmered dangerously close to the surface. He was like the Southern version of Millweed, back in Maroon Creek, harboring some unseen chip on his shoulder that he took out on those below him, namely me.

In his defense and the defense of all the Southerners who expressed less than enthusiastic feelings toward Northerners, the packs of Yankee golfers who came down could be pretty obnoxious. There was a running joke that the club was called Secession because *it* had seceded from the South—sworn its allegiance to New York, Chicago, Philadelphia, and wherever else the wealthy Northern golfers came from.

They came in packs, what I would come to know all too well as buddy trips—weekend golf getaways that were like bachelor-party reunions. Anywhere from four to twelve guys escaping the wife and kids, getting way too loud and drunk, putting each other in headlocks, pinching the waitresses' asses, using the word *fuck* as a verb, adverb, adjective, and noun, often in the same sentence: "Fuck you! You're so fucking fucked, you fugly fuck!"

But these packs of overgrown frat boys paid well, so Joe tied a neat little bow around his loathing, put it in his back pocket, laughed along with them, and gratefully and humbly accepted the greenbacks they palmed him. But God save the next caddie who bumped into him and loosened that bow, because Joe's anger would come popping out like a mad, axe-wielding jack-in-the-box.

Believe me, I know. I untied that bow regularly with the dexterity of a Christmas elf.

My trouble with Joe caused some of the regular Secession caddies to give me a wide berth because they knew all too well how the wrath of Joe could be doled out in relentless, unforgiving measure. They'd worked hard to carve out their niches in Joe's system and wanted no part of his bad side nor

When I confronted John about it, he shrugged. "It didn't seem that heavy to me."

"That's 'cause you're a freak of nature!"

Carrying one heavy bag and one light bag is even worse than carrying two heavy ones. By the end of the round, I felt I'd developed scoliosis, my back bent permanently to the right.

When we stepped off the eighteenth green, the player who owned the heavy bag asked me what the caddie fee was. I told him $28.50. (The caddie fees at Secession were so low that working there after Maroon Creek felt like being demoted from the major leagues to AA ball.) He nodded and dug into the bottom of the bag's large side pocket—the place where most of the weight had been. I hadn't bothered to check why it was so heavy, because there was nothing I could've done about it. I figured it was just a bunch of extra balls.

But it wasn't extra balls. It was a giant freezer bag with something shiny in it. I didn't really focus on it until I heard John laugh. A loud booming laugh. And believe me, that was something, because John never laughed. I turned and looked closely at the bag. It was full of change. *Years* of change. Quarters, nickels, dimes, even pennies! It looked like the jar that had been my savings bank when I was a kid.

The guy handed me the bag and held out his hand to shake mine. "Thanks," he said, beaming. "You did a great job!"

I looked at his hand. I looked at his smiling face. He was dead serious. He'd just had me carry around a bag of change and was now trying to pay me with it. I was too stunned to object and when the guy walked off, John howled, "We literally carried around our weight in gold!"

I shot him a mean look. "That would've been fine if it was actually *gold* and not damned nickels and pennies!"

John and I argued about who was going to cash in the bag of change and then how we were going to divvy up the money. We couldn't agree, so finally we just auctioned it off in the caddie yard to the highest bidder and ended up getting fifty bucks for it.

It turned out to be $88.73.

I carried around $88.73 in change for two hours for a lousy $25. Unbelievable.

Timmy and I became the closest friends of the four of us, by far. He was a lovable little sweetheart of a man. And when I say little, I mean like five-foot-two little. He had this giant, extra-long Killer Bee driver that was nearly as tall as he was. He could hit the shit out of it too. We were allowed to play the course only on the first Monday of every month (yet another reason I pined for Maroon Creek). On those Mondays, Timmy and I often teamed up against Alden and John, and we usually beat them like a drum, because Alden thought he was way better than he actually was and would let his ego get in the way of common sense, and John just quietly accepted whatever teams were agreed upon because he knew the winners had to pay for the drinks afterward anyway, and that's all he was interested in.

We drank at Stewbies, a marina and restaurant on the Intracoastal Waterway where snowbirds docked their boats to refuel and rest on their way south for the winter. Some stayed for weeks, some for months. I made friends with one couple who were in the middle of an around-the-world sail. They'd just crossed the Atlantic and were relaxing for the winter in Beaufort before setting out on their second leg, through the Panama Canal into the Pacific. I spent many evenings enjoying sunset drinks on their boat and listening to their stories—having their sails torn to shreds in a gale off the Azores, losing their engine in the windless doldrums of the mid-Atlantic, catching tuna and eating sashimi that was so fresh the meat was still warm. I shared some stories of my own and was flattered by how much they enjoyed them. They made me feel I was on my own around-the-world sail. I liked that romantic vision of caddying as a vehicle that carries you to beautiful far-flung places, the golf courses like ports where you dock for a while, fix your sails, replenish your supplies, and then set sail again the following season for another destination.

My experience in Beaufort was very much like that. It was a place I might never have visited if I hadn't come there to caddie. Caddying enabled me to stay there for six months, immerse myself in the place, and really get to know the people—the whole Low Country culture, with its shrimp boils and oyster bakes, its backwoods barbecue joints and old stone churches. Its miles of waterways and marshes were dotted with fishing boats and sailboats and shrimpers, even diving boats, from which divers descended their anchor lines into the murky water to collect prehistoric megalodon shark teeth from the mud. The local arts scene was rich with painters and writers whose works were displayed in galleries and bookstores along Main Street.

If you drove east toward the coast, way, way out across island after island, bridge after bridge, through the rustic little town of Frogmore (after which the famous local dish Frogmore stew was named—shrimp, sausage, potatoes, and corn all boiled together in a giant pot with Old Bay Seasoning), you eventually came to a beautiful sandy, oak-forested island right on the Atlantic called Hunting Island, where the ocean waves crashed right into the forest at high tide and the beach became wide and smooth and hard packed at low.

One time Timmy and I took our golf clubs out there and played up the beach for a good mile, picking the little pointed remains of tree stumps for holes—stumps that had been submerged at high tide and were now ringed with a small water-filled depression that acted as a perfect hole. We carried three clubs: a seven iron, sand wedge, and putter, sometimes putting from as far away as fifty yards on the smooth hard sand. The ball always broke sharply to the sea, and the longer shots bounced and rolled that way, too, so you had to aim dangerously close to the trees to keep the ball in play. Afterward we blasted drivers up and down the beach—standing three hundred yards apart and trying to bounce our drives off each other's feet. Hunting Island had campsites, too, and I spent many nights under the oak trees at the edge of the sea, sleeping to the sound of crashing waves.

There were two peak golf seasons in South Carolina. There was the fall, from late September, when the humid summer heat finally abated, until December, when the cold crept down from the north, and there was the spring, from the beginning of February until the heat returned in mid May. In the fall, I rented a room from one of the waitresses at Stewbies, a sweetheart of a girl named Mary, who was also a part-time nurse. And then in the spring I found a single-room cottage out on one of the islands. It was right on the edge of the Intracoastal Waterway, surrounded by acres of woods. A friend who owned a little fishing boat would pick me up on a dock just down from my house, and we'd speed off through marshes, anchor at the mouth of one of the many small channels, and cast our net just as the tide turned and started to rush out, dragging all of the shrimp out with it. Our net would come up popping with translucent shrimp. We'd pour them into the live-bait wells in the back, and on the way home, as the dropping tide exposed the massive, muddy oyster reefs, we'd hop down off the boat, carve oysters out of their shells, and eat them right there on the reef.

On Masters weekend, we boiled the shrimp in a huge pot at my cottage, sat on my screened porch, and watched the tournament against the backdrop of the oak and pine forest and the glittering waterway. The birds in the forest around us echoed the birds on the TV above the fairways of Augusta.

Watching the tournament that year, 1999, was very special because Timmy and I had gone to a practice round earlier in the week—the first time I'd been to Augusta. We drove the winding oak-shaded roads up out of the Low Country, through the little town of Yemassee, where we stopped for some amazing barbecue. We crossed I-95 and kept heading west into the pine-scented South Carolina hills that rolled right into Augusta on the Georgia–South Carolina border.

The town of Augusta stood out in trashy, mass-consumerist contrast to the gentrified confines of the tournament. The road to the club was basically one long strip of chain stores—Waffle House, Pizza Hut, Hooters—and a ton of cheap hotels, whose parking lots had all been transformed for the week into the golf equivalent of a Grateful Dead show. Camper vans and RVs were set up everywhere, pop tops extended, generators buzzing. People were grilling and drinking and lounging in beach chairs on the pavement. More industrious souls were hawking everything from hats and T-shirts to time shares and golf-club memberships. There was even a mock cabin of a corporate jet in one parking lot to lure people into purchasing shares of NetJets. It was mayhem. This was years before John Daly got taken to the hospital after passing out in a Hooters parking lot (claiming that he'd been sleeping with his eyes open), but I saw at least a hundred other people who looked as though they were about to suffer the same fate.

Timmy and I bought a pair of tickets from a scalper and sprinted the last hundred yards to the gate in excitement, like two little kids running to the entrance of Disney World. We arrived at the turnstile huffing and puffing. Took one last deep breath, smiled, high-fived each other, and pushed through into a hushed world that was so strikingly different from where we'd just come, it felt as though we'd passed through a star gate or time machine, been beamed to one of those peaceful garden planets in the old *Star Trek* episodes.

The crude chaos vanished, and we found ourselves walking through a row of shaded pines out onto grass that was so perfectly groomed, it looked like AstroTurf. We had not come in through the famous Magnolia Drive but instead through a side gate and so were standing behind the tenth tee looking down a fairway that I should've recognized after years of seeing it on TV. I could describe a hundred shots that had been played there over the years—long bounding drives, clutch curling putts, great escapes from the pine straw and the talcum sand—but it looked nothing like what I'd imagined. The fairway was as steep as a ski run. It plummeted down the hill toward Rae's Creek. And the fairway was as wide as a superhighway. In fact, the entire property was much hillier and more open than it appeared on TV, the screen having flattened and cropped everything. The greens, especially, were so warped and pitched, they made the infamous Stanwich greens seem tame by comparison. From where we were standing, we could see clear across eight or more holes—ten and eighteen, one, two, and three, seven, eight, and nine, even seventeen peeking through a row of pines way, way down beyond the seventh green.

The practice round was a great time to see the course, because it was uncrowded and informal. We moved around with ease, rarely waited in line for food and beer, and even managed to find a private little spot behind a hedge, where we smoked a bowl and kicked back in the sun as distant cheers rose and subsided in the pines. It was a heavenly afternoon.

We headed home pretty early, retraced our route back down into the dark, dank Low Country. Sometime after dark, when we were back under the thick, bearded canopy of oaks, we passed an old graveyard and decided to pull over to have a few nips from a bottle of whiskey we'd bought for the trip.

Timmy was buzzing pretty good at this point. He'd done some damage to the whiskey bottle already, and his cheeks had reached their usual late-night luster—not so much a bar tan as a bar *burn*.

The graveyard was deserted. The road was deserted. Clouds passed over the moon. Shadows passed over the headstones and tombs. The iron gate was ajar, its bars topped with Gothic spearhead finials. The place exuded vampiric energy.

We found a row of headstones in the soft grass. Timmy leaned against one and I leaned against another, and we passed the whiskey bottle back and forth and watched the moon duck in and out of the clouds.

I howled like a werewolf.

"Don't do that."

I howled again.

"I'm serious!"

And he was serious. I could tell by his voice. There was genuine fear in it.

I didn't do it again. But when I got up to take a piss, I decided to play a trick on Timmy. I walked way off into the woods, then circled around behind the graveyard, snuck up behind him, and waited.

After I'd been gone for way longer than it would take to piss, Timmy called out, "John?"

I didn't answer. It was hard to keep from chuckling. I was so close behind him that if I'd breathed too loud, he'd have heard me.

After another couple of minutes, he shuffled nervously. Craned his neck. Peered through the dark. "John! That's not funny!"

I waited silently. Trying desperately not to chuckle.

When he called my name a third time, I jumped out from behind a headstone and yelled, "Boo!"

Timmy shrieked. He tried to jump to his feet but fell over and spilled the whiskey bottle. When he finally got his feet under him and turned to me, I saw the look of genuine terror on his face. Tears welled up in his eyes. "Why did you do that?"

My smile vanished. I immediately regretted it. I hadn't meant to really *scare* him, just make him jump. But it was obvious that I'd done much more than that. I'd stirred up something deep inside him, jolted open a dark door that was best left closed.

This became more obvious when we got in the car. Those tears didn't subside. They didn't quite pour out, but they glistened in his eyes, and Timmy began to gush a torrent of fears and shames—how small he was, how he was a failed golfer (the thing he was best at), and how he'd never amount to anything but an old drunk caddie, how his incredible knowledge of golf history—a nearly photographic recollection of every major tournament winner and runner-up, even their scores and the specifics of their rounds—was just a glorified parlor trick.

He went on and on.

I tried to comfort him, but he was so drunk and disappointed, so deep in his own dark thoughts, that he was just mumbling to the air, to the God who would never listen to him. He didn't even know I was there anymore.

Sometime later he passed out; he roused only long enough to make it from the car to the couch he slept on in a little side room in one of the caddie's houses.

Years later, after I'd moved on and lost touch with Timmy, I found out from another caddie that he had died. I don't know if it was from drinking specifically, but sadly I've no doubt it was from the broken heart drinking opened up, the terrible, unresolvable sadness behind his kind eyes.

This was my first glimpse of the dark side of caddying.

6

THE TURN

ATLANTIC GOLF CLUB, SHINNECOCK HILLS,
NATIONAL GOLF LINKS OF AMERICA,
THE HAMPTONS, NY,
1999–2001

Deep down in my heart of hearts, I knew that my "adventure" was just beginning. OK, it wasn't even that deep down. I loved the romantic vision the sailing couple wintering in Beaufort had of caddying as a round-the-world voyage, and I was very excited to pick the next "port" and throw my sails open to the wind. I wouldn't have given it a second thought or a moment's worry if it hadn't been for my dad. I knew he didn't approve of my continuing to caddie. To him it was just short-sighted self-indulgence that wouldn't lead to any good in the end. I disagreed with him on this point, but I didn't yet have the confidence to completely trust my convictions and I didn't dare use my "book" as an excuse again because I hadn't written a word down south, and whatever momentum I'd been riding from my first published story six months earlier had pretty much evaporated. I placated the warring sides of my conscience by taking what amounted to a "half-step," choosing for my next destination a place that was close enough to home and New York City—the "real world" and my family—that should I have a change of heart, I could easily reverse course. A place that was also, conveninently, a golf and caddie mecca—the Hamptons on eastern Long Island.

There are actually very few golf courses in the Hamptons, but the handful includes the National Golf Links of America, Shinnecock Hills, the Maidstone Club, and the Atlantic Golf Club. That's like having Magic Johnson, Michael Jordan, Larry Bird, and Kobe Bryant on the same team. I caddied at all four, but my "home" course became Atlantic for the simple reason that it was the first to offer me the job. This was not a poor decision. Atlantic granted the caddies four-day-a-week playing privileges, and the members paid us Maroon Creek–level tips. I have no idea what the bag fees were, but we averaged well over two hundred bucks a loop. It was like being called back up to the majors—Aspen-by-the-Sea.

Atlantic was known as the Jewish club at the other, non-Jewish (read: WASPy) clubs. And while this was somewhat true—Atlantic did have a lot of Jewish members—it was more accurately the club that was finally built to accommodate all of the wealthy golfers who, Jewish or not, had no chance of getting into the area's nepotistic, old-guard clubs. The Hamptons' population has grown so much that even the children of the members at those old-guard clubs are no longer guaranteed admission. That's why several more clubs have been built since. Incredibly, Atlantic, founded in 1990, is now considered somewhat old school.

From my caddiecentric point of view, Atlantic was also distinguishable for being the only black caddie yard in the Hamptons, probably because it was located right next to a historically black community in Bridgehampton.

This might not have been notable—lots of clubs have black caddies—if they hadn't all been Antiguan and Jamaican and so many of them related to one another—like the four brothers and their mother (who also caddied), two uncles, some other cousins, and close family friends, all from the same Antiguan town (I eventually learned Antigua isn't big enough for this to be much of a coincidence). I will quickly add here that I am *not* suggesting that the Antiguans were related to any of the Jamaicans. No, no, no. The foolishness of that idea was driven home many an afternoon when our peaceful coexistence was broken suddenly by some indiscernible slight, and the caddie yard instantly erupted into an inter-island war. Under duress, their island tongues, normally very beautiful and lyrical and somewhat easy to follow, became more and more frantic and fragmented, until they were shouting insults at one another in machine-gun patois.

"Galang a left mi!"

"Mi Gaan!"

"Cha! Babylon stepper! 'im boasie! Big Bout Yah!"

"Bumba Clot!"

"If you no wan' 'im go deh, den tek 'im out bwoy."

"Yaman! Dat bwoy 'im fine 'im mamma yard!"

And so on, louder and louder, until all the members on the range turned around to see what the hell was going on and the head pro himself had to step in to stop the fight. The head pro was the only one everyone immediately calmed down for. He was the big dog.

"Sorry, pro."

"No problem, boss."

"Mi fine."

And it would be back to peaceful coexistence as though nothing had ever happened.

Because Atlantic was a fairly new club (not even ten years old when I got there, having opened for play in 1992), many of the islanders had been there from the beginning, so the Atlantic yard was very much *their* yard. Ironically, because they were truly blood-relative family, I suddenly felt deprived of *my* new "family"—the independent, unattached, wandering souls, those who had no one to go home to at the end of the day, no spouses or kids or cousins, so gravitated toward each other and congregated in the bars after work, as Timmy, Big John, Alden, and I had done at Stewbie's down in Beaufort. We'd spent our evenings together and our days off playing golf together. When I expressed this sentiment to a Jamaican named Purple when we were out on a loop one day, he patted me on the back, smiled broadly, and said, "John bwoy, the key to happiness is a cold Red Stripe and good woman to keep your balls empty and your belly full!"

There were a few of us wanderers at Atlantic, though, like the kids from Ireland the caddie master, Lenny, invited over for the summer. The Hamptons have long been a summer destination for Irish kids coming of age. I have no idea how that tradition began, but you'd see packs of them in early June hovering around the pay phones with newspapers in hand calling every room-for-rent listing in the classifieds. This made them none too popular among the seasonal American employees, like me, who were also looking for rooms. But it was hard to feel ill will toward them, because, next to Canadians, the Irish are the friendliest people on earth. And besides, I found a room in the caddie convent.

The club provided housing for the regular golf staff on the property. The Antiguans and Jamaicans had their families and their community. The Irish kids slept piled on top of each other like puppies in some tiny, overpriced basement apartment. There were a couple of local kids who lived with their parents or families. The remaining few—the unhomed, the wayward souls—we had the convent.

The convent was a once proud, now drooping, weathered old mansion—a real-life House of Usher—named Maycroft. It was built by a wealthy New York family in the late 1800s on forty waterfront acres just across the bridge from the historic whaling village of Sag Harbor. At some point in the early twentieth century, a particularly religious or charitable family member gave the house to the Episcopal Church, and it became at various times a convent and a private girls' school. Eventually, in the early 1990s, the last of the sisters died, and, unable to decide what to do with the place, the Episcopal Church started renting the rooms out to seasonal workers. Once word got to nearby Atlantic, the tenants ended up being mostly caddies. The last caretaker for the sisters, Georgia, became our caretaker. God bless her soul.

There were only six bedrooms in the wing that served as the old dormitory, so we were a small group, which rotated over the years. My first summer, there was an old black gentleman, Dennis, who was nicknamed the King. And when I say *gentleman*, that's exactly what I mean. The King was in his sixties. He was tall and dignified and always had a smile on his face and a kind word to say. He was always dressed real sharp and drove a big, old-school Cadillac. He represented the best of caddying to me, how to do it right and make the most of a long career: develop long-standing relationships and devoted clients. I don't think he even carried bags anymore, just offered valued advice and companionship and always that warm smile and chuckle that could disarm the surliest curmudgeon. This was no small feat. It is a tricky business aging gracefully in the caddie world, because when the body begins to break down, walking all those miles day in and day out becomes increasingly difficult. And unless you've done some very "un-caddie-like" forward thinking and put aside a chunk of your money every season for decades you have no choice but to keep working until you drop because there's no retirement plan—no health insurance nor benefits of any kind. Yes, I've heard stories of generous and charitable members taking care of their favorite loopers for life and I've seen golf clubs slowly transition faithful, longtime loopers into ranger and locker room jobs when they can no longer carry the bags, but these are the exceptions, not the rule. Sadly, many more times I've seen the dark, flip side of that— old penniless caddies wasting away in some crappy old trailer or RV somewhere, subsisting on whatever charity their fellow caddies and remaining family members provide.

Down in Beaufort there'd been an ex–Tour caddie named Kevin who lived in an old trailer in the woods near Secession. He drank and chain-smoked menthols as he rattled and wheezed to anyone who would listen about his glory days out on the big Tour when he caddied in major championships for famous players who apparently didn't know or care that he existed anymore. The only people who did care, it seemed, were a few Secession caddies, myself included, who stopped over to play cards with him in the evenings and donate cigarettes, beer, and food.

So in contrast to that heartbreaking scenario and the sadness that had surfaced in Timmy in the cemetery, it was uplifting to find myself living with not one but two older caddies still enjoying and profiting from the game—the other being a soft-spoken fifty-something-year-old Midwesterner named Johnny. Granted he was a little younger than the King, but Johnny'd had open-heart surgery a few years back and was still carrying the bags! His son was an aspiring Tour player, and Johnny spent part of the off-season caddying for him on the mini-tours. Johnny loved country music, and I have fond memories of sharing a few beers with him in the evenings after work as we hit balls in the field in front of Maycroft, the doors of his pickup truck open wide and Willie Nelson and Waylon Jennings blaring from the speakers. He got so into the songs; he sang along and swayed to the music, totally transported, any concerns about his health or uncertain future laboring on the links temporarily forgotten in the warm glow of a blissful summer evening.

The remaining four of us were young and carefree, not thinking past the summer. There was Shane, a happy-go-lucky member of the staff who was a regular golf partner of mine on our off days. Lisa, a local waitress and aspiring writer whose parents had a house across the cove. And Steven—the only straight male ballet dancer in New York—who was out teaching Pilates for the summer and teaching himself to play guitar on the porch in the evenings. I'd been playing for a couple of years myself, so we gamely plucked away at acoustic classics by the Grateful Dead, Bob Dylan, and Neil Young.

Sag Harbor was affectionately known as the un-Hampton because of its authentic local and historic charm—its Cape houses and crumbling walls, its meandering streets and waterfronts, its Old Whalers' Church, single-screen movie theater, five-and-dime store, family grocery, and so on, a refreshing contrast to the increasing pomp and pretension of the neighboring towns.

The locals would argue with me, of course, say that the pomp and pretense were ruining Sag Harbor, too. I once had a woman cry in my arms at the Corner Bar because her family had been driven from the home they'd owned for generations by escalating real estate prices and property taxes. She tearfully told me about lamplighting for eels as a kid in the creeks off Three Mile Harbor and riding her bicycle for miles down the middle of empty roads that had now become deadly gauntlets of speeding, cell-phone-distracted supercars. By the end of her tale, I was in tears, too.

I love that old America. It's what I loved about Sag Harbor and all of the Hamptons—those beautiful old parts that still remained. The small, untended farm stands piled with baskets of tomatoes and corn and potatoes, the prices neatly printed on an index card next to the jar where you placed your money and took the change you were due. The brackish ponds spanned by little stone bridges where kids lured blue crabs into their nets with chicken legs tied to lines of garden string. The miles of dune-backed beaches marked by the silhouettes of fishermen surf-casting for striped bass in the autumn dusk.

Georgia, the caretaker, grew up in the Hamptons. She remembers when this was the complete picture, the whole cloth, as opposed to a tattered patchwork of remnants. And she, like many of the locals, had a hard time appreciating the parts that remained because it was painful for her to see it so diminished. That's why she loved Maycroft. Even on its last legs, in its crumbling state of disrepair, it was a reminder of quieter times when people actually came to the Hamptons to *get away* from the city, as opposed to bringing their black Mercedeses, spike heels, fruit roll-up dresses, and pushy attitudes with them.

Maycroft has since been sold and completely renovated, so now that remnant is gone, too. I feel very fortunate to have lived there for the two seasons I did. It felt like a time warp back to the days when open space and waterfront access were the norm, not the exception. And in the moonlight, what we called the Maycroft moon, when the fields lit up all around the house, the shadows of grazing deer standing as still and evenly spaced as haystacks, it was possible to imagine ourselves living at the turn of the previous century, the mansion's chipped paint, missing shingles, and sagging roofline temporarily retouched by the moon's soft brush. It was also easy to imagine we were living at the turn of the century when the old coal burner in the basement blew out, sending soot shooting through the vents, and the old electrical wiring shorted out for days, forcing us to walk those spooky hallways by candlelight beneath the imposing gaze of the mother superior's portrait, her eyes following us like the Mona Lisa's.

In the evenings, after work, the caddies turned the main field into a driving range and I designed an eighteen-hole wedge course around the property—out to the main road and back through the trees behind the carriage house (which still hosted a preschool), down past the dilapidated teahouse, all overgrown with honeysuckle and ivy, to the weathered, warped, clamshell-littered dock, and finally back up the hill past the huge elm to the row of gravestones beside the house where the sisters were all buried, including the mother superior, whose headstone became the eighteenth hole.

We rode our bikes into town at night and called on all the bars along Main Street (what we dubbed the Sag Harbor crawl), then weaved home giddily under the stars, often with soaking hair and sandy feet, our shoes draped over the handlebars because we'd stopped to jump off the bridge into the deep channel that flows in from Sag Harbor Bay to the spacious cove behind Maycroft. The same cove that John Steinbeck lived on and immortalized in the opening chapter of *Travels with Charley.*

One of Atlantic's assistant pros lived across the cove. He had a dock of his own and a water-ski boat. He picked us up at our dock in the afternoons to go skiing, out to the bridge and back, and then we "après-skied" in town—tied up at the public dock and walked across the street to the local Mexican restaurant for margaritas.

On occasion he lent me the boat to take into town myself, and one night I invited one of the Irish caddies, Kieran, to join me. Kieran was very personable, even by Irish standards. As he put it, he had no problem talking to *birds*. He was what you'd call a good "wing man."

We tied up at the public dock and did the crawl, and at some point Kieran happened to mention to two attractive girls that we had a boat. Whatever positive light they already saw us in became positively radiant, and they both chirped "Yes!" when we asked them if they'd like to join us for a moonlight cruise.

We sped out across the sparkling bay, the girls sitting side by side up front, pressed against the bow rail, their feet dangling out over the water, their arms raised in the wind.

We cut the motor in the middle of the bay and drifted between town and the sandy spit of Ram's Head Island. We popped cold beers from the cooler and clinked bottles under the stars. Before long we decided to go skinny dipping, and in a flurry of flying undergarments and big splashing cannonballs, we were all in the water. All, that is, except for Kieran, who was still inexplicably standing fully clothed on the boat.

One of the girls splashed at him and yelled, "A shy Irishman! That's a first!'

"I'm not shy. I can't swim."

This I could not believe. "You're from a fishing village on the Irish Sea and you can't swim?"

"Do you have any idea how fockin' cold the Irish Sea is?"

The girls splashed him again. "Well, if you're not going to swim, then take off your clothes and sing us a song."

Kieran shrugged, stripped down to his tighty whities, stood up on the bow, his pale frame like a ghost in the moonlight, and sang.

I went home on Saturday night as drunk as drunk could be.
I saw two hands upon her breasts where my old hands should be.
Well, I called me wife and I said to her, "Will you kindly tell to me
Who owns them hands upon your breasts where my old hands should be?"

"Ah, you're drunk,
You're drunk you silly old fool.
Still you can not see
That's a lovely nightgown that me mother sent to me."

Well, it's many a day I've traveled a hundred miles or
     more,
But fingers in a nightgown sure I never saw before.

Kieran sang verse after hilarious verse. We nearly drowned laughing. Keiran so won us over with his crooning, as did the amazing light show put on by the phosphorescent jellyfish that ignited like swarms of fireflies when we swirled our arms under the water, that we never wanted the night to end. We sped back under the bridge into the cove, the entire boat wake glowing behind us like a comet's tail and the girls flying again up on the bow. We docked at Maycroft and ran up across the field through the gravestones to the convent. The girls giggled in nervous delight as we climbed the spooky spiral staircase under mother superior's imposing gaze.

Kieran took one of the girls into a bedroom off the main hall, and within seconds of closing the door, her voice shook the crucifixes and porcelain statues of the Virgin Mary. "Oh, Keiran! Oh!"

Her friend looked at me with a wicked grin and threw me down on another bed in the soft moonlight filtering through a stained-glass nativity scene. . . .

The next day, Kieran and I were laid out in the caddie yard, sleeping on full-length reclining beach chairs we'd purchased at Kmart. There were many ways Atlantic reminded me of Maroon Creek, and this was one of them—burning the candle at both ends. Going out big at night, and then paying for it the next day. Especially on weekends, when everyone was out from the city and we wanted to be out, too, but this was also when the members played golf and we made our bread and butter, so we had to be up bright and early, ready to caddie with a smile. A bit of a catch-22.

I'd lived the last five years on a reverse schedule, working weekends when everyone else was having fun and off during the week when they were all back at their desks. I wanted badly to be a part of that weekend fun, part of the "group"—the beach barbecues and clambakes, those glorious, languid August afternoons playing volleyball and Frisbee on the beach with friends as opposed to pulling thirty-six in the hot sun after two hours of sleep every Friday and Saturday night. But it was slowly dawning on me that I wasn't willing to give up those quiet, unhurried weekdays for it—those Monday afternoons when I'd just finished an early loop and was walking down the peaceful Atlantic driveway to the caddie parking lot, the sun high in the sky, my pocket stuffed with cash, three and a half days of freedom ahead. Three and a half days of empty beaches and empty fairways—I would surf in the morning and play eighteen in the afternoon through those gentle rolling glacial hills fringed with swaying fescue, the ocean glittering way, way down across the farm fields as the late afternoon sun did its hypnotic Hampton trick, the one that has drawn painters and photographers from all around the world.

Being allowed to play all week on such a beautiful course after being paid so handsomely over the weekend felt like stealing. We certainly doted on the members, but they doted on us, too. A typical day of caddying at Atlantic consisted of a leisurely foursome of ladies playing a late-morning round (often playing only nine and paying as much as $200 for two hours' work), then treating the caddies to whatever we wanted for lunch at the halfway house—even a lobster roll if we desired (I often did). Before paying me and saying good-bye they'd stuff my pockets with cookies and snacks, smile and say, "In case you get hungry later, sweetie." It might not have been an exclusively Jewish club, but it was definitely a Jewish *mother* club.

Not all of the loops were forecaddie jobs, but many of the afternoon ones were. I might get a husband-wife two-some in a cart or perhaps just a husband out for a quick nine before some lawn party or big charity dinner that night. And my main responsibility in these cases was to provide a little instruction, retrieve errant shots, and keep the solo players company. And for that I could easily earn another two hundred. Then on Sunday evening and Monday morning, they'd all vanish back to the city and turn the keys to the kingdom over to us. *Take good care of the course while we're gone! We'll be back next weekend!* They were like the dream parents we all wanted as kids.

On one of these morning loops with the ladies, I was out with another caddie—a local police officer named Bob. As we walked up the fairway on the long par-four fifth hole, we found a small pouch lying in the fairway. One of the la-dies picked it up and opened it and pulled out a rolled plastic bag. She unrolled the bag and sniffed the contents. "What is this? Tea?"

I took the bag, opened it, sniffed it, too, and stealthily pocketed a pinch. "Definitely tea."

One of the other ladies gave me an incredulous frown. "That is *not* tea! That's *marijuana!*"

Bob took the bag from me. "I'll take care of it, ladies."

"Where did it come from?"

The ladies looked around as if the drug smuggler might be hiding in the grassy dunes beside the fairway. One of them even looked up at the sky, perhaps suspecting it had fallen from a plane. Bob and I didn't have to look anywhere, because a Jamaican caddie named Tommy G (the G being short for *ganja*, the Jamaican word for pot) was strolling the green in front of us with the pin in his hand, reading putts as a trail of smoke from his "cigarette" drifted behind him.

Bob rolled his eyes. "I can't imagine."

As Bob and I walked out into the next fairway to fore-caddie, he said, "OK, give it to me."

"Give you what?"

"I saw you pull a piece out back there."

"A *piece*, Bob? Really? It's called a *bud*."

I pulled the tiny bud from my pocket and handed it to him.

I don't know whether Bob ever talked to Tommy about it. We had no proof it was his bag anyway, but with a name like Tommy Ganja, he was kind of incriminating himself. Even so, Bob knew there was no point in hassling caddies about smoking pot, because if you did, there wouldn't be any caddies left in the yard. Especially a yard full of Jamaicans.

The season chugged along at a leisurely, fairly consistent pace with pleasant lulls in the middle of the week, until the mad late August/early September rush when business in New York slowed down and many of the bosses and fortunate employees headed out to the shore for their annual summer holiday. We went thirty-six a day for seventeen days straight—one caddie per foursome because there weren't enough of us to carry all of the bags. This two- or three-week stretch pushed the Atlantic yard to its limit, but as exhausted as we became, we loved it because of the money. It was a gravy train—a minimum of $500 a day right through Labor Day.

Once the dust settled and the members returned to the city, I had more cash in my pocket than ever before in my life. I decided to take a break from Atlantic and head over to caddie at Shinnecock because their yard had finally thinned out with the departure of the kids heading back to school and the lifers migrating south for the winter, and I was dying to get out on those famous fairways. Shinnecock gets tons of guest play in the fall. It's a destination course, a once-in-a-lifetime experience on par with Pebble Beach and Augusta National, and the fall season there is one of the gems of the caddie circuit. It's an opportunity to work and play at arguably the finest course in the country and make one last fistful of cash before the winter sets in.

I first visited Shinnecock Hills in 1986 with my dad to watch the US Open—the first of Greg Norman's many final-round meltdowns. He shot 75 on Sunday and ceded the tournament to forty-three-year-old Raymond Floyd, who became the oldest American winner in the tournament's history.

Shinnecock is a timeless place—the clubhouse and course are just as they've been for nearly a century (more for the clubhouse)—and walking those fairways again brought back a flood of memories from that weekend when my dad and I walked them together.

I called him after my first loop there and gushed over

the phone about how amazing it was. I recalled many of the shots we'd seen. Tour pros hitting woods dead into the wind on their approach to the long, towering par-four ninth, barely reaching the green, their balls almost falling backward in the face of the gale. They missed short and bounced back down the steep hill that fronts the green. They drifted to the right and left like little deflated balloons and dropped into the deep grass and bunkers surrounding the green. Such a different reality from the Tour today when the kids bomb it 350 and hit wedge into everything.

My dad listened very patiently, but when I was finished he just asked, "What are your plans for the winter?"

It was a rhetorical question. We both knew I had no plans for the winter. It was just his way of letting me know that he wasn't at all pleased with my indecision. My return to Shinnecock as a caddie in my late twenties wasn't nearly as romantic for him as it was for me.

But the coming winter was easy to ignore, because I couldn't have picked a more beautiful fall to work at Shinnecock. The Indian summer lasted right up to the New Year—three glorious months: October, November, December. And after Election Day, when the club officially closed, the Shinnecock caddie master granted us unlimited playing privileges, seven days a week, sunrise to sunset. Even for me, despite the fact that I'd been caddying there for only a month. We called this the winter membership.

When I wasn't caddying, which was basically every day after Election Day, because most of the members were back in the city and there was no more guest play, I rolled out of bed with the single goal of playing thirty-six. I stopped at Cromer's Market on North Sea Road. Picked up a bacon, egg, and cheese sandwich and a coffee. Played a quick three-hour eighteen. Grabbed two slices and a Coke for lunch at the pizza parlor down the street and played another eighteen till sunset. I must've played close to a hundred rounds in those three months.

My friend Carlo came out to visit from San Francisco. We got a rare loop over the weekend and then teed off at National, right next door to Shinnecock, on Monday morning. It was only days until National closed for the winter, so we were the only ones on the course. We reached the turn in just over an hour, but instead of continuing to the back nine, we hit our drives from the forward tees on ten over the trees into Shinnecock's third fairway. Amazingly, we both made four on this 450-yard hybrid hole. They'd turned the water off for the winter at Shinnecock, so the fairways and greens were brown and firm. The course was difficult enough with the water on. Now it was downright nasty.

It was a game of attrition. The conditions were far too difficult to attack the pins (if it is ever possible at Shinnecock), so we played strategically and tried to avoid a big mistake. That pair of pars when we crossed over was a rarity, but it hardly mattered, because we were playing a match. It was all about trying to outsmart each other and resist temptation. Knowing when to play for the pin and when to play for a bunker—and I mean that literally, because bunkers were the only places a ball was guaranteed to stop.

The lack of water had another consequence. All the spigots and drinking fountains on the course were off, too. When we crested the hill at the short, treacherous par-three eleventh (famously called the shortest par five in the world by Johnny Miller or Jack Nicklaus or someone), my throat had turned to sand. From that vantage point, we could see National's iconic windmill miles away, as tiny as a model on a toy train set. Our car was parked behind it. I suddenly became concerned. "Gosh, we've walked a long way," I croaked.

Carlo suggested burning a joint to take our minds off our thirst. I don't know why I thought that was a good idea. Smoking pot to alleviate thirst? Three holes later, my dehydration reached medical levels, or at least it seemed that way now that I was stoned. I dropped my clubs in the middle of the fifteenth fairway. "I'll be back."

We knew there was a small housing development somewhere behind the trees next to fifteen because Carlo had parked there during the 1995 US Open and snuck through a hole in the fence. Amazingly, I found the very same break in the fence and managed to scramble through it with only minor abrasions from brambles and branches and frayed metal ends of the fencing. I did get pretty darned dirty, though, crawling through the piles of dead leaves, and I emerged onto the neat little residential cul-de-sac on the other side looking like I'd just escaped from *The Blair Witch Project*.

The first door I knocked on was answered by a little old lady who took one look at me and said, "Lord have mercy, sweetie! Where did you come from?"

"Shinnecock."

"The golf club?"

Her image of posh, private Shinnecock clearly didn't mesh with my bedraggled looks. But her maternal instincts took over.

"Wait here."

She disappeared into the house and returned minutes later with a paper cup filled with ice water. And it wasn't just any old paper cup, it was one of those giant, wax-coated milk-shake cups you get at a shake shack or beach club in the summertime. She'd even put a lid and straw on it. I thought I was hallucinating.

"You got another one of these?"

When I reemerged from the woods, Carlo was waiting patiently right where I'd left him. He marveled at the milk-shake cups, the straws, the crushed ice.

"What the hell! Is there a Dairy Queen back there?"

"No. Some lady gave me these."

"She had milk-shake cups with lids and straws in her house?"

"Yup."

We both broke down laughing at the absurdity of it, polished off the water and ice in seconds and, feeling completely rejuvenated, continued our match.

When we reached Shinnecock's third tee, we fired our drives back over the trees into National's tenth and played in from there—the famous finishing holes that trace the edge of Sebonac Inlet, up over the hill past the windmill, and out onto the bluff overlooking Peconic Bay.

We called our hybrid creation the Double Helix because of the way it looped in around itself like an infinity symbol or a strand of DNA—quite possibly the greatest contiguous thirty-six holes in the world.

When we holed out on eighteen high on the bluff above the molten sun-kissed waters of the bay, the windows on National's huge stone clubhouse lit up like flames behind us, Carlo smiled and said, "This is why we can't quit caddying! How else would we be able to do this? Even on the remote chance they were actually willing to let us join a place like this, how many years would we have to work to afford it? How many hours and years after that to sustain it? Yet here we are, just a couple of caddies with the two best courses in the world all to ourselves."

In five sentences, Carlo articulated what I'd been grappling with since I'd moved back from Colorado. He'd expressed the value of the life we were living in a way I hadn't been able to. I knew I wasn't caddying just to research a book—yes, I was buying myself the time to write, but the story I wanted to tell, what inspired me, was the life that caddying provided—the privilege to play the Double Helix, the freedom to hitchhike across the West, to travel and to live in San Francisco, Beaufort, the Hamptons, and wherever the road led me next. The fact that I didn't have any idea where I was going next was part of the thrill.

I remember thinking of my dad in that moment, wishing I could psychically communicate exactly how I felt standing there on National's eighteenth overlooking Peconic Bay and any number of equally sublime moments on and around the links. I know he would've appreciated them all, but I also know they wouldn't have changed his perspective that caddying was a permanent vacation and that one day my carefree lifestyle was going to lose its luster and my nonexistent résumé would read *inexperienced, indecisive, unreliable*. Shortly after that day with Carlo something happened that would drive my dad's point home, and show me very clearly what was at stake as a result of my transient life. I fell in love.

Of course, Cheryl was attracted to me in the first place because of the very passion and adventurous spirit that fueled my noncommittal existence, and that first summer we enjoyed together everything that makes the Hamptons so special—the sunsets, the miles of beaches, the quaint farm stands and cozy ponds. It was like living in a Keats poem. We lit fires on the beach at night and slept on the sand under the stars. We kayaked on Georgica Pond and rode horses through the trails in the Northwest Woods. We sailed on the bay. We even played live music together out in the local clubs because Cheryl was an amazing singer and piano player. I wrote like fifteen silly love songs on the guitar—duets that we sang together à la Elton John's "Don't Go Breaking My Heart" and the Captain & Tennille's "Muskrat Love."

Our relationship rekindled my dad's hopes, too. He started using his old trademark dorky terms of endearment that I hadn't heard in years. When we visited for the holidays and Cheryl told him how wonderful she thought I was, he proudly called me a "chip off the old block." And our last night in town before we headed back to the Hamptons, he took me aside and offered to treat Cheryl and me to a "romantic dinner for two" so I could save "my nickel." I have no doubt my family truly loved her, but it was also painfully obvious that they saw her as their last best chance to rein me in. Cheryl had a power over me that they didn't.

If that wasn't enough, I also happened to caddie on two separate occasions (once at Atlantic and once at Shinnecock) for the headmaster of a local private school who asked me if I'd interview for a teaching position. It was like the universe, my guardian angels, the three Fates, and their uncle Destiny were all kicking me in the butt, saying, "Hey, kid, if you want this, we'll help make it happen, but you've got to make up your mind and commit to one path or the other. No more of this waffling, half-ass, sorta-kinda crap."

All the values my father stood for were now staring

me boldly in the face in practical and emotional reality. If I wanted to take my relationship with Cheryl to the next level, I couldn't just ship off and leave her to go globe trotting for six months here and there. As much as Cheryl admired the life I'd lived and would have loved to join me, she had one overriding reality that made that impossible—she had a daughter.

I looked long and hard into my heart. I meditated. I walked alone on the beach, consulted some of the older caddies and my friend Georgia. But the fact that I had to think about it at all spoke volumes. Cheryl could see the indecision written on my face and hear the longing to travel again in my voice. In many ways she knew me better than I knew myself—the man she'd fallen in love with was still in the process of finding himself, just beginning his journey. So as much as she wanted me to stay, she didn't want that to translate into holding me back. She was the one who ultimately encouraged me to go.

I think my decision to head back out west was even more heartbreaking for my dad than it was for Cheryl and me. To say he was disappointed is an understatement. From that point forward we basically stopped talking. We didn't stop exchanging *words*, our words just became very formal and efficient. I may not have realized it then, but my dad's silent disapproval would turn out to be a far more powerful force than his words of advice and encouragement had ever been.

7

LIFER

Cheryl and I cried in each other's arms in the driveway. It was February. You could see right into the heart of the forest. Eastern Long Island's twisted, leafless scrub oak, gray and forlorn, a reflection of the way I felt on the inside. A place I didn't want to look.

I drove full speed up the Montauk and Sunrise highways, past the landmarks of the last three years of my life. Leaving was like prying myself from Cheryl's loving hands finger by finger. Once I hit the Long Island Expressway, I gripped the wheel and stared straight ahead, my foot pressed to the accelerator, the radio silent, as if her hands were still reaching for me and if I slowed or wavered, they would catch me and drag me back.

I was still crying when I passed the city and crossed the George Washington Bridge in the slow afternoon traffic.

The first few ridges of the Alleghenies in eastern Pennsylvania looked like the Swiss Alps after living so long on the low sand hills of Long Island. As I crossed the rocky gorge of the Delaware Water Gap and snaked up, along the tops of pine trees and open snowfields, the lights of the farmhouses blinking on in the gathering darkness, I felt the first familiar glimmer of that old wanderlust, the first ray of confidence. But it wasn't until I got to the Rockies and the Southwest desert—Boulder, Aspen, Moab, Flagstaff, Sedona—places that were filled with the very memories that had been drawing me back out west, that the nagging doubts about my decision began to lose their grip on me. I felt the first real confidence that I'd made the right decision.

I was headed to Los Angeles. I didn't have a job nailed down, but I figured they had to play golf in Southern California in the winter, and I had a couple of friends out there to help me get started. In hindsight, I think I also wanted to put as many miles between me and the East Coast as possible, to make sure I didn't turn around and head back to Cheryl.

I spent most of my meager savings on the monthlong cross-country trip. I visited old friends in Boulder. Skied again in Aspen. Hiked the canyons in and around Moab. So when I finally arrived in Los Angeles, the need to find work was pressing. Fortunately, my friend DeWitt was out of town for a month and gave me the keys to his bachelor pad a half block from the beach in Venice.

Venice Beach was culture shock. A world apart from the tidy, quiet Hamptons. It was brash and bawdy. Graffiti and attitude. Crowded with skateboarders, surfers, hippies, and homeless people. There was even a homeless guy living in DeWitt's garage, which made it a challenge to park, because if he was sleeping when I got home, I had to wait while he lifted himself feebly up onto one elbow and shuffled his cardboard bed over a couple of feet like a struggling pupa in his grimy sleeping bag. I had to pull in beside him without running him over. It was more stressful than parallel parking in Manhattan.

There was a posh side to Venice, too, but it was flip-flops and T-shirt posh—actors, writers, producers, and musicians, all in expensive eyewear and designer jeans. There wasn't a polo shirt or pair of khakis in sight. If anybody played golf in the neighborhood, they did a real good job of hiding it.

I tried to have fun. I forced myself out of my shell one night when I realized I was sitting alone at the end of the bar, crying into my third beer and watching *SportsCenter* on mute. I slid down a few seats and said hello to a couple of girls. I even asked one of them to dance. And for a second, I actually felt happy.

When the song was over, we stumbled out onto the patio to have a smoke.

"So, what do you do?" she asked.

"What do I *do*?"

"Yeah, like what's your job?"

"I'm a caddie."

"A *golf* caddie?"

"Yes."

Her interest in me immediately cooled. "You know, you really shouldn't tell people that."

When we went back inside, she started talking to someone else.

I returned to my beer. The Lakers beat the Celtics in overtime.

I stopped in at all the best golf clubs in the city: Riviera, Bel-Air, Los Angeles Country Club. Getting a caddie job had always been so easy for me, simply a matter of showing up, that it never occurred to me it might be different in a city of three million where every waiter, bartender, busboy, and yes, caddie was an out-of-work actor. Hell, even the cashier at the grocery store had his head shot leaning against the register. I've never met so many healthy, eager, educated, underemployed people. And that's not even counting the tens of thousands of Mexicans streaming across the border looking for under-the-table cash—exactly what caddying provided.

I visited Los Angeles Country Club first and was sitting in the yard waiting to meet with the caddie master, when the Mexican fellow sitting next to me said, "Look around you, hombre. What do you see?"

I looked around. "Caddies?"

"Mexicans, man. Notheen' but Mexicans. You in the wrong place, *güero*."

"Do Mexicans even play golf?"

"Ever heard of Lee Trevino?"

"Isn't he from Texas?"

A scuffle very nearly ensued. And seeing that I'd managed to pick a fight with another caddie in the first ten minutes, the caddie master thought it best I try a different yard.

The Bel-Air caddie yard reminded me of the old-school East Coast yards around New York City, like Baltusrol and Winged Foot. It was packed with veterans: old black guys shining their shoes and smoking Kools, old white guys reading the racing papers, young guys spitting chew and playing poker. The caddie master was actually willing to take me on, but he couldn't promise me much work because I'd be the new guy; I'd have to sit. Maybe a loop or two a week. Definitely not enough to live on. I left Bel-Air concerned.

That night I tried to remain optimistic, tried my best to smile. I'd read somewhere that the simple act of smiling can breed confidence. I went back to the same bar and started talking to another girl and this time when she asked me what I did, I said, "I'm a writer."

"What do you write?"

"I'm writing a book about caddying."

"Do you have a publisher?"

"I published a story in a golf magazine."

She was not impressed.

I quickly learned that being an aspiring writer in L.A. has about as much cachet as caddying. Everybody and their uncle is a writer.

Riviera shot me down, too. Oddly enough for a course nicknamed Hogan's Alley (after the legendary pro who started his career as a caddie) and one that hosted a US Open, a PGA Championship, a US Senior Open, and countless Los Angeles Opens, Riviera didn't really have a caddie yard, just a couple of guys hanging around the cart barn hoping for the odd loop. It was as inexplicable as the Olympic Club's shoddy yard had been. And just like Olympic, Riviera isn't some quiet members' club. It's a golf factory. They probably get more rounds than any other private club in L.A., and tons of guest play. It would be a great course to have a veteran caddie who knows all the greens and history and where the famous shots from the tournaments were hit. I said as much to the caddie master. He just shrugged.

After Riviera I was downright depressed.

I went out drinking again and burned a few more crumpled dollars on cheap beer. This time a girl sat down next to me and struck up a conversation. I nearly cringed when she asked, "What do you do?"

"What the hell is it with you girls out here and this 'What do you do?' crap? What difference does it make? I'm a golf caddie! I carry golf bags! There, I said it!"

Her eyes lit up. She smiled so brightly, she nearly burned a hole through my forehead. "My brother's a caddie! Where do you work?"

"Well, nowhere at the moment. I can't find a job."

She tried not to laugh, but her face turned purple. She put her hand over her mouth so she wouldn't spit out her drink.

"What's so funny?"

"So, you're an *aspiring* caddie?"

I had to laugh at that, too, but it must've come out like a pathetic whimper, because she hugged me and said, "I'm sure you're the best caddie in the world!"

She told me her brother used to caddie at Sherwood Country Club and that he used to make *a lot of money* there.

I hadn't even thought of Sherwood—a Jack Nicklaus course tucked up in the mountains about an hour north of the city, where Greg Norman used to host his Shark Shoot-out and where Tiger Woods now hosted his tournament.

I called them first thing in the morning and all but begged the caddie master for a job. He liked my desperation and told me to come see him on Tuesday.

My "training loop" at Sherwood—the one that would determine whether I was hired or not—coincided with De-Witt's return, and because I barely had any money left, I went to the one place I could afford to live: Malibu Creek State

Campground. I hadn't planned on camping out when I came to Los Angeles, and at first I felt pretty down about it. I loved camping, but it's one thing to plan a camping trip; it's another to be forced to camp because you are broke. I think that's more accurately called being homeless. I comforted myself with the fact that Malibu Creek was a lot closer to Sherwood than Venice, and staying there gave me an entirely different perspective on Los Angeles.

L.A. may be all hell and smog, but it's also a beautiful city. Bordered on one side by ocean, another by mountains, and a third by desert—real desert with cactuses and Joshua trees and towering red mountains that have swallowed mule trains whole. And the Santa Monica Mountains rise three thousand feet right out of the sea with only a sprinkling of homes on their flanks. The rest are covered in sage, yucca, sycamore, live oak. And they've got red rocks of their own, glowing hoodoo spires and sandstone chutes that rush with water in the wet winter. This is where Mulholland Drive snakes northward into nothingness, where you see the silver eyes of coyotes flash across the road at night.

It's no wonder L.A. became the movie capital of the world. In Malibu Creek they filmed *MASH*, *Tarzan*, *Butch Cassidy and the Sundance Kid*, *Planet of the Apes*, and countless others. In other words, Malibu Creek is equal parts Korea, Africa, Bolivia, and postapocalyptic Earth. And it really is. I can totally see the MASH chopper circling in against the rocky peaks, the doctors rushing out to treat the wounded, a lion stalking up through the swaying field grass, Tarzan wrestling a croc in the little palm-shaded swimming hole, or Butch and Sundance galloping up the dusty trails, six-shooters whizzing off the rocks.

These films all predate the campground, but the campground itself was worthy of a film, something like *National Lampoon's Vacation* meets *La Bamba* meets *Hair*. There were families singing "Kumbaya" around the fire, Latinos swilling beers and blaring mariachi, and gypsies dancing, twirling fire sticks, and giving each other henna tattoos. In the campsite next to me, there was a woman sleeping in a Rolls-Royce. I tried to say hello, but she dived into the backseat and clicked the power locks as though there was a murderer on the loose and I might be him. As I lay in my sleeping bag and gazed at the stars, I tried to imagine what she was doing there. I played each scenario over in my mind—she'd stolen the car and was running from the law, she'd lost her memory like the girl in the movie *Mulholland Drive*, she was hiding out from mobsters in Vegas she owed a ton of money to . . .

• • •

Despite its rural location, Sherwood obviously was still very much a high-profile L.A. club. Starting with the entrance— cameras, guys with walkie-talkies, and a huge, automatic wrought-iron gate embossed with the Sherwood logo. I guess this is understandable, given that it is also an expensive housing community, but coming from New England, where you can drive into almost any exclusive golf club without so much as a toot of the horn, it seemed a little over the top. Hell, Shinnecock Hills even has a public road cutting right through the fairways. On the twelfth hole, the members have to wait and wave your car through before they hit their second shots.

The guard checked the list on his clipboard. "Let's see . . . Mr. Dunn . . . Here you are! Caddie trainee."

He filled out my temporary pass, placed it in my windshield, and said, "Welcome to Sherwood. Keep your eye on the ball."

I had no idea how prophetic that advice would be.

The clubhouse was like a brick Georgian battleship—sprawling and discombobulated like a high school or community college that has been added on to over the years. But this community college had a lot of very rich students. The parking lot was filled with Porsches and Ferraris.

I parked on the side, where I'd been told to, and walked up to the valet. There were a few caddies milling around in their maroon Sherwood aprons. I didn't notice anything particularly unusual about them, except maybe that they all had model good looks and were between the ages of twenty-one and thirty and in suspiciously good shape. No smokers, no potbellies, no old guys, no facial hair. In other words, no typical caddie characteristics. But it was a small sampling. And besides, having just turned thirty-one, I was within that demographic myself, so in an odd way, it was comforting. Very different from Bel-Air, for example.

Jeff, the caddie master, a twenty-eight-year-old from Ohio, couldn't have been a nicer guy. When I walked into the office, he had his feet up on the desk. He was yucking it up with a couple of other caddies; they were giving each other shit. He might've been the boss, but he was very much one of the guys. The caddies in his office looked just like the caddies out front—clean-cut, in great shape, superconfident. It was more like a casting call for *The Stepford Caddies* than a real working yard.

Another even more athletic guy, whom I was sure I recognized, walked in right behind me and asked, with tongue planted firmly in cheek, "Is the Great One here yet?"

And then it dawned on me. I was looking at Russ Courtnall, a nineteen-year NHL veteran. And the Great One he was talking about was Wayne Gretzky. I only knew this because I played junior hockey and used to follow the NHL religiously during the height of Courtnall's career. (I think I even still have his hockey card.)

Minutes later the Great One himself showed up, and one of the caddies who'd been standing in the shack gave him a big high five and started giving him shit like they were old pals, which in fact they turned out to be. This was Jimmy, Gretzky's regular caddie. There seemed to be a very relaxed, personal relationship among the members and caddies.

It's not as though close relationships between caddies and members are unusual. Some members spend more time with their caddies than they do with their spouses. But I immediately sensed a rare egalitarian vibe to Sherwood. It reminded me of the blurred social lines I'd experienced at Maroon Creek Club, where the members partied with the caddies and invited them into their homes and on fishing trips to Cabo and blowouts to Vegas.

But, alas, I was not part of the gang yet. It was Training Day for me. And just like any other tight-knit group one wants to join, there is bound to be an initiation. Dare I say some hazing?

The first thing that was different about Sherwood was that my training didn't actually involve carrying bags. Jeff handed me five putters (two of the pros had decided to join our threesome), a pin sheet, and a bottle of sand-and-seed mix to fill in divots. He showed me two hand signals: the traditional "safe" sign and an emphatic double arm pump that meant "not safe," as in gone. He told me to run out into the center of the fairway, watch all five tee shots, snap out the signals, and then begin calculating yardage to the front, back, and pin as quickly as possible.

Just at that moment, a ridiculous-looking custom golf cart sped toward us up the eighteenth fairway. It was red with a long hood and huge hood ornament and golden rims. It had an air conditioner in the roof, a tinted windshield, stereo system, bar, the works—like a mobile version of Rodney Dangerfield's golf bag in *Caddyshack*. And it was *flying* up the fairway.

But the weirdest thing about this spectacle was the caddie sprinting next to the cart, his arms pumping, feet pounding, lungs straining. He looked like an Olympian.

"What the hell is that?"

Without blinking, Jeff said, "That's Tom. He's a division-one soccer player. He's racing the cart."

"And you want me to run like that?"

"I want you to try."

I could see the sadism gleaming in his eyes.

It suddenly dawned on me why everyone was in such good shape, why there were no old guys or smokers or potbellies. This place was like the Caddie Olympics.

I started running. Five balls came whizzing at me before I even turned around. I snapped out signals as crisply as a major league umpire. I raced around and paced off yardage, but before I'd even calculated two of the balls, the carts were on top of me. They were all souped-up jobs, just like the red one on eighteen.

The first guy asked, "What's my yardage?"

"One seventy-eight."

"What's it to the back?"

"One ninety-three."

Another voice interrupted me.

"Which one's the Titleist 3?"

"It's this one. No, wait, it's that one. Sorry."

Right in the middle of that last reply, the first guy hit. The ball whizzed past me like a rifle shot. I ducked and then ran back and seeded his divot. I barked out the rest of the yardages and ran around frantically seeding those divots, too, like a gardener on steroids. I didn't even make it to Jeff's ball before he hit. I was already sweating through my shirt.

Just at that moment, another custom cart, this one white with a little flag fluttering on the back of the roof like a land yacht, drove past on the adjacent eighteenth hole. There was a caddie sitting in the cart with his feet up. He was holding a drink. He sipped the drink.

Jeff saw the longing in my eyes. I was like a mongrel dog rooting through trash cans who sees a poodle drive by in the passenger seat of a Range Rover.

Jeff said, "You can only ride in a member's cart if you're his *regular*."

The word *regular* reverberated off of the inside of my head like an incantation. Being someone's regular was clearly the key to this kingdom.

Jeff interrupted my little reverie.

"Now run to the green. Mark, clean, and replace all five balls. Read each line and hand each player his putter."

Jeff took off in his cart. I chased after him doing my best impression of a division-one soccer player.

• • •

Sherwood wasn't a typical caddie yard in many ways—most blatantly in that there wasn't really a yard. By this I mean there wasn't a physical place where the caddies hung out, because most of the loops were either already taken by regulars or preassigned the night before. The caddies showed up an hour or so before their loops, prepped their carts, and headed out to the range with their players. The few of us who didn't have loops—the *standbys*—stood out front at the valet, greeted the members and their guests when they arrived, and pulled bags from the trunks of cars. Under no circumstances was a golfer allowed to carry a bag past us.

My first day officially on the job, I walked out to greet a guest who'd self-parked. I offered to take his clubs.

"That's all right. I've got them," he said.

I nodded politely and stepped aside. Another caddie rushed forward, gave me some serious stink eye, and grabbed the bag right off his shoulder.

When he returned to the valet, he hissed, "Never let a guest carry his own bag."

About an hour later, the actor Will Smith arrived with a guest who was also carrying his own bag.

I jogged out to greet them. "Welcome to Sherwood. May I take your clubs for you?"

"It's all right. I got 'em."

"No. No. I insist."

I actually placed my hand on the strap and started to

pull. A tug of war ensued. Will Smith stopped, put his hands in the air, and deadpanned, "Don't mess around with these caddies, man. They're serious. Just give him the bag and step slowly away."

The guest released his bag.

I walked triumphantly past the other caddies.

As I was strapping the bag to Will's cart beside the driving range, a beautiful six-foot blonde walked up said, "Will you tell Joe I'm here when he arrives?"

I had no idea who Joe was, but I just smiled and nodded and said, "Yes, of course."

When I got back to the valet, I told one of the caddies about it, and he said, "Do you know which Joe she's talking about? Pesci."

About five minutes later, a black Cadillac Escalade pulled up. The caddie elbowed me.

"That's Joe. Go get 'em."

Joe jumped down out of the huge truck. He couldn't have been more than five five. He was holding an unlit cigar. He popped open the back. I reached in for his clubs. "Your guest is here, Mr. Pesci."

"My guest?"

"Your lady friend."

"My lady friend?"

I could actually feel my foot going into my mouth, but somehow I managed one more sentence.

"Tall, attractive blonde."

Pesci started nodding. Not a nice affirmative nod but one of those spastic nods when somebody's about to explode and tear your head off. A Joe Pesci nod.

He stepped up into my face. I've never felt so awkward

being taller than someone in my life. I actually felt my-self wilt.

"You're fuckin' funny. You know that? No, seriously, you should be a fuckin' comedian!"

He poked his cigar into my ribs. "That's my wife, you asshole."

He stormed back to the driver's door cursing. "Lady friend? Tall, attractive blonde? Where do they find these ass-holes?"

There was dead silence at the valet until he pulled away, and then every caddie there fell to the ground laughing. I mean, they were crying. I hung my head pathetically, Joe's bag dangling from my shoulder.

One of the caddies stumbled over and slapped me on the back. "That was like a scene straight out of *Casino*, dude!"

Welcome to Sherwood.

I dealt with my newbie status by showing up at the crack of dawn and hustling my ass off when I was lucky enough to get a job. I became Super Caddy. I sprinted up the fairways to scout tee shots. I jogged backward while players were hitting to keep ahead of the carts. I snapped out signals like a traffic cop. Cleaned balls like a precious-egg collector. Responded to every question with "Yes, sir," and "No, sir."

Almost everyone at Sherwood played in carts, but even during the traditional walking loops, I ran down the fairway, the bags thumping against my legs, the straps slipping off my shoulders, sweat pouring down my back and dripping off the end of my nose. Anything to ingratiate myself and nail down a regular loop. I was running hard during one loop that hap-pened to include Laird Hamilton and Gabrielle Reece, the professional surfer and professional volleyball player. I was huffing and puffing up the steepest hill on the course, be-tween number five and six, sweat raining off of my forehead and arms. They pulled up beside me and asked, "Want a lift?"

"No. I'm fine."

They looked at me like I was crazy. And when two of the world's fittest athletes look at you like you're crazy for running up a hill, you probably are. I'd become the soccer player I'd seen racing the cart that first day.

Sherwood wasn't really set up as a walking course. It was a mountain valley with a river running through it, the steep, rocky wall of the Santa Monicas rising two thousand feet on one side, the smaller foothills curling around the other to form a sheltered cove. Some of the smaller hills had been lopped off, effectively turned into mesas, to accommodate palatial mansions that lorded over the merely single-digit-million-dollar homes beneath. The course wasn't hemmed in by houses like courses in Florida and Arizona, but the narrowness and steepness of the valley caused the routing to be a little squeezed and strung out—a couple of long walks between tees and greens and a couple of steep hills to climb.

The hill between the fifth green and sixth in particu-lar was so steep that a tram up it wouldn't be unreasonable. There were stairs next to the green to provide a shortcut, but they were as steep as a Mayan temple. And when the warm weather finally came, those steps were a favorite sunning spot for rattlesnakes, little mottled brown coils you saw only when they were three steps above you and inches from your nose, an encounter that hopefully didn't startle either party and cause the snake to strike or the caddy to tumble backward down the stairs.

These standoffs ended one of two ways: with the caddie retreating and taking the long route around or bravely sweeping the snake away with a club. Neither option was very appealing. But exhaustion and inconvenience are powerful forces. During my lone encounter, I opted to sweep. I heard the rattle fire as the snake dropped into the grass, and I leaped up the stairs like a kangaroo.

The early mornings at Sherwood were particularly beautiful: mist rising in ghostly sheets from the river, silent shadows of owls gliding through the trees, the moon and stars hanging like jewels above the mountains.

Only one other caddie showed up at dawn. He was not new like me, but rather the runt of the old pack. Chip was a nervous little guy, like a skinny, hairless rabbit, all elbows and knees and involuntary facial tics. Even after a year at Sherwood, he still didn't have any regular loops.

Like me, Chip was forced to show up early to survive—to pick up one of the unassigned loops, which weren't on the tee sheet and therefore didn't have a caddie attached to them. There was usually one unscheduled group that arrived early each morning looking to get out ahead of the crowds, but there were rarely two, so there was a big difference between being first and second on the list. It was often the difference between working and not working.

I'm afraid my arrival disturbed poor Chip's routine and added a little unwanted competition. Before me, he'd been able to show up almost at his leisure, well after dawn, and still be first. But one day he came around the corner and found me standing there and suddenly he was second. I got the early loop and was on the course in less than an hour and finished three hours after that. Chip was still waiting when I got in. He was not pleased.

It became a daily battle, both of us arriving earlier and earlier, sometimes a half hour or more before dawn, the sky still brilliant with stars, the valley heavy with cold.

This often happens in caddie yards that reward jobs on a first come, first served basis. The caddies end up sleeping in their cars or on benches bundled in towels. And I did catch Chip sleeping in his car a couple of times. One time I snuck past him, banged on his passenger window, and sprinted for the pro shop as he scrambled to get out of his car. That *really* pissed him off. The next day he was standing out front at 4:30 a.m.

"I will stand here all night if I have to!" he threatened.

Caddie masters usually stop the madness before the caddie yard turns into a campsite. They make a rule that no one can sign in before 6:00 a.m. But at Sherwood it was only me and Chip, so nobody really cared how early we got there. And honestly, I think they enjoyed the fact that there was a new guy tormenting Chip. It added a little spice to the daily routine and threw a little cruel fuel on the postadolescent fire.

I eventually picked up a couple of regulars and no longer had to wake up in the freezing dawn. But I remember those early loops fondly, being off the course before noon, the whole day ahead of me. If I couldn't get a second loop (which I rarely did), I'd take the road that led out of Sherwood, past horse ranches with white post-and-rail fences and little corrals shaded by cottonwood trees, hook a right at the junction, and head west up over the mountains—a dizzying, disorienting climb that switched back and forth along the edge of precipitous drops, the green fairways of Sherwood popping in and out of view, farther and farther below.

The mountain range eventually crested in a hanging

valley. The road straightened out and dipped down through groves of live oak. A lucky few had homes up there, the best ones perched right where the road began to drop down the other side toward the Pacific, with sweeping views of the sea, the little thumb of Point Dume, and the ink smudge of Catalina Island. From there I literally glided to the beach. Seven miles straight downhill in neutral to La Piedra, El Matador, and Leo Carrillo state beaches to surf and sit on the deck of a little seafood shack called Neptune's Net, where surfers sipped Corona tallboys and bikers thundered up and down the PCH. I ordered towering plates of peel 'em and eat 'em shrimp, surfed till dusk, and then snuck into the Leo Carrillo campground to shower.

It was during one of these afternoon sojourns that I noticed a For Sale sign marking the end of a dirt road up on top of the mountains. The dirt road crossed a meadow and disappeared over a ridge. It was a little overgrown and rutted from rain but looked passable even in my hatchback. I turned onto it and bumped through the window-high weeds and up the steep slope, my wheels spinning in the dust. The road topped out on a saddle between two peaks above a small oak grove. Beyond the oaks, at the bottom of the valley, was a fenced meadow and beyond that, rolling hills of sagebrush that piled up against the flanks of three-thousand-foot Boney Mountain—a jagged, toothy ridge that held the setting sun in its silhouetted jaws.

I didn't even bother driving back down. I unrolled my sleeping bag, set up my beach chair, cracked a beer, and sat back in the expansive silence, only a pair of house lights in view, far across the darkening valley.

Thus began what I refer to as my Siddhartha period—a

life in complete contrast to the material world of the golf course and the city below. Admittedly, it was not at all what I expected when I set out for L.A. I'd imagined myself working somewhere in the city, living somewhere hip and lively, like Venice, making lots of friends, being part of the scene. Not living in isolation on top of a mountain with my thoughts (and the owls) my only companions.

The caddies didn't quite know what to make of me. Many of them grew up in the local suburbs—alumni of the high school golf, soccer, and wrestling teams. It was not your typical vagabond caddie yard where at least one person living out of his car was to be expected.

Still, they were Southern California kids. They grew up within an hour of the Valley, Hollywood, Compton, Venice, just over the mountains from the coast, where traveling surfers in camper vans are a regular sight. It's not as though I was camping in Connecticut, where, if people discovered me, they were likely to assume I was a serial killer and immediately call the cops. Californians are hardwired for a certain minimum level of open-mindedness. They're used to transplants and transients, people from different walks of life. Even my closest neighbors, the Zachas, who lived about a quarter mile away on another hilltop, smiled on my presence. They invited me for dinner and sunset drinks on their patio. I played chess and Ping-Pong with their son Chase and went surfing with their other son, Andrew. And at night when I sometimes grew introspective and lonely, I'd climb the hill to their stables, write at the desk in the tack room, and talk to the horses, comforted by their warmth and restless physical presence.

But I was an irresistible target for the caddies. And the

one who ribbed me the most, Jocko, actually became a good friend and the only caddie who ever camped with me. He teased me relentlessly. "Hey, Grizzly Adams, how's *My Side of the Mountain?*"

"Crocodile Dundee! Throw another shrimp on the barbie!"

Privately, though, he admitted he actually thought it was cool that I was camping, and one day he showed up at work with his sleeping bag and said, "Let's party at your house tonight!"

He loved it, even though we barely slept, because he jumped at every rustle and hoot and squeak. And even I have to admit it could literally get a little wild up there some nights—owls perched on the roof of my car, coyotes hunting mice in the tall grass, I even had a groundhog run full tilt into my sleeping bag one night, apparently fleeing the coyotes. When he hit me he was as stunned as I was. I sat up and flipped on my headlamp. He'd been knocked flat on his back. He rolled over, blinked his eyes at me, and ran back the way he'd come. Apparently I was a lot scarier than the coyotes.

Jocko's absolute favorite way to make fun of me was to quote the Chris Farley skit from *Saturday Night Live*, the one in which he plays motivational speaker Matt Foley. "My name is Matt Foley. I am thirty-five years old. I am divorced, and I live in a van down by the river!"

I tried in vain to defend myself. "I'm thirty-one and I live on top of a mountain."

But that only encouraged him. "You are a writer!" he said and turned to the other caddies. "We got ourselves a writer here! Hey, Dad, I can't see real good. Is that Bill Shakespeare over there?"

And on cue, the caddies piped up: "From what I've heard, you're using your paper not for writing but for rolling doobies!"

"You're gonna be doing a lot of doobie rolling when you're living in a van down by the river!"

They got endless amusement at my expense. But that was fine. At least I finally felt like one of the guys, and after enough time had passed, even Jocko tired of the joke. Then I made the fatal mistake of selling my hatchback and buying a minivan, and it started all over again. "My name is Matt Foley. I am thirty-five and live in a van down by the river!"

Fortunately, there were far more interesting and entertaining people than me coming and going every day. Like this one member, Casey, a skinny thirty-eight-year-old with tattoos and bleached blond hair, who rolled up in his Porsche with a wad of cash wrapped in a rubber band. Every time he arrived, he held it up and said, "If you can guess how much money I'm holding, you can have it."

It was a roll of Ben Franklins at least three inches thick.

The caddies shouted guesses. "Five thousand." "Six thousand." "Seventy-five hundred."

Then Casey peeled 'em off one by one.

". . . eighty-one, eighty-two, eighty-three hundred bucks."

A collective groan. Puddles of drool. Material worship.

The only caddie who remained silent was Doug, Casey's regular. He'd seen this same act too many times. Found it pathetic. Just shook his head silently and carried Casey's clubs out to the range.

They were an odd couple, Doug and Casey. The same age exactly, but opposite in every other way. Doug was a natural golfer. Casey played every day and was still a hack. Doug was honest and had no money. Casey was a total scammer with tons of money. Doug was lacking in confidence he should've had. Casey was brimming with confidence he had no right having.

But Doug put up with his shit because Casey paid him well.

This is not uncommon. There's a whiff of prostitution to caddying. Sometimes we're paid for our services. Sometimes we're paid for our companionship. Sometimes we're paid to take people's shit and stroke their egos, especially with guys like Casey who don't even really need a caddie. They always take a cart, so they don't need anyone to carry their clubs. They've played the course hundreds of times, so they don't need anyone to read the numbers off the sprinkler heads or the slope of the greens. They don't need anything. They want a companion and a confidant. And they're willing to pay for it.

So Doug took the money and rode in the cart by Casey's side, just like the caddie I admired so much that first day when I was running around like a maniac on my training loop. It was definitely a good gig. Easy money. But it wasn't always as romantic as I first imagined. Casey could be a total jerk. Like the day he showed up with a new tattoo—a pinup girl inked on his leg.

It bore a striking resemblance to his girlfriend, and Doug, being nothing if not a gentleman, said, "That's a really nice drawing of Gina."

Casey responded, "That's not Gina. It's a stripper I know in Vegas."

That's exactly the kind of inexplicable lack of respect and tact that drove Doug crazy, made him consider dumping Casey for good. But in the end, he didn't have to because one day Casey mysteriously disappeared. Rumors swirled about money laundering, embezzlement, the mob. There was no love lost, but the caddies were sad to see him go, because now there were no more chances to win that wad of dirty money.

The whole member-caddie relationship was even trickier with women—unhappy wives, divorcées, cougars. Doug had one of those, too. The same qualities that had attracted Casey—Doug's natural golfing ability, his humility, his integrity—attracted Susan. She'd already been married to a rich egomaniac. There was no luster left to the society thing. She took Doug to her second home in Scottsdale to caddie for her in the member-guest tournament out there and it wasn't long before their relationship developed beyond the golf course.

A caddie-member love affair is an odd arrangement to say the least, especially for a genuine guy like Doug, who tries to see the best in everyone. He wasn't in it disingenuously; he felt genuine warmth for her, but even he admitted that he let it go way further than he would have if they had met on a level playing field outside the club.

At first, they had the best of both worlds. He was paid handsomely for easy, enjoyable work—spending afternoons with Susan, caddying some, but also playing the role of therapist and confidant, the golf cart parked in the shade of a sycamore, sharing a drink and conversation, the cares of the real world far, far away. She represented the tantalizing promise of a life beyond caddying, and he, the promise of a life beyond the material bullshit and judgment of society. Those are both powerful promises in a place that worships youth and superficiality and material wealth as much as Los Angeles.

I call it the caddie confessional. Sitting there in the cart or walking side by side up the fairway, we may not be in separate cubicles or have a mesh window between us, but there is an invisible fence—an extension of the fence that surrounds the club. We are on the inside, but we are from the outside. There is the illusion that secrets are safe with us, as though we are priests.

And this is true to some extent. We will most certainly tell the other priests (caddies), just as Doug told me, but we would rarely risk confiding in other members for fear of putting our jobs in jeopardy.

This arrangement is great for spilling one's guts or having an affair, but it's very difficult to take the next step and become a genuine couple in the public eye. If it had been true love, it might've worked. But it wasn't, and Doug eventually had to extricate himself from the relationship.

He tried to go back to just being Susan's caddie. He worked for her when she played in a group with the other girls—safety in numbers. But they all knew what had been going on, and even that finally proved to be too awkward. So suddenly Doug found himself in the odd position of not having any regulars. And this was when he began seriously thinking of giving up caddying.

I was amazed he was still a caddie as it was. There was nothing wrong with him. He wasn't a heavy drinker. He wasn't running from anything. He wasn't a recluse. And he wasn't an aspiring Tour player either. He didn't exhibit any of the usual caddie symptoms, the typical reasons we keep caddying even when it's no longer in our best interest.

Doug started at Sherwood when he was in his twenties, back in the golden era of the 1990s, when the golf course first opened and the housing development began. The club offered guaranteed cash to attract caddies and build a program quickly from scratch. This happens a lot at new clubs. You need a caddie program; you provide guaranteed money. And the golfers usually pay the caddies full anyway, so the caddies make double. But this doesn't last forever. Once the membership fills up or, in the case of a public course, the hotel and tee sheets are consistently booked, once the "caddie program" is established and sustainable, the club pulls the subsidies, and the money drops back to normal rates. The lesson here is, it's good to get in at the beginning.

But in the case of Sherwood, the money didn't drop much, because the club's opening in the early nineties coincided with the beginning of the tech boom and resurgent California real estate market so everyone was flush and feeling very optimistic and generous. Those early golden days at Sherwood lasted a *very* long time. It wasn't until I got there in the new millennium that the bubble, if it didn't exactly burst (this is Hollywood after all), began to leak significantly and for those feeling a little less buoyant, exorbitant caddie fees were dead weight.

But it was a good run and it's easy to see how a guy like Doug could wake up one day a decade later and say, "Holy shit! I'm almost forty and I'm still a fucking caddie!" And I think that's one of the reasons he was so drawn to me—I was doubling down on the life he was contemplating getting out of. We talked about this a lot over beers and rounds of golf on our off days. We went back and forth debating the pros and cons of caddying, but during the height of the summer season when loops were still plentiful there was very little urgency to these conversations. They were more like passing fancies—along the lines of "When I grow up I'm going to be a . . ." This was a pattern I'd become all too familiar with—each successive season providing another excuse to put off any serious decision making because calmer, clearer days were always only months away.

But when the fall rolled around, Doug decided to finally step up and make a move. He invited me to Thanksgiving with his extended family, and there were many toasts to his decision to join the family real estate business. I raised my glass, too, but not without some introspection and, honestly, a little self-doubt. I'd already made my move and this was it. I was a caddie. And one living on top of a mountain, no less.

At Christmas, another Sherwood looper named John invited me to join his family, and while they were incredibly warm and welcoming, I could see the bewilderment and sympathy in their eyes when I told them where I was living. I can't deny that I thought a lot about my own family that night, gathered around a similar table three thousand miles away. Of course, I could've gone home and spent the holidays with them. Even though my dad was now giving me the major silent treatment, I was always welcome. But staying in California for Christmas was my way of sticking to my guns, of owning the path I'd chosen for myself. And as lonely and misunderstood as I honestly felt at Christmas, I reminded myself how lucky I was to be living and working in California, spending my mornings on a world-class golf course with the who's who of Hollywood and my afternoons on the beaches of Malibu. Surely when people dream of "greener grasses" the life I was living isn't far from what they imagine. It certainly wasn't far from what I had in mind when I decided to leave the East Coast for good. Except, maybe, for the hedgehogs and coyotes.

8

GOLF BUMS

BIGHORN GOLF CLUB,
PALM DESERT, CA,
2003–2005

I wasn't planning to stay at Sherwood forever, but I didn't know exactly where I was headed next, either. I had worked very hard to earn a couple of steady loops and was feeling as at home as it is possible for a technically homeless person to feel. But apparently it wasn't my destiny to settle down yet. My decision to move out west was, after all, a decision to *move*, not just trade one permanent residence for another. At least that's what I told myself three months after Christmas when I suddenly found myself fired from Sherwood.

When I look back, it's actually amazing that I'd never been fired from a caddie job before—a fact that has less to do with my behavior, good or bad, than with how *hard* it is to get fired from caddying. However, there are certain lines a caddie cannot cross, and at Sherwood I strode across one of them.

First, let me say that when people ask if I've caddied for

a lot of jerks over the years, I always respond, "Yes, there were some real jerks, but ninety-nine percent of the people were great." And I mean that. I find that to be true about life in general. Most everyone is very decent. And the golf world is no exception. In fact, I think golfers may even feel more goodwill toward their caddies than toward the average person because of our shared passion for the game. I think most players respect us for our complete devotion. We are like those wandering holy men in India, the sadhus, who offer guidance and good luck. But every once in a while, we run into those who don't feel they need any guidance or luck, whose bitterness has caused them to scorn the Golf Gods and their earthly representatives, the caddies. In these rare cases, we become the whipping boys, the scapegoats for their frustrations, for we are a constant vexing reminder of the failings and imperfections that the game so glaringly and un-flinchingly lays bare.

I'm the first to admit that caddies are far from perfect. We all misread putts, misjudge yardages, lose balls and head covers, and sometimes even leave clubs behind—the wedge next to the green or the putter leaning against the bench on the tee. But I find that we tend to be mirrors of our play-ers. We end up giving them what they expect. And by this I do not mean some lofty standard they hold us to; I mean the preconceived notions and predisposition they bring to the game and to the role of the caddie. There may be a bias toward the type of caddie they think we are: the salty old Scot, the congenial Southern black, the clean-cut college or mini-tour player. Perceptions are as varied as the players, but one thing remains the same: if you think something is likely to turn out a certain way, the odds increase dramatically that it will.

I got that final fatal loop, the one that abruptly ended my tenure at Sherwood, from one of the longtime veteran caddies. We'd nicknamed him Houdini because of his knack for disappearing from bars without so much as a good-bye. The caddies would all be out together enjoying a post-work bonding sesh. One minute Houdini'd be there yucking it up with us, gracing us with his charismatic presence, and the next he'd be gone, and we'd all raise our glasses and shout, "Houdini!"

His disappearing acts were a form of self-preservation. They kept him from going over the top, staying too late, drinking too much, saying something he'd regret. In other words, they helped him stay out of trouble, and I should've seen that he was clearly trying to avoid trouble when he Houdinied out of the loop that day. I should've been suspicious of the smooth, smiling way he offered it to me: "Looking for a loop, buddy, old pal?" But I figured it was just a low-dollar loop, that's all. And by Houdini's standards, that didn't necessarily mean it was all that bad, because he was used to getting paid handsomely.

But the second I met the player, the host of the foursome, I knew I'd made a mistake. The guy was a jerk. His snideness was evident immediately in his limp, disinterested handshake and the offhand remark he made about Houdini's absence and how I'd "better be good." He said it in a way that had the intonation and vocal pitch of a joke but wasn't funny because there was no humor in it, no smile behind his eyes. All his comments and jokes were that way. Dripping with

sarcasm and negativity. Barbs to me and his playing partners that on the lips of another man might be considered a
friendly ribbing but coming from him were loaded with real
disdain.

I'd dealt with my share of megalomaniacal assholes,
but most of them were good at being assholes. They might
throw a club or yell at you after a bad read, but on the next
hole, they'd seek your advice again immediately and pay you
a compliment to bolster your confidence. They were comfortable in positions of power and knew just how much they
could get away with and when to throw you a bone to keep
you happy. And in the end, they paid you. Because every successful asshole knows that's the bottom line.

But this vindictive little shrimp knew nothing about the
art of being an asshole. He never backed off or threw me a
bone. He second-guessed everything I did—every yardage,
every read. And he did it with that same high-pitched, nasal
tone that's meant to be funny but isn't funny at all.

"I don't know. . . . You sure about this one, John? You
really sure it's a ball out left? The one on the last hole didn't
break as much as you said!"

"That's 'cause you hit it five feet past."

He didn't like that response at all.

Eventually I gave up arguing with him. I grew quiet and
distant and gave him only bare-minimum information. As I
said, I was a mirror. Right from the second I met him, this
guy was pissed that Houdini hadn't showed up. He assumed I
was a poor substitute who had been dumped on him, and he
ended up getting exactly what he expected. At the end, he
paid me the bare minimum fee: $90. Seventy bucks less than
I'd made for a foursome all year.

When I carried his guests' bag out to the parking lot and was asked the rhetorical question, "Did you get taken care of?" (to which the correct answer is a polite "Yes, I'm taken care of, thank you"), I heard myself say, "Actually no, your cheap-ass host totally stiffed me. Gave me ninety bucks."

I have no idea whether his guests were sympathetic or not, if they recognized what a jerk he had been, but they dug into their wallets regardless and scraped together another $80 or so. I thanked them joylessly and walked back to face my fate.

Caddies called this the *shakedown*, hitting up golfers for more money after being stiffed. It was strictly forbidden, and when I walked back into the cart barn and saw Jeff, the caddie master, the first thing I said was, "I just got fired."

And sure enough, two days later I got called into the head pro's office. He and Jeff were sitting there. They were not smiling. "You already know what this is about."

This wasn't the first firing offense I'd committed at Sherwood. Months earlier, in December, I'd swung Tiger Woods's clubs right in front of the security camera in the bag room. They were standing irresistibly just inside the door after a practice round during his annual tournament. It was like they had a SWING ME sign hanging on them. I popped the head cover off the driver and sniggered when I saw the unmistakable shape of the Titleist 975D head with the Titleist logo on the bottom sanded off and stamped with a Nike swoosh (his new sponsor). And the Nike irons were dead ringers for his old Mizunos, too. I swung them all. I even took the cover off his putter—the one club, a Cameron Newport, he refused to replace—and gave it a couple of strokes dangerously close to the cement floor. All while smiling at the camera in the corner, wondering if there was some rent-a-cop on the other side who had any clue this was Tiger's bag. Apparently not, since I never heard anything about it.

But now that I was actually fired, none of that seemed very daring or funny. It was not a happy moment. I genuinely liked Sherwood and was just starting to feel at home there. I had made some good friends and secured several regulars who came to my defense and vouched for my character, but Jeff already knew my character; that wasn't the issue. The shakedown is forbidden, and the member's word is the final word, no matter how much of a shady asshole he is. A caddie is expendable. Period.

I would later realize that moving on from Sherwood was a blessing, that I hadn't left the East Coast just to settle down somewhere else. As I said, Sherwood was not a destination for me; it was a stepping-stone. Getting fired just forced me to take that next step quicker than I anticipated.

My only real regret is that I didn't tell that prick off to his face. There is a legendary story about a Sherwood caddie who was out on a loop with an especially condescending movie star. The caddie had been out with him several times and had had it with the entitled jerk's attitude. It was especially bad on the first few holes that morning, and the caddie reached his breaking point, couldn't take it for a second longer. At the top of the hill at five he said, "I'll get off here, thanks."

And the movie star asked, "Why? Are you going to forecaddie?"

"No. I'm done. I've had enough of your bullshit. I'll tell Jeff you need another caddie."

And he walked in without looking back. Turned in his

apron and kept walking right out to the parking lot to his car. Drove away and never came back.

That's how I wish I'd gone out.

. . .

Fortunately, it was late February, the height of the golf season out in the California desert. On a tip from a friend, I called Bighorn Golf Club in Palm Desert. The caddie master didn't even hesitate, "Come on out. You can start tomorrow."

Palm Desert is in the Coachella Valley about two hours east of L.A.—an area generally referred to by Californians as the Desert and everyone else as Palm Springs. But Palm Springs is just the most famous of the dozen or so towns that checker the forty-five-mile-long valley, framed on one side by the jagged, crumbling red-rock peaks of the Santa Rosa Mountains and the other by the massive plateau of Joshua Tree National Park.

"The Desert" feels like a bit of a misnomer, too, because even though the place is very much a desert, almost every inch of it is covered with grass. And I'm not talking about wispy dune grass, but the thick green stuff you see in a Scotts Turf Builder commercial. Thousands upon thousands of acres of it—fairways and lawns kept lush by the constant click and hiss of sprinklers. They even water the sidewalks here.

Most of that water is piped up from a giant aquifer under the valley, and some of it comes from old water rights to the Colorado River. The Coachella Valley may be a desert, but it has *tons* of water. There are even waterfalls up in the red-rock canyons fueled by torrents of snowmelt from 10,800-foot Mount San Jacinto.

San Jacinto lords it over the valley like a gatekeeper between L.A. and the Desert. It blocks the smog and ocean
weather, and when there is a storm pushing in from the Pacific, you can see it piled up against the mountain's shoulders, dumping snow on its peak while golfers in shorts play in
eighty-degree sunshine beneath it.

I am not a fan of the Desert's gated communities and
suburban sprawl, nor of most of its cookie-cutter golf courses
and faux Mediterranean malls, but there is no denying the
natural beauty of the place, especially in the spring, when all
of the cacti bloom—the prickly pears with their little yellow
and pink roses, the Spanish bayonets with their white waxy
wedding-cake bouquets, the long spindly ocotillos with their
red feathered tips like Indian paintbrush. And I've seen few
prettier sights than the full moon at dawn pinned to the blue
velvet sky above the snowy shoulder of San Jacinto as the sun
rising opposite sets the face of the mountain aglow—purple,
pink, red—a blend of sky and snow and red rock.

The Desert is a golf town in the same way that, say,
Aspen or Vail are ski towns. There are hundreds of golf
courses, most of the fairways lined with homes—usually
second homes owned by snowbirds and retirees and wealthy
families who vacation here, and resort hotels with their own
golf courses and spas with "golf treatments," like the Golfer's
Facial ("a firm, relaxed putting stroke starts with a firm relaxed face"). There are restaurants and bars with golf names
and themes, like Mulligan's and the 19th Hole and Arnold
Palmer's, which even has its own putting green in the back.
Droves of college grads, aspiring Tour players, dropouts, and
golf bums come to work in these places for the winter. You
see them in caddie yards and cart barns and pro shops all

across the valley. Every dollar they earn, every free moment, is spent on golf.

I'd been caddying for fifteen years and worked in nearly a dozen yards by the time I got to Bighorn. I was confident I knew everything there was to know about caddying and had seen it in all its various forms. No place was perfect, but I'd had it pretty darned good at several clubs, like Atlantic and Maroon Creek, where they were very liberal with the money and the playing privileges. But even those places had their weaknesses—namely, having to sit and wait for hours on end to get a loop, sometimes all day, thirty or more idle men in close proximity. It could drive you mad. Sherwood had solved this by preassigning loops so you only had to show up one hour before your tee time. I can't overstate what a difference this made for morale, especially over the length of a season, as those hours of waiting can add up to entire weeks of your life. On the other hand, Sherwood rarely let us play the course and made us run around like track stars, up and down those steep hills. So as I said, every place has its advantages and disadvantages.

But Bighorn took the caddie experience to a whole new plush level. To start with, not only were the loops preassigned, but they were recorded on a hotline every night so you just had to call in after six and all the caddies' names and tee times were listed. We were also allowed to order lunch at the restaurants on both courses and only had to pay five bucks for a huge club sandwich or cheeseburger with fries and a Coke. We were allowed to play almost every day, as long as we performed "divot duty," driving around nine holes with a bucket of sand and filling all of the fresh divots. One spring during a Pac-10 tournament, the kids tore up the course so badly that the caddie master, Brendan, felt sorry for us and said that if we came every evening during the tournament and sanded the tee boxes and landing areas, we could play unlimited golf the rest of the season without filling any more divots. It was only March, so that meant a solid two months of playing golf every day whether you worked or not. Many afternoons I just showed up at my leisure, ordered a cheeseburger, hit balls on the range (we were allowed to practice, too), which was stocked with brand-new shining Pro V1s, and then teed off and played a casual eighteen holes in a cart.

As if that wasn't enough, there was another caddie perk at Bighorn that was so unheard of, I'd never seen it in all my days nor honestly even thought of it as a possibility (and, believe me, I spent *plenty* of time sitting around the caddie yard thinking about how this job could be better). The caddies at Bighorn had their *own* golf carts. And I don't just mean to play in—we actually *caddied* in carts. I tried to imagine what came after that. Caddies with their own caddies?

But there was a reason behind our being allowed to use carts; it wasn't just a luxury. The carts enabled us to race out ahead of our players to forecaddie. This was especially necessary at Bighorn, because the fairways on both courses (there were thirty-six holes) were hemmed in by desert scrub and rock, so a shot that drifted even slightly off-line could bounce or ricochet wildly in any direction. There was simply no way to tell where it ended up unless you were standing right next to it when it landed. Even then there was no guarantee you were going to find it or be able to play it, but at least the odds were dramatically increased.

When I say the caddies raced out ahead, I mean *raced*. My training loop, with a caddie named Kris, was frightening—

like a roller-coaster ride at Six Flags. Kris took me out on the Mountain Course, which, as its name suggests, is mountainous. These are desert mountains, so we're not talking about grassy slopes with wildflowers that you can run and tumble down like in *The Sound of Music*, but hostile piles of jagged boulders that look like the remains of a mining excavation or meteor strike. And there are cactuses poking out between the boulders—spears of Spanish bayonet, spiked arms of ocotillo, and my favorite, the jumping cholla—a cactus that actually jumps out and pricks you.

Put it this way: I can't think of a landscape more inhospitable to flesh and bone and balata. Those rocks could tear the cover off a Pro V1. I had no desire to find out what they would do to me. And there we were hurtling down curling, forty-five-degree-angled, five-foot-wide cart paths in a vehicle with no doors, six-inch wheels, and a plastic steering wheel. It seemed the height of foolishness.

Kris was talking to me the whole time, yelling over the whooshing air and humming tires. I assume he was describing the course, but I didn't hear a word he said. I was too busy gripping the steering column and cup holder as that bizarre, grassed over, mansion-lined moonscape blasted by me in jarring, high-speed montage.

The first thing that amazed me was the fact that people were willing to spend millions of dollars on homes that were so close together that their air conditioning units fogged up each other's windows. And so close to the edge of the fairway that golf balls pinged off their roofs and patios like hailstones. And because they were built up the side of the mountain, almost every inch of the patio and pool areas, and often most of the indoor and outdoor living areas, were visible from somewhere on the golf course, a tee box or elevated green or mound beside the fairway.

It's amazing that this didn't deter women from sunbathing topless by their pools, and during one of my first loops, when I was standing on a mound next to the third fairway as my four players prepared to tee off hundreds of feet above me, I found myself looking down on two college girls sunbathing by a pool no more than twenty yards away. They were sprawled out on lounge chairs, the straps of their bikini tops dangling by their sides.

The last thing on earth I wanted to do was interrupt their amphibian bliss, but being two hundred yards from the tee and twenty yards from the left edge of the fairway, they were directly in the path of a well-struck snap hook. And in two short holes, the four apes I was caddying for had hooked everything they'd hit, including their putts. "Um . . . excuse me . . . ladies?"

One of them stirred, lifted her head an inch and tilted it my way. "Oh my God, there's a guy standing right there!"

Her friend tilted her head. "Is that a caddie?"

"Sorry to bother you . . ."

"Is he talking to us?"

"I just wanted to warn you that my players are teeing off and they have a tendency to, um, hook the ball. . . ."

"He's definitely talking to us."

"This is so embarrassing. Make him go away."

"He's kind of cute."

"Gross! He's a caddie!"

"It's not like Daddy's place in Bel-Air. The caddies here are cute."

"If I yell Fore! please place your hands over your head

like this"—I imitated the crash position they teach you on an airplane—"and turn away from the tee."

My first player was already standing over his ball, waggling aggressively. I couldn't see his grip from that distance, but I could tell by his wide stance and hunched shoulders that his right hand was rotated all the way under the club—what is known as a strong grip. He had hook written all over him.

I glanced at the girls again. They'd settled back into their slumber. Hadn't registered a word I'd said. Were just hoping I'd go away.

My player swung.

The ball took off like a rocket. It stayed straight for about a hundred fifty yards and then turned sharply toward me as though it was on a string. At the top of my lungs I yelled, "Fooooore!"

The girls did exactly the opposite of what I'd told them to. They turned and looked right at me. When they saw me duck, they screamed and covered their heads. The ball whizzed right over all of us and hit the huge metal barbecue behind them with a deafening clang. It ricocheted off the patio furniture and plopped into the pool.

The girls screamed, "Holy shit!"

They jumped up, so rattled they made only a halfhearted, unsuccessful effort to hold their tops to their chests. They ran, boobs exposed and bouncing, across the patio and disappeared into the house.

"Sorry about that!" I called after them.

Just to add insult to injury, my fourth player skipped one off their roof. I heard the distinct *tic tic* of the ball bouncing down the road, but thankfully no broken glass or car alarms.

The first player came racing up in his cart.

"Is that first one playable?"

Um . . . no.

• • •

For those first couple of weeks, I camped in and around the valley—in Joshua Tree on one side, in the Santa Rosa Mountains on the other, and beside a reservoir in La Quinta. I actually went sledding a couple of mornings up in the pine forests behind San Jacinto before driving down into the valley to caddie, and that made the whole desert experience that much more surreal. Then one day after work, a caddie named Phillips poked his head through my van's sliding door unannounced. (I soon learned that Phillips poked his head into a lot of things unannounced.) He asked me if I needed a place to live. Told me his girlfriend was looking for a roommate. This turned out to be his ex-girlfriend, who was in therapy to get over the trauma of their relationship. I moved in, and Phillips started hanging around again, much to Sarah's consternation.

I could see how she made the mistake of getting involved with him. He was very charismatic and full of energy and ideas. I could also see why she wanted to get rid of him, because under his gregariousness and charm, he had a simmering fatalism, a chip on his shoulder, the kind you usually see only in the older lifers who are caddying to escape some misfortune—a broken marriage, a dead-end career, the law, personal demons—guys who find solace in the mobility, anonymity, and quick cash caddying provides. But Phillips was still in his twenties and wasn't trying to escape anything.

He seemed to come from a good family. His granny lived in one of the nicest golf communities in the desert, where he'd grown up playing. He was extremely golf knowledgeable, and the members seemed to love him. He worked a ton and was constantly being given free golf equipment and getting hooked up to play at clubs all over the valley. From my perspective, he seemed to have it pretty good.

But then he'd spew pessimistic absolutes like "People are all the same!" and "You can't trust anyone." My favorite was "Golf ruins lives." He said this to me one afternoon right after we'd just polished off a couple of cheeseburgers in the Bighorn clubhouse and were cranking a fresh stack of Pro V1s on the driving range before going out to play. I looked around at our beautiful surroundings and tried to imagine how they were ruining us.

"You're such a drama queen, Phillips."

"Don't hate the player; hate the game!"

But he wasn't all fire and brimstone. He had a passionate side as well, and to his credit, he really took advantage of the freedom of caddying. He was always doing cool things like playing great golf courses, going to concerts, racing dirt bikes, rock climbing in Yosemite, snowboarding up in Tahoe. I hate to admit it, because he could be so damn dark, but he reminded me of myself—of all the doubts I'd struggled with through the years and the passion for life that had helped me persevere. He was like the devil and angel, one on each of my shoulders, voicing both my pessimism and optimism. But I was well on my way to getting past the pessimism. I was finally making some legitimate headway with my writing and seeing parts of the world I'd always dreamed about. I'd just gotten back from Australia, and I was headed to Baja California and the Pacific Northwest at the end of the season. I just wanted the dark side of Phillips to shut the hell up.

His problem stemmed in part from the fact that he viewed himself as a failed golfer, a far-fetched belief, given that he never practiced nor exhibited any of the mental toughness and discipline necessary to even sniff success. But golf is unique among sports in nurturing delusional self-appraisals, because unlike tennis, say, which is also technically an individual sport, it is possible to play golf alone—to measure yourself without actually competing against another human being. In other words, it's possible to experience flashes of the game at the highest level—even if it's for just a single round—and believe that is your true potential. And maybe it *is* your true potential, but it's a huge leap to go from shooting a lone 65 on a Wednesday afternoon to doing it four consecutive times in a tournament. To shoot the equivalent of that 65 on *any* day in tennis, you'd have to actually *beat* somebody significant, and that would at least be a real accomplishment. Success in a recreational round of golf is little more than a tease.

But boy, is it a powerful tease, and there were guys all over the valley who had traveled here from every corner of the country and Canada, too, to try their luck at the professional game. I'd seen a few of them in other caddie yards across the country—at Sherwood and Secession—and I knew there were many in Florida, the country's other big winter golf destination, but the Desert was crawling with them. These were the golf bums, and they came in all different shapes and sizes and skill levels. And levels of delusion, too.

There were those who were sober and disciplined and

dead serious in their quest but didn't have a tenth of the talent necessary. There were those who had the talent but were far from sober and serious. They tried to float on talent alone. They could effortlessly shoot those recreational 65s and even fire an occasional low score in a mini-tour event, but sadly, they never buckled down and put in the effort required to take it to the next level. These guys were the real shame, because when they were finally washed up for good, that window of opportunity closed, many of them resigned themselves permanently to the caddie ranks. And in these cases, I could see Phillips's pessimistic point of view that "golf ruins lives," because even if they got a good caddie job out on the big Tour, earning a hundred grand a year, it's got to be a hard pill to swallow, caddying for and supporting someone else who has succeeded at the profession you failed at.

But it wasn't golf that ruined their lives, it was themselves. Failures like this certainly aren't exclusive to golf, but golf holds out the tantalizing hope of success a lot longer than most other pursuits. It's hard to imagine a thirty-year-old basketball or football or hockey player who's never come close to making the pros thinking he still has a chance. Yet there are plenty of those guys still chasing the golf dream in the Desert, and by the time they finally realize they aren't going to make it, they've wasted so many years trying, they've blown their chance to build a career in most other fields. That's why so many of them end up being caddies. Golf is the only thing they know.

I feel the most sympathy for the guys who get close, who really grind and get a taste of the big show—play in a Tour event or two, enjoy some success at the mini-tour level. You see them every other year in the Desert when PGA West hosts the PGA Tour Qualifying School Finals. Their futures pinned to every shot and putt, the pressure gnaws at their swings and putting strokes and the brave game faces they put on. You can see the nervous tics and twitches leaking through cracks in their armor. Like this one guy on the seventeenth tee of the PGA West Stadium Course during the final round of the 2004 Q School. He'd tasted the Tour—had conditional status and lost his card. And now here he was on the brink of getting it back. He just needed to par the last two.

He was standing on the tee of the short, rock-rimmed island par three affectionately known as Alcatraz. There was a devilish little crosswind that couldn't make up its mind. He was conferring with his caddie, tossing pinches of grass that swirled in different directions. Finally he selected his club and glanced at the pregnant girl standing next to me. She smiled and patted her belly. I don't know if she meant to do it, but this was clearly his wife and with that little pat, she'd just said, *Do it for the baby.*

I started to get nervous just standing next to him. His swing was a touch less than smooth, a little punchy, but he managed to hit the green and two-putt for par. The pregnant girl was biting her nails like crazy, but she smiled supportively every time he looked her way. Honestly, I couldn't even bear to watch the eighteenth. I wished her luck and walked over to eleven to follow another group. And if I couldn't even stand watching him as a random spectator, I hate to think how nervous she felt.

I had mixed feelings about watching these guys trying for the Tour. On the one hand, I didn't envy the grind. On the other, I admired them for playing golf for a living. It seemed more noble than just being a caddie, even if many of them were going to end up being caddies anyway. There was something romantic about the pursuit of the dream even if you ultimately failed to make it a reality.

But seeing all these golf bums go at it also gave me a sense of relief that I suffered no such illusions. In that spring of 2004, I had one goal—to save enough money for a road trip with my new girlfriend, Amanda, down to Cabo San Lucas on the tip of the Baja Peninsula, 1,000 miles south of San Diego. I would be a different kind of golf bum—one riding in a cart at Cabo del Sol with a margarita in hand and snuggling with my girl on the beach at night in our tent. And then we'd turn around and drive 2,500 miles north to the tip of the Olympic Peninsula and cross over to Vancouver Island by ferry. Amanda's family had a summer home up there. We would see a huge swath of the Pacific coast of North America, much of it for the first time, and then I was planning to caddie for the remainder of the summer at Bandon Dunes Golf Resort on the southern Oregon coast—an absolutely stunning place that I'd visited only once, years earlier, but never forgotten. Every loop at Bighorn that season was motivated by the promise of that trip. Every dollar that wasn't spent on food or rent went into my Baja fund. So in the end, I didn't really envy the golf bums at all, because I had an upcoming tour of my own that I was guaranteed to make with just a few more months of hard work.

9

CADDIE HEAVEN

BANDON DUNES GOLF RESORT,
BANDON, OR,
2004–2006

When I first arrived in the Desert, I often camped at Lake Cahuilla (named after the Cahuilla Indian tribe), a small man-made 135-acre reservoir that helps feed the vast network of canals and pipes that irrigate the Coachella Valley. There is no swimming or boating allowed on the lake, so I was very surprised to see a sailboat on a trailer at one of the campsites. I went over and struck up a conversation with the fellow who was sitting on board enjoying a beer as if his boat was actually anchored in the water somewhere.

He turned out to be a caddie named John, who'd lived on his sailboat for years—most of them while it was still in the water. But when he started working in the Desert, it no longer made sense to pay the steep docking fees out on the coast, so he hauled the boat, trailered it, and was now living on it here. High and dry.

This odd sight brought me back to my winter in Beaufort, South Carolina, when Timmy, Alden, Big John, and I used to drink at Stewbie's Marina on the Intracoastal Waterway and I made friends with the couple who were sailing around the world. I'd adopted their appealing vision of my caddie life as a voyage—each golf course a port where caddies from far and wide congregated for the season to replenish our "supplies" (read: bank accounts), hobnob with locals, and share our impressions of other ports we'd visited—Shinnecock, Maroon Creek, Bighorn, etc. According to the couple, this wasn't all that different from touring sailors wintering in, say, Honolulu, Cape Town, or Antigua.

And here at Lake Cahuilla, I'd stumbled upon a literal version of this metaphor—a caddie who was actually towing a sailboat from course to course. He was like a character straight out of a Tom Robbins novel—the landlocked sailor. The flawed, slightly less courageous, but no less noble caddie adventurer. Crossing oceans? Having your sails torn to shreds off the Azores? Pah! That just makes you a plain old sailor. But towing a boat on the I-10 and living on it in the Desert? Now, that's pure caddie.

I camped for only a couple of months before meeting Phillips and renting a room from his ex-girlfriend Sarah. And it was a full year later when Amanda and I set out on our three-month, 3,500-mile Baja–to–British Columbia road trip that ended for me at Bandon Dunes Golf Resort on the Oregon coast. From our campsite on the beach on the tip of the Baja Peninsula, we watched the tiny jeweled constellation of the Southern Cross rise from the moonlit waters of the Sea of Cortés, and then two months and twenty-five hundred miles later, we both saw our first northern lights storm sweep across the gulf islands between Victoria and Vancou-ver, British Columbia. As Amanda said so poetically in the moment, "We drove all the way from the Southern Cross to the northern lights!"

Bandon was the perfect "port" for me to summer in at the end of our Pacific voyage, because it was only a day's drive south of our final destination in Washington's San Juan Is-lands. At the end of June, I dropped Amanda at the small airport in Eugene, Oregon, to fly back to Southern Califor-nia, then drove the final two hours down to Bandon, where I was planning to spend the rest of the summer caddying. I camped the first night at a little RV park on the Coquille River just a few miles from the golf resort. It was a favor-ite camping spot for salmon fisherman, and even though it wasn't salmon season yet, there were already several boats trailered there, mostly aluminum skiffs with outboard mo-tors. But there was one boat that caught my attention be-cause it was the only sailboat in the campground. I thought that was interesting in and of itself, and then I realized I was looking at the same sailboat I'd seen at Lake Cahuilla a year earlier, the one owned by John the caddie. And sure enough, there he was, enjoying a beer on the deck after a hard day's work on the fairways of Bandon Dunes. I hurried over and said hello. "Hey, John! Did you sail up?"

"Nope. Trailered."

"How was the trip?"

"A little rough coming up the I-5, boat blows around pretty good when those sixteen-wheelers go by."

I nodded solemnly and tried not to chuckle, because I doubt John would've appreciated my take on the voyaging caddie who tows his boat instead of sailing it, nor how funny it sounded that a sailboat "blowing around" was a problem. The last thing I wanted to do was spoil the moment, because I'd just pulled my own boat (van) into port and was genuinely glad to be enjoying a beer on his deck, "anchored" there on the grass five minutes from Bandon Dunes.

I don't know what the most popular destination is among touring sailors, but I can tell you Bandon Dunes was about to become the most popular one for caddies. When I arrived in late June 2004, the first course had already been open for five years, the second for three, and the ground for a third had just been broken. Riding the wave of its success, the resort was plowing forward. They were building new lodges and restaurants and roads to meet the growing demand. The caddie yard was no exception. They'd recently hired a new "professional" caddie master to shepherd the yard from its humble local beginnings into a humming high-volume operation, one the likes of which the caddie world had never seen—*hundreds* of caddies from all across the country. But that was still a couple of years away. When I got to Bandon, the caddie shack was a pair of temporary trailers left over from the construction of the second course, and the caddie yard was still staffed heavily with locals.

On my first loop, I went out on the original course, Bandon Dunes, with my new boss, caddie master Ken Brooke, and the designer of the course, a young Scotsman named David Kidd. It was quite an introduction being out there with the architect himself, hearing about all of the challenges, choices, and last-minute changes during construction, such as owner Mike Keiser's purchase of the adjacent property while they were still routing Bandon, allowing David to expand his original plans and build four holes on the new land—

five, six, seven, and eight. The adjacent property was now home to the second course, too—the Tom Doak–designed Pacific Dunes. I felt guilty even glancing over at Pacific as we played the holes that border it, because it had stolen some of Bandon Dunes's thunder, even been hailed as "the greatest golf course in the galaxy." David was justifiably feeling a little snubbed, and I was afraid if he caught me looking that way, it might ignite his short Scottish fuse. "Yes, that's focking Pacific! Go ahead, take a good, long look at it!"

I did. I couldn't resist. Pacific was as much a visual master-piece as a strategic puzzle. It was wild and rough-hewn—much darker and tougher looking than open, smooth-contoured Bandon. It literally looked as though they'd just stuck flags in the ground, which was amazing, considering that almost every inch of it had been shaped by bulldozers and back-hoes. On Bandon I could see the machine work—the star patterns around the greens, the perfectly round mounding lining the fairways and neat sod-stacked bunkers. Bandon looked shaped on top of the terrain. Pacific looked cut out of it. And as I would soon discover, because the caddies worked equally at both courses, this was not just an aesthetic differ-ence. Pacific's wild contours produced an equal amount of wild bounces, which probably explains why, even though it was the critics' darling, most golfers still preferred Bandon. I would've said that to David, but it was my first day, so I didn't know what any other golfers thought yet. Besides, his salty, sardonic demeanor suggested more than a hint of pleasure at playing the victim.

I was especially fascinated by the huge green mounds and long reefs of razor-sharp gorse (a spiky Scottish plant) that frame the fairways and greens on both courses, giving them a maze-like quality and adding some intimacy to the otherwise open and exposed linksland. The gorse isn't native. It was brought to Bandon by a Scotsman a century ago, either as a nostalgic bit of the homeland or as natural fencing for his sheep. There is no doubting its effectiveness for the latter. If you fenced me in the gorse, I wouldn't be able to get out. The stuff is impenetrable. I said as much to David and he snapped back, "You should try hackin' fairways out of the bloody stuff!"

"Why didn't you just burn it?"

"They wouldn't let me. Fire hazard. This town burned to the ground twice, you know."

"So how did you do it? With tractors?"

"With a lot of beer. That's how."

And that's pretty much the way the round went—me asking a million stupid questions and David giving me wiseass answers that I wasn't sure were true or were at my expense for his entertainment. But I hardly cared if he was making fun of me or not, because I was experiencing that blown away, blissed-out feeling that all first-time visitors to Bandon experience—being so gobsmacked by the scenery that whatever's happening on the golf course (the score, the conversation, a crappy caddie, or curmudgeonly player) hardly matters. Somebody, owner Mike Keiser or David Kidd, depending on whom you ask (I'll let you guess who David says), resisted the obvious temptation to build the hotel out on the bluff overlooking the ocean, so when you finally reach the bluff at Bandon's fourth you see only golf holes stretching in either direction.

The buildup to the "reveal" is palpable. You first see the ocean from the elevated third tee on the inland side of the property—a panorama of fairways, sea, and sky—then you dip down behind the dunes again. The real kicker comes when you turn the corner at four and the ocean is suddenly right there in front of you, the green framed against the infinite backdrop of the Pacific. It's as if someone flipped the switch on an IMAX projector. And that first day was one of those rare bluebird summer days on the Oregon coast when the steady, twenty- to thirty-knot north wind inexplicably vanishes and the restless green sea lies down and turns a brilliant arctic blue. What you would call a perfect day.

But the sea has a hundred moods, and I would come to appreciate them all. Those holes along the bluff are arguably even more dramatic when it is stormy and steel gray and shafts of silver light pierce the clouds and illuminate patches of the dark, choppy sea. Or when the fog is in and you can't see anything but can still feel the presence of the sea—hear it rumbling and smell the salt and kelp much more keenly in the misty stillness. But on that cloudless, windless first afternoon, I looked at the miles of uninhabited coastline—not a single human structure in view—and I asked my new boss, Ken, "Why doesn't anyone live here?"

He said, "Wait till tomorrow."

True to his word, the next day the fog was socked in till noon. It swallowed everything—the fairways, the greens, the balls. And then, as if on cue, right at the strike of noon, it suddenly broke and and the wind cranked up as if a director had yelled, "Start the wind!"

In minutes the flags were rattling in the holes, sand was blowing out of the bunkers like glass dust, and we were screaming at each other from five feet away. The poor people down on the beach trying to enjoy the first day of July were bent against the wind in sweaters and windbreakers or hunkered down behind the dunes so their picnic lunches wouldn't fly away. That's why Oregonians don't call this the beach. They don't say, "Let's spend the weekend at the *beach*." They say, "Let's spend the weekend at the *coast*." And by this they mean the *storm coast* where the Arctic and Pacific currents clash and whip up storms that'll rip a roof off a house. Entire trees wash ashore and waves pound the jetty at the river mouth with such ferocity, it's hard to imagine anything less seaworthy than a Coast Guard cutter getting in and out of here on most days.

That's why no one lives here.

And frankly, it's amazing that people fly here from all over the country to play golf. They brave the harrowing propeller-plane flight into the tiny North Bend airport, a flight that ends with a big bank turn out over the glorious Pacific and an ominous drop into the fog, where you bounce, leap, and jostle through purgatory until you punch out the bottom and everyone gasps because you're only a hundred feet above the black water, speeding up the Coos River toward a runway that looks like a fishing pier.

But they do come. In droves. And credit goes to the resort's owner and founder, Mike Keiser, for somehow knowing they would, for having faith that all of the American golfers who travel to Scotland every summer to brave the wind and rain and walk miles on brown concrete do it because they actually *like* it and would be just as happy to do it here as there. Credit him for trusting golfers' taste and intelligence enough to resist building an easily marketable signature course stamped with Jack Nicklaus's or Arnold Palmer's name, choosing instead to build a pair of true links courses—

the first designed by an unknown and untested Scot and the second by a barely more recognizable American (Tom Doak is famous now *because* of Pacific Dunes). Perhaps most daring of all, he decided to require every golfer who comes to Bandon to walk the courses—carry one's own bag, pull it on a trolley, or take a caddie. You can take a cart at Bandon only if you have a bona fide medical excuse, and even then, you *still* have to take a caddie.

Keiser was like a beautiful, high-maintenance woman playing hard to get, gambling that the less accessible she is, the more interested the men will be. That's a dangerous game. A woman that bold better be *fetching*. But Keiser's confidence was understandable. I can imagine him visiting the property for the first time when it was still grazing land for sheep— standing out on that bluff where the fourth green sits today, and basking in the golden glow of the Pacific marveling at the thunderous surf and miles of empty beaches (maybe even feeling that the presence of Scottish gorse was a sign from the Golf Gods that this was the place), and *knowing* in his heart of hearts that every golfer who watched his ball bound and soar along the edge of those bluffs (and sometimes over the edge) would never be able to forget it and forever want to return. Boy, was he right!

This is the reason I was at Bandon and the reason my new boss was, too. With the great success of the first two courses and the third on the way, it was unlikely that Keiser was going to stop there. He owned enough land for five or six courses, and if he was going to hold firm to his walking-only policy on every one of them, he was going to need caddies. *Lots of them.* I'm not saying Ken would've hired me if I was a deaf, mute gorilla, but if I'd been just slightly better than that, say, a cute chimpanzee, he probably would have. When we shook hands on eighteen, I was officially a Bandon caddie.

I walked back to my van all smiles, the midsummer sun still high in the sky. I rounded the corner past the temporary trailers that were acting as the caddie shack, and whom should I find leaning against my van? Phillips.

"Need a roommate?" he asked.

"If you like wet grass and snoring salmon fishermen."

"I *love* snoring salmon fisherman!"

So Phillips and I split a site at the campground where John's boat was "anchored." It was a simple place—a little old lady's house down by the river. Just a few acres of grass with some basic water and electrical hookups, firepits, and picnic tables. Her son had constructed a cement bathroom that was almost sanitary, as long as you showered in sandals and didn't make actual physical contact with the walls. It was $10 a night. Combining resources, we could pay a month's rent in one morning and still have money left over for lunch.

At first the little old lady was very welcoming to us "caddie folks." She was surprised and superhappy to suddenly find her campground full all summer as opposed to just the months surrounding the fall salmon season. Like most everyone else in Bandon, she'd never heard of a *caddie* before. She put her hands on her squat little hips and shook her head in disbelief when we told her what we did for a living.

"And why can't these golfers carry their own bags? Are they handicapped or something? Is this one of them *special-needs* places?"

"No, ma'am. They *can* carry their bags. They are *able* to carry their bags. They just choose not to."

"Jiminy Cricket! A perfectly healthy man who's too lazy

to carry his own golf clubs! We never would've won the Second World War with the bellyachers in this country today!"

I decided not to get into nuances of the game, like green reading, because I could hear her already. "They got eyes, don't they?"

To say Bandon (population two thousand) wasn't a golf town before the resort's arrival is putting it mildly. Their one golf course had been a muddy field with nine flags in it. And the only town near Bandon that had a "real" eighteen-hole course was the *big town* twenty-five miles away—Coos Bay (population fifteen thousand). So when the resort first began looking for caddies, meaning *anyone* with golf experience, the pickings were slim.

This area had once supported thriving fishing and timber industries. Coos Bay had been a major sawmill and port, so many of the locals who became caddies had been fishermen, lumberjacks, mill workers, and longshoremen. One of the older guys, nicknamed Wyatt, who'd been a longshoreman, told me the Coos River used to be so choked with logs floating down from the clear-cuts up in the hills that you could walk across it. And the guys down in the mills and on the wharves in town couldn't pull 'em out and saw 'em up fast enough to load the trucks and barges that shipped them off to ports near and far.

There are still a couple of working mills along the river, and you still see the occasional truck rumbling along Route 1 between Bandon and Coos Bay with its trailer full of pine trees stripped and stacked like matchsticks. But the most obvious remaining evidence of the industry are the clear-cuts beside the road. They are poorly hidden by a single row of trees intended to keep them from startling passing motorists.

From the air you can really see them. The denuded hills look like a company of fresh marine recruits crowded together in the barber shop, some of them already completely bald, others on their way.

Pro timber folks call the forest a renewable resource, a crop. I guess by renewable they are referring to the stubble of Christmas trees sprouting up in the sea of stumps. And maybe they're right, maybe one day those sprouts will become proud trees, and those stumps will rot and feed the forest floor, and all of the loam and lichens and fungi and grubs and insects and a million other essential components that constitute a forest (as opposed to a Christmas tree farm) will return. Fifty or a hundred years from now these hills will once again qualify for the term *ecosystem* and once again be loggable. In the meantime, the timbermen and longshoremen have turned to another more immediately renewable resource: golfers.

Bandon is a port, too, but tiny by comparison—just a small fleet of near-shore fishers that trawl daily for halibut and ling cod and the like, and some small recreational boats that cruise the Coquille River. The town's main remaining industry is cranberries. You see the huge square bogs dug into fields along the back roads outside of town, and after the harvest in September, Bandon throws a three-day Cranberry Festival with a Cranberry Queen and booths piled with just about every cranberry-inspired food item you can think of. But most people who'd visited Bandon before the resort remember it as a charming little tourist town—a fish-and-chips and salt-water-taffy stop on the summer RV circuit. When I first saw it, the historic four-block downtown reminded me of Montauk or Block Island in the 1970s (where my family

spent some of our summer vacations)—the streets lined with
mom-and-pop shops selling myrtle wood carvings, kites, and
weather vanes, families fishing for Dungeness crabs on the
docks and eating ice cream at picnic tables overlooking the
harbor. And it's still that way. The silver-haired septuagenari-
ans on RV tours still sit silently across from one another in the
restaurant booths, their hands folded neatly in front of them
on red and white checkered tablecloths, their bags full of ce-
ramic lighthouses and huckleberry jam stowed safely beside
them. But now in the evenings you see a new element—what
might to the untrained eye appear to be packs of insurance
salesmen or dentists roaming around at a convention or, in
their edgier, more boisterous incarnations, packs of old frat
brothers reunited for a weekend in Vegas. (Remember those
buddy trips I mentioned in South Carolina?)

For caddies there is no mistaking these guys. We can
identify them a mile away by their visors and V-necks, logoed
shirts and pleated shorts, their ankle socks or, if they happen
to be going sockless, ankle sock *tans*. These guys may indeed be insurance salesmen and dentists, but that's not what
unites them; that's not why they are here. They are here because they are golfers—and by golfers, I don't mean guys who
just *play* golf; I mean guys who *travel* to play golf, who are the
core constituency of the golf-resort circuit. You see them in
Pinehurst, Myrtle Beach, Pebble Beach, Palm Springs, Cabo,
Kiawah, St. Andrews, etc. And now you see them here, in
this tiny, middle-of-nowhere coastal town that you'd miss if
you blinked, a place not a single one of these guys would've
ever set foot if it weren't for Bandon Dunes.

I don't think anyone except for Keiser, and probably not
even him, realized the extent to which they would come.

It didn't happen overnight, but being so small, Bandon felt the impact immediately. In the beginning it was mainly the restaurants and bars that noticed the increased business, because these guys aren't much for shopping (unless were talking about logoed golf swag). But now that the two courses were established and there was a third on the way, the resort's repeat business was kicking in, the net was widening. Guys were starting to bring their wives and even occasionally their kids, basically doing whatever it took to get to Bandon, because most wives were amenable to only one buddy trip a year. On several occasions when I was looping for couples, the husband confided in me quietly off to the side that he'd spent his buddy trip that year somewhere else and then talked his wife into coming here. Very crafty.

But Bandon actually *is* a romantic place to bring your wife or girlfriend. It's even a nice place to bring older kids who like to golf. And so what if that means spending one precious afternoon in town shopping or walking on the beach? Bandon is a genuine slice of small-town Americana, and the beaches here are some of the most rugged and beautiful I've ever seen. They stretch for miles, lined with cliffs, littered with driftwood and tide pools, studded with rock chimneys that rise from the surf like totem poles, their goblin faces staring out to sea. Rivers rush down out of the hills, tumble through rock quarries, plummet in misty plumes from hundred-foot cliffs. I lobbied my players to explore the surrounding area so many times, you'd think I worked for the Bandon Tourist Commission. I told them to take a short break from their three- and four-day golf marathons, just one afternoon to see some of the place.

My pleas fell mostly on deaf ears that first summer, except

for one player who came cheerfully striding up to the first tee on the final morning of his stay, slapped me on the back, and said, "Thanks for the recommendation, John! We went out last night, and you are *totally* right. This place is *amazing*! We went to the strip club up in Coos Bay, and I swear that's the first time I ever paid a girl to put her clothes *back on*!"

That's not exactly what I meant.

In any event, the resort's increasing popularity did eventually translate into more tangible gains for the local economy—into more nautical-themed napkin sets and bags of chocolate cranberries sold. But it would be a mistake to attribute this purely to golfers because there was another force to be reckoned with, an *x* factor or side effect, a hard-to-calculate by-product of a "walking only" golf resort: the caddies.

The local folks probably didn't notice the new arrivals so much at first, because we blended in pretty well with the roughnecks who were already there, the original local caddies and the remaining lumberjacks and fishermen. We drank at the same bars, stayed at the same crappy motels, camped out at the same dingy RV parks. We were like their long-lost cousins, following golfers the way they follow trees and fish. Sure, we looked a little different, with our visors and polo shirts, but we drank and gambled with the same vigor and shared their libertarian attitudes and solitary, wandering ways.

That first afternoon, Phillips and I were at a bar in town celebrating our new job when a big, bearded tree of a man sitting next to us leaned over and said, "You fellars are a couple of them caddies." He didn't say it like it was a question. He said it matter-of-factly. He nodded and raised his beer. "You're all right."

He called to the bartender, "Buy these fellars a round."

"What do you do?" I asked.

He flexed his massive arm and said, "What's it look like I do? I fell trees."

We traded stories over several pitchers. The bar grew steadily busier as caddies came in off the links, fishermen off the water, cranberry farmers off the bog. There weren't more than a handful of women in the place, and they were all pretty rough looking. I mentioned this to our new friend. He asked, "You know what a Bandon hickey is?"

"I have no idea."

"It's when a lady takes you home to her double-wide, gets down on her knees next to her water bed, pulls out her teeth, and starts to give you a hummer. When she sets them teeth on the dresser and really gets down to business, you reach over her shoulder and grab 'em. You grab her teeth and"—he made a chomping motion with his fingers—"and you bite her on the neck with 'em!"

A great booming laugh erupted from his barrel of a chest. He slapped me on the back so hard I spit out my beer.

"Get it? You bite her with her own damned teeth! That's a Bandon hickey!"

I thought it was pretty funny, but Phillips *loved* it. He was roaring. Laughing so hard he almost fell out of his stool. When we stumbled out of the bar sometime after dark into the damp, misty streets, the shops all shuttered, the boats bumping restlessly in their slips, he drew a deep, satisfied breath, spread his arms wide, and said, "I love this place!"

At first the love seemed to be generally reciprocated, too, even by the local caddies, who had every reason to fear our competition. We must've seemed to them as the early white men did to the Indians—the fur trappers in their moccasins and coonskin hats. We blended in well enough and were accepted in small numbers, but once word about the abundance out west spread to caddie yards near and far, it dawned on the local Indians that there were a *lot* of us white men coming, and suddenly they got a little concerned. And so did the local proprietors and police, too. Once our invisible positive impact—more quarters in the Laundromat machines, increased business for the taxi drivers, an uptick in the sale of socks and medicated foot powder and pizza—was obscured by our more visible negative impact—our propensity for drinking and gambling and gathering in large numbers at the local bars, spilling out into the streets and causing a loud late-night ruckus. Once we reached a critical mass and could no longer be ignored, the word *caddie* finally, permanently took hold in the local consciousness.

I imagine the sheriff calling a meeting one morning and pointing to a dry-erase board where he'd written:

"CADDIE"

An employee of Bandon Dunes Golf Resort who carries golf bags for golfers who are, for some reason, unable or not allowed to carry their own.

Similar in drinking habits and public debauchery—urinating, copulating, marijuana smoking, and general loud disorderliness—to lumberjacks and fishermen, but deceptively benign in appearance—clean shaven, short hair, polo shirts, pleated slacks.

Important Note: caddies are similar in appearance to the Very Important People known as golfers, who also travel in packs and sometimes publicly urinate and make general loud disturbances.

Approach all preppy, polo-shirt-clad suspects with care. We do not want to upset any golfers by suggesting they might be caddies.

It wasn't long before drunken late-night revelry became a problem at the campground, too. And when the police came looking for a couple of caddies who'd caused some trouble in town, it dawned on the little old lady who owned the place that we weren't just benign little buttercups sprouting on her lawn, but more like patches of crabgrass threatening to spread and take over the place. Suddenly that sweet woman became a foul-mouthed tank, and her fiery redheaded son, who'd kept his booze-ignited temper in check at her bidding, was released upon us.

Phillips and I quickly packed up and moved across the street to the state park, where we'd been showering anyway because its bathrooms were like the Ritz-Carlton compared to that old lady's moldy cinderblock spigot. The state park's handicapped bathroom, in particular, was so spacious, you could do yoga in there if you wanted to. It had a bench and a full-length mirror and blow dryers and everything. One morning I emerged all coiffed and able-bodied, the picture of health, and some persnickety old hen nodded at the handicap sign and gave me some serious stink eye. I stared right back.

"What? I'm mentally handicapped."

The state park rangers were on to the caddies, too. We were the ones sneaking in to shower without paying, overstaying the two-week limit, overflowing the two-cars-per-campsite limit, and of course, overextending the 10:00 p.m. noise curfew. I don't know if they powwowed with the police or not, but I think at some point they realized they had an infestation on their hands that was much more problematic than crabgrass—an invasive species like lamprey eels or Brazilian waterweed or European bark beetles, one that cannot be eradicated so must be understood and managed. When Phillips and I first checked in at the campground entrance, we responded to the ranger's suspicious questioning with bright, innocent smiles.

"Yes, sir, there are just two of us. Only camping for two weeks, sir. Affirmative, only have two vehicles. Well aware and *grateful* the noise curfew is ten p.m. Need our beauty sleep!"

We dealt with the two-week limit by alternating between Bullards Beach State Park, right next to the golf course, and Sunset Bay State Park, forty-five minutes north of the course near Cape Arago—the major headland you can see from the fairways along the bluff. True to its name, Sunset Bay is a little horseshoe of sand with rock walls on either side that jut out to sea and form a passage or channel that at the height of summer frames perfectly the setting sun. And when the surf is up, huge plumes of spray explode off the rocks, reflecting the evening sky as they rise—purple, red, pink, gold—like a natural version of those fountain light shows in Vegas.

It is quite a sight and one of the most photographed scenes on the Oregon coast, but from a caddie's point of view, there's an even more beautiful part of Sunset Bay that is rarely if ever photographed—the nine-hole golf course tucked back in the wooded valley behind the campground. In my romantic mind, it was like a poor man's Augusta National, with fairways cut through the pines, its own humble, meandering version of Rae's Creek, even an homage to the famous par-three twelfth with its shallow sliver of green. Phillips and I would start a fire in the metal ring in our campsite, pack a couple of beers into our golf bags, and walk barefoot up the gravel road to play a quick nine while the fire burned down into coals perfect for cooking fish and potatoes and corn on the cob wrapped in foil.

Phillips was totally in his element at the state campgrounds. He loved hobnobbing with all the RVers cruising the coast. The families down from upstate—sometimes a full four generations of them all camped together in an assortment of pop tops and tents, a tablecloth thrown over the picnic table, and folding chairs arranged around the fire. He and his very cute pit bull mix, Sierra, would roam the campground, strike up a conversation here and there, and the next thing you'd know, he'd be sitting down to dinner with a family, a paper plate in his lap heaped with barbecued chicken and baked beans, Sierra next to him slopping up her own generous serving. Phillips would charm them with tales of his adventurous caddie life—how he and his *best buddy* John were camping here while looping at the amazing nearby Bandon Dunes. People were genuinely excited to hear about the Dunes because there was a buzz on the RV circuit that the sleepy little town of Bandon had a fancy new golf resort. When I returned from work or dinner or a sunset round of golf, Phillips would wave excitedly and say, "John, come on over and meet my new friends Dale and Jeanie and Bettie and Bobby. They're down from Corvallis for the weekend! I told them they've got to go play the Dunes tomorrow and that we'd love to caddie for them."

I'd shake my head and grumble under my breath, *Has he told you how golf ruins lives yet?* But then I'd smile and play nice, because I had to admire his industriousness. I'd never seen a caddie drum up loops at a campground before, and besides, how could I begrudge Phillips his love for this noncommittal, transitory camaraderie when I enjoyed it so much myself—meeting people while traveling, bonding over shared experiences and new discoveries. It wasn't all that different from caddying at the Dunes, where we were assigned a new group of golfers every three or four days, most of them first-time visitors not only to the golf resort but the entire Oregon coast. And because I was new that summer, too, I saw everything from the same fresh perspective. When we made that cinematic turn at four on Bandon and my players' jaws dropped, I was right there with them feeling just as awed and inspired.

One afternoon one of my golfers and I were standing side by side on Pacific's fourth tee gazing out to sea (both courses reach the sea at four) when suddenly, no more than two hundred yards offshore, an impossibly large gray shape exploded from the water and launched into the air. It rolled over with a giant paddle of an arm extended as though it was waving at us and then it crashed back into the water with a great splash. My player shouted, "Holy shit! Did you see that?"

I yelled, "Oh my God, that was a whale!"

As much as I encouraged golfers to get out and experience the Oregon coast, I had to admit, you could experience a lot of it right there on those links. This was not some hermetically sealed golf experience. There were no picket fences or privet hedges, no checkerboard mower lines or flower boxes beside the tee. There wasn't even a single human habitation anywhere in sight. And the game out there was just as wild as the scenery. The ball hurtled downwind and bounced around on that rippled, weather-sculpted terrain like a pinball. As amazed as my player had been by that whale, he was even more blown away when I handed him a nine iron from two hundred yards.

"I thought you said it was two hundred?"

"I did, but it's blowing thirty and the fairway is as hard as concrete and you *do not* want to go over. Trust me."

A two-hundred-yard nine iron sounded superhuman to him, beyond even what Tiger Woods would hit. He tried to resist, "How about a *seven* iron?"

But I insisted. I blocked the bag and held the nine out in front of me until he relented. I made him promise to trust the club and not overswing. He promised, and when that ball soared, bounded, rolled, and then somehow miraculously curled to a stop thirty feet behind the pin, the unconvinced cock of his brow lifted into a full arch of trusting joy—a big, beaming smile that said, *You the man!* For the rest of the round, he accepted every club I handed him without question, no matter how insane it sounded.

This was the beauty of caddying at Bandon. First, it was such a spectacular walk that no amount of bad golf could spoil it. Second, the playing conditions were so different from almost anywhere else in the United States—much closer to the links of Scotland and Ireland—that the adjustments and compensations you had to make for the wind and firm, undulating turf were unfathomable to most players. I was familiar with the conditions only because of all those autumn rounds I'd played at Shinnecock after they turned the water off. Bandon and Pacific made the caddies look like heroes; I could save a first-time visitor ten strokes, no exaggeration. I had one stubborn guy out on Pacific who wouldn't listen to me for the first six holes. He argued with everything I said and ended up bunkered on every hole—left, right, short, long—sometimes twice a hole. When he ignored the far right line I gave him off the sixth tee, hit it down the left side instead and made triple, he looked as though he'd just gotten pummeled in the first round of a prize fight. We'd played only 6 of 108 scheduled holes, and he was already nine over.

"I know you probably don't believe me," he said, "but I'm a five handicap!"

"I'll believe you're a five handicap if you believe that I've been caddying for fifteen years and I know what I'm doing."

He nodded. "OK. Fair enough."

I told him if he followed every instruction I gave him starting right then and there, no arguments, no second-guessing, I would get him in under 85, and we would break 80 that afternoon. He surrendered. He became clay in my hands, a little rigid at first, but as the bounces and breaks started going our way, he became softer, more pliable, and our round started to take shape. When we reached sixteen, we were still nine over.

On the sixteenth tee he said, "We have a chance to break 80!"

"We did until you said that."

"Oh, come on. This hole is only 310 yards, and eighteen is a par five."

"This 310-yard hole is the hardest par on the course. Five is a good score here."

"Five? I'm going to make *three*!"

His newfound confidence I'd worked so hard to nurture turned him against me, especially after he hit a perfect drive. When I told him to hit his approach shot—a seventy-yard sand wedge—into a collection area to the left of the green, he laughed in my face. "Miss the green *on purpose*! With a *sand wedge?*"

"If you put it in that collection area, we can get out of here with a four."

"I told you, I'm going to make three."

He went straight for the pin and, I'll give him credit, he hit a beautiful high sand wedge, but the wind took the spin right out of it, and it bounced over that skating rink of a green and buried in the face of the back bunker. The resulting lie was so bad, he hit himself in the leg with the next shot and didn't even finish the hole. We barely spoke on seventeen and eighteen, but on the final green, he hung his head and said, "I promise to listen to you this afternoon."

He did, and we shot 77.

This was such a different dynamic from all of those private courses I'd worked, where the members played every week, some of them for years. Those courses were extensions of their backyards. They knew them as well if not better than the caddies. Yes, most of them politely deferred to us on yardages, reads, club selection, etc., but that was more ritualistic than substantial, because they could just as easily have calculated everything for themselves. And while I'm sure it was always a joy to be out on their home course, especially if their home course was, say, Shinnecock, they'd played those fairways so many times, the experience rarely if ever qualified as *exhilarating*. It was often *pleasant* and sometimes, if they played well and the weather and company were fine, even *very* pleasant—enough to elicit a spontaneous pat on the caddie's back or a wink that exuded self-satisfaction in that fine moment. But I never once saw the expression of childlike wonder that regularly appeared on the faces at Bandon, and I rarely felt the genuine glowing admiration and gushing gratitude for my caddie skills that I felt at Bandon—admiration that translated into a real enthusiasm and curiosity about me and my life beyond the links.

"Are you from here? How did you get here? What is it like to live here? Do you get to play out here?"

And when I told my players about my 3,500-mile Baja-to-Vancouver road trip and pointed to Cape Arago and said, "I'm camping in a cove just north of that headland and, yes, I play out here all the time, almost every evening," I saw a sparkle of envy I'd never seen in a golfer's eyes before. I heard them say time and time again, "I'd love to trade places with you for just one summer."

And I've no doubt they meant it. Bandon was exotic, fresh, and exciting. It represented something beyond the routines and rituals of everyday life, beyond the familiar scope of normal existence, no matter how posh and privileged that existence might be. I felt its pull just as strongly as the golfers, but Bandon held a different charm for me. Yes, I loved the remoteness and ruggedness and freedom of the place, but as a caddie I'd always felt free, and I'd traveled to many remote places in the off-seasons. It was the sense of *belonging* that was new and unexpected.

When I'd worked at private courses, most of the members treated me wonderfully, bent over backward to make me and all the caddies feel at home. At some of the clubs, we enjoyed such generous playing privileges that we actually played more than the members did—like at Bighorn, where in the midst of hitting a stack of Pro V1 range balls and playing a sunset eighteen in a cart, it was easy to forget we were just caddies. But when I dropped the cart off and walked back to the caddie parking lot at the end of the day, past the kids splashing and screaming in the club swimming pool, past the million-dollar houses with their lush lawns and well-tended gardens, I was reminded how far removed this world was from my life outside the gates. The road I was traveling in my beat-up old van didn't ultimately lead anywhere near here. I wasn't a day or dollar closer to actually joining a club like Bighorn or even buying a house in the same town. This was only a temporary stop. I was here only because I was the help.

The caddies were technically the help at Bandon, too, but Bandon is a public golf resort, and at the end of the week, it was the guests who went home. We we were the ones who stayed. We were the ones who came to intimately know every nuance of wind and weather, every bounce and break, because in addition to caddying out there every day, we were granted unlimited playing privileges. The powers that be—Keiser and Ken—believed that a caddie's pride in and knowledge of the golf course are essential to the "traditional walking experience," so they allowed us to play whenever there was an empty tee time. My favorite time to play was sunset, preferably alone, as I always had, going all the way back to those childhood rounds with Lumpus in Fairfield. And Pacific was my favorite course. I'd grab a beer at the halfway house out by the fourth tee, lie back in the lee of a dune overlooking the ocean and let that amazing scene wash over me, maybe even doze off for a few minutes in the silky fescue grass. Then I'd tee off any hole that was open, and if it was quiet, I'd play cross-country golf, reimagine Pacific as if I'd designed it myself. My favorite pair of "hybrid holes" actually crossed over to Bandon and back—a par three from the upper tee on Pacific's tenth down to Bandon's sixth green and then a par four from the middle of Bandon's seventh fairway back up Pacific's tenth to the upper green. But nothing compared to playing backward off of Pacific's fourteenth tee out into the undeveloped dunes that would eventually become the fourth course. I plotted an entire eighteen through those sandy wastes, and years later I watched with envy when Tom Doak returned for an encore and dug that plot up like a kid in a giant sandbox with life-size Tonka trucks. I was proud that he routed at least one hole exactly as I had—the uphill par-four fourteenth that climbs what had been a windblown dune to a green perched on the very top. Once there was grass on it, it was a hell of a lot easier to climb but nowhere near as romantic.

I felt just as much at home away from the course. The Oregon coast had long been a refuge for the unfettered, the off-kilter, the nonconformist, and when that first fall finally rolled around and I decided to trade my tent for a solid roof over my head, I moved in with two like-minded souls—a wild-mushroom harvester, Michael, nicknamed Migs, and his Pilates instructor girlfriend, Kaetlyn. Migs and Kaetlyn lived in a pair of A-frame cabins way back in the woods behind town, beyond the cranberry fields at the end of a dead-end dirt road. Migs had cleared the trees around the cabins so they had a cozy little field hemmed in by towering pines (and one giant redwood that had somehow migrated up from California). There was a stream running through the property that we pumped our water from, and Migs cleared a plateau on the other side of the stream, pulled out all the stumps, tilled it, and planted grass. When the grass grew in, he did what any clear-thinking man would do—he mowed it short and cut a golf hole in the center of it. Voilà! A 135-yard par three with the back tee conveniently located right next to the barbecue. We spent many an afternoon grilling salmon and Dungeness crab, swilling beers, and firing golf shots across the creek.

Kaetlyn named their home Rivendell after the Elven Valley in *The Lord of the Rings*. They were not wealthy, but they owned their little piece of paradise. Bandon was remote and sparsely populated enough that real estate was still affordable, and it was possible to buy a beautiful home on a wild-mushroom harvester's and a Pilates instructor's income—though I found some humorous irony in the fact that Migs, who had moved all the way from Staten Island to middle-of-nowhere Oregon, made at least part of his living by selling the mushrooms he harvested—porcini, chanterelle, matsutake—to fancy restaurants back in New York. And Kaetlyn had recently added a "golfer's workout" to her Pilates offerings. So their life "off the grid" was powered by an extension cord. (Not to mention my rent, which came straight from "the man.")

But it was that very extension cord, the unlikely presence of the resort in that far-flung corner of the country, the last wild coast, that made it possible for the caddies to carve out a life for ourselves, too—buy or build that dream home near a golf resort we could call our own, where we were as close to being members as anyone. A resort that offered such good golf—arguably the best collection of courses in the world—that it was booked solid for the six months of the dry season—April to November—and even attracted a small but steady amount of play in the rainy months. In fact, February on the southern Oregon coast is renowned for offering up weeks of fine weather when the sea, exhausted from throwing a two-month temper tantrum, finally lies down and takes a little nap. And golfers from the cities within driving or direct flight distance—San Fran, Portland, and Seattle—live close enough to take advantage of the breaks in the weather. So for the caddies who had been migrating north and south with the seasons for so many years that they felt like Canada geese, Bandon offered the tantalizing prospect of a place to finally rest their heads—an affordable, unpretentious place where they could make a living for themselves without having to move every six months, a place to truly call home.

I still returned to Bighorn in the winters, for several reasons, including having a girlfriend in California and the fact that I spent all my savings traveling during the shoulder seasons, so I couldn't afford to work part-time in the winter. But those three summers I lived at Rivendell were some of the happiest of my life. My room in the main cabin had a potbellied stove and a desk overlooking the garden. Kaetlyn's cat, Issie, would curl up at my feet next to the fire as I wrote and sometimes her greyhound, Siddha, too. Kaetlyn had an old-fashioned Singer sewing machine and one of those fancy fabric tables for stitching patterns, and she would spend many mornings, before going to teach Pilates, sewing and listening to audiobooks. I would lie in bed on my off days, drifting in and out of sleep for hours to the hum of her machine and a soft woman's voice reading some romantic story, like *Girl with a Pearl Earring*. I slept more peacefully at night there than anywhere else, too, especially in the cool autumn months when raindrops pattered on the wooden roof and the fire dipped and swayed in the stove, dancing to the wind in the chimney pipe.

I often imagined having a place just like Rivendell to call my own, and just knowing that it was possible in Bandon made all the difference. It made caddying seem less like a path permanently beaten through the rough and more like one that might actually reach the green someday. But I wasn't ready to lay my head down just yet. I had a few miles left in my shoes. After all these years, I was finally beginning to take the long view, to see the arc of my caddie journey as a whole, and there was one glaring omission in my résumé: I'd never been to Scotland, the birthplace of the game I loved so much. Caddying had carried me up and down both coasts of North America and right across the middle of the continent, too, but for it really to become a bona fide "round-the-world sail," I had to cross the ocean.

10

LINKS

By my third summer in Bandon, the caddie yard had swelled to over three hundred, and Keiser had built us a brand-new caddie "shack" with a TV lounge, cafeteria, showers, and locker room. The veterans' loops were scheduled a week in advance, and a fleet of shuttle buses drove us to and from the three courses. The grounds crew eventually even built us our own *caddie putting green* in the center of the parking lot. Keiser was so good to us, I was starting to think he was a reincarnated looper.

The playing privileges and preassigned tee times were the best perks by far and, honestly, I could've done without the rest of it—I actually preferred the old dilapidated trailers and the smaller, down-home and dirty yard, it seemed more authentically *caddielike* to me. But the one advantage to working with three hundred guys was that if you wanted to know the ins and outs of any yard in the world, all you had to do was listen. One morning I heard a distinct Scottish burr coming from the smoking area, and I zeroed in on the source. It turned out to be a caddie from St. Andrews over for a few months during their off-season. I had long had my sights set on Scotland. Frankly, it was embarrassing that I called myself a "golf writer" yet had never been there. I have no idea what more convincing I felt I needed, but when I heard that caddie from St. Andrews pronounce the name *Old Course*—"Aye, there's nothing quite like the *Ooolde Courssche*"—it sounded as sweet to me as water over river stones, like the way Sean Connery said "Pussy Galore" in the movie *Goldfinger*.

I knew immediately I couldn't put it off any longer.

Ken e-mailed the St. Andrews caddie master, Rick Mackenzie, on my behalf and put in a good word. When a month went by and neither of us heard back, Ken offered to e-mail him again. But I feared, now that it was June, Rick would have hired all the guys he needed and might say no, so I decided to just fly over and show up, figuring he couldn't possibly be cruel enough to reject me if I was standing right in front of him.

I caddied at Bandon until the end of the month and flew over in early July. I took the train up from Edinburgh across the Firth of Forth, along the edge of the North Sea to Leuchars, the nearest station to St. Andrews. When I stepped off the train onto the platform, a Royal Air Force jet taking off from the neighboring base blasted over the station, rattling the windows and blowing blue rings from its afterburners.

The bus into town trundled past rolling hills and farm

fields, through the old mill town of Guardbridge and into the cobblestone streets of St. Andrews—the Auld Grey Town, with its towering stone arches, slate-roofed cottages, and crumbling castle ruins. I would soon be living in one of those cottages myself, but that first night I stayed in a B&B down on the Scores—the road that traces the rocky cliffs along the North Sea and dead-ends behind the Royal and Ancient Clubhouse. It was one block from my door to the Old Course.

Only two times in my life have I felt such butterflies seeing a course for the first time—at Pebble and at Augusta. But St. Andrews is very different. It is a public course in the truest sense, an extension of the town itself. Golfers walk right off the fairways into the streets, and pedestrians walk right off the streets onto the fairways. When I rounded the corner of the Royal and Ancient Clubhouse behind the first tee, a foursome of golf-hungry Americans was waiting patiently while a woman pushed a pram across the fairway to the East Sands, the beach where they filmed the opening scene from *Chariots of Fire*. And right next to them, on the adjacent eighteenth green, the players coming in bowed and doffed their caps to a small crowd that had gathered to watch and cheer everyone's final shots and putts.

The scene before me completely contradicted the American stereotype of golf as an exclusive game played in private sanctuaries. Even the hoity-toity members of the Royal and Ancient Golf Club, having just finished lunch, emerged from their venerable clubhouse, wiped the remaining Yorkshire pudding crumbs from their sweaters, and descended the few short steps from their door to the same first tee used by the general public. There they waited patiently, just as the Americans had, for yet another group of beachgoers to cross the fairway.

I felt I'd stumbled upon a separatist movement—a utopian, social-democratic golf experiment. But then I came to my senses and realized that *I* was the one who was part of the separatist movement. This is where golf had originated; these were the descendants of the people who *invented* it. If anyone had a right to say how the game was supposed to be played, they did.

I followed the road out along the first fairway between the caddie shack and the beach. A brisk wind was blowing in off the North Sea, stirring up whitecaps on the dark water. Choppy waist-high waves gnawed restlessly at the entire length of the East Sands—all the way out to the point where the Eden Estuary flows in behind St. Andrews's four oldest courses—the Old, the New, the Jubilee, and the Eden. The courses, routed side by side, all run out to the estuary and back, but only the Old starts and finishes right in the heart of town, in front of the Royal and Ancient Clubhouse, the Hamilton Hall dormitory of St. Andrews University, and the golf shops and hotels along Links Road. This is because the other courses were added later, tacked onto the sides of the Old. By later I mean, in the case of the New and Jubilee, the 1890s. It sounds pretty funny calling a course that's been around for more than a century the New, but it is new compared to the Old, which was first played in the 1400s.

I cut in to the second tee beside Swilcan Burn and walked up the fairway, away from town, toward a group of golfers playing with caddies. One of them, an American whose ball lay in the fringe a yard short of the putting surface, was squinting down at the grass.

"Where's the green?" he asked.

I knew what he meant—the fairways and greens here are such a similar cut and color—a smooth, mottled green and brown—that it's difficult to tell where one ends and the other begins, but that question was just too loaded, too typical of a dumb American for his caddie to resist. "It's tha' bit o' grass with the flag in it!"

Everyone roared, including the guys on the third tee and the bystanders like me. The poor fellow hung his head and blushed. Watching the playful dynamic between the Scottish caddies and visiting Americans was too much for me to take. There was no way I was going to walk an entire eighteen without wanting in on the action. I turned and ran back to the first tee.

The caddie shack was in the midst of its usual midday chaos: golfers asking for caddies and the caddie master, Rick, scrambling to provide them. There was no mistaking Rick, because the yard was empty and he was simultaneously trying to placate the golfers ("We called ahead and *specifically requested* an *experienced* caddie!") and convince the old veterans coming in off the course to go around again right away—in looper parlance, known as *turning and burning*. My timing couldn't have been better.

During a short lull, I introduced myself. "Hello, Rick, my name is John Dunn. I e-mailed you in May from the States about caddying this summer."

"Ah, yes. The American writer. Sorry, I meant to e-mail you back, but as you can see, we're very busy."

"If you need someone to work this afternoon . . ."

He eyed me up and down. "Do you know the Old?"

I lied. "Oh, yes. Just finished walking it. Followed a group of players with caddies. Took lots of notes."

He disappeared from the window and returned with an apron, a yardage book, and a towel. "You're on the tee."

I thought if I showed up I would get the job, but I didn't think it would happen that quickly! I smiled and practically skipped to the tee. I also said a prayer. *Please, dear God, don't give me some know-it-all who wants the exact yardage to every bump and bunker.*

Even in that short two-hole walk, I could tell that the Old was the one course in the world you did not want to go out blind on. It wasn't hilly so much as pocked and rumpled like an unmade bed, and on many holes you couldn't even see the fairway from the tee or clearly make out the shape of the green from the fairway. And the place was littered with bunkers positioned so counterintuitively (like across the entire middle of the fairway and on the backside of some random knoll) that no amount of innate golf sense could steer you through them. I wasn't just afraid of guiding a player's ball into a bunker, I was afraid of falling into one myself.

I walked up to the first tee, where the other caddies were gathered. I smiled and nodded, trying to appear amiable, but none of them smiled back. They looked me up and down in my fresh apron and towel and my brand-new St. Andrews visor. Their stony expressions needed no translation. *Who's this jackass dressed up like a St. Andrews caddie?*

A Spanish tour guide walked over. (Tour guides often arrange tee times and caddies for groups, drive them down to the course, and see them off at the first tee.) With a heavy accent, he said, "I sorry to inform you gentlemen, but the players in this a group is from España. No one speak a much Englis. If you just please point and wave your hand, they will be very happy."

Then he introduced each of us to our players. Mine was a beautiful woman named Sonia. She was twenty-eight, had lustrous, shoulder-length black hair, shining brown eyes, a freckled nose, and long gorgeous legs that sprouted from her tiny pleated skirt. She looked exactly like the Argentinean tennis player Gabriela Sabatini. Sonia held out her hand, giggled nervously, and said, "I spake a no Englis!"

Even if she did want to know which way a hole went, she couldn't ask me! I looked to the heavens and whispered with utter sincerity, *Thank you, God!*

It's not unusual for caddies to be a little territorial and inhospitable toward new hires, especially in the middle of the season, because new caddies mean fewer bags for the old caddies. It's simple math. So I wasn't surprised when the two older Scots in our group paid me little attention. I guess they figured that the best way to get rid of me was to ignore me, because I couldn't possibly survive the Old on my own. I was thankful there was a young English caddie in the group named Norman, who saw me as more than just an opportunistic bag thief. He took pity on me and patiently answered my hundred questions. The best part was, I could ask him out loud right in front of our Spanish players, "Where does this hole go?" and they had absolutely no idea what I was saying.

But even with Norman's help, I added about thirty strokes to Sonia's score and unfailingly guided her into at least one bunker or gorse bush per hole. I would tell her "Zapatero" (the socialist prime minister of Spain) for left and "George

Bush" for right. If I had to fine-tune her aim, I put my hands on her hips and moved her a little bit more to the left or right. The tall, dashing, dark-haired fellow who kept glowering at me turned out to be her fiancé.

I was at my worst on fourteen, when I steered Sonia right into Hell Bunker, an aptly named pit that is not only punishing, but invisible from the fairway. She'd followed my instructions perfectly—aimed straight for the pin and hit her best five wood of the day. She was very pleased with herself. We walked merrily down the fairway enjoying our now fluent wordless communication. She handed me her club and smiled. I shined it and put it back in the bag with loving care. She pointed to the town in the distance, took a deep breath and sighed. I smiled and nodded and sighed right along with her. All was right with the world. That is, until we crested a little knoll and found our path to the green blocked by a great sandy moat in which, barely visible at the bottom, snuggled against a ten-foot face of stacked sod, was her ball. Sonia turned to me puzzled. Had she spoken English, this is likely when she would have asked: "John, how come you aimed me straight for this gigantic bunker?"

But she didn't speak English so she just accepted the wedge I handed her, climbed gamely down into the sand, and started swinging. One, two, three. She paused for a breath. Looked up at me exasperated, hands on her hips. Four, five, six. She was now so covered with sand her thick brown hair looked blond. But for all her efforts, the stubborn ball had barely moved, she'd only succeeded in digging a trench behind it. This was more than even beautiful, patient Sonia could take. She bent down, picked her ball up, threw it out of Hell Bunker and cried, "Inferno!" Which is probably exactly how that pit of despair got its name in the first place.

I felt terrible, but I have to admit, that little tantrum was the single cutest thing I've ever seen. Even the Scottish caddies, who made looking grumpy an art form, cracked a smile. At the end of the round, Sonia gave me a big, sandy hug and told me, through the tour guide, that I was the best caddie she'd ever had. I can't even imagine who the worst was.

Golfers will tell you the real locals' bar in St. Andrews is the Dunvegan, and it's true, the Dunvegan has a ton of history and many Open Champions have raised their pints there, but the summer I was in St. Andrews, the bar where the caddies hung out was the Pilmour. So that's where I headed to celebrate the successful navigation of my first loop on the Old. Once the Scottish caddies had a couple of pints in them, they seemed to forget that I was just a rotten bag thief. Their stony visages melted from within as the scotch and beer slowly warmed their bellies and cheeks. By the third drink, they were downright friendly, but a lot harder to understand, too. One of them sat down next to me and said, "Gar bar argh me yar America! Grot doan laird gore Tiger Woods. Em nye dot flog Augusta National."

America, Tiger Woods, Augusta National? It was like a word-association game.

I nodded solemnly and said, "Aye. Tiger Woods. Augusta National."

I decided to leave out America, figuring that was probably redundant. The caddie sitting on my other side nudged me and said, "Makin' friends with Cartgate, are ya?"

"Who?"

He nodded to the caddie I'd just been speaking to, "Cartgate Kenny. He's named after the Cartgate bunker on the third hole."

"Why's that?"

"'He fell into it while caddying one day, clear from the top. A good six feet that! And with his man's clubs on his back no less!"

"*Fell* into it?"

"Aye. His golfer turned 'round to ask Kenny for a read, but couldnae find 'im. Poor bastard looked everywhere. Finally he says, 'Where's Kenny gone?' That's when he heard Kenny say, 'Down here, sir!' And he looked over the edge, saw 'im lying in the sand." The caddie burst out laughing. "Isn't tha' right, Kenny? Backed clear off the edge of tha green and landed flat on tha bastard's bag!"

Kenny raised his glass and smiled. He said something that sounded exactly like the last thing he'd said minus the recognizable part. But it hardly mattered if I understood a single word, because we'd downed enough pints now that our sparkling eyes and raised glasses said it all. *Caddies! Brothers! One for all! All for one!*

Sometime later I received a huge slap on the back that almost knocked me out of my seat. I was expecting it to be yet another burly Scotsman feeling congenial in the glow of a good buzz, but when I turned around, I was amazed to find myself looking at a little blue-eyed, blond-haired girl. By the look of her ruddy cheeks and shining eyes, she'd thrown back a few pints herself.

"You coming to Aikman's?" she asked.

"Aikman's?"

"Aye. They say all roads lead to Rome. Well, in St. Andrews, all roads lead to Aikman's!"

"They do?"

"Oh, stop your havering and get off your fannybaws! You comin' or no'?"

And with that she marched out the door. I downed my pint and rushed to catch up.

The girl, who's name was Dawnie, turned out to be a caddie. Female caddies aren't unheard of; I'd met a few over the years. There'd been a Scottish girl from Dornoch down at Secession and a collegiate champion golfer at Bighorn, and there were quite a few girls at Bandon, but Dawnie was the first girl I met who *acted* like a caddie. She drank and swore and jawed with the best of them. In a bar full of boozing Bravehearts, she'd proved to be the alpha. She got me to jump to attention in three sentences and now I was following her up the street. And she wasn't kidding about all roads leading to Aikman's. Packs of merrymakers were marching toward the bar from every direction—from North Street, South Street, Market Street, and both ends of Greyfriars Gardens. Music poured out the windows, and people stumbled out into the night and stumbled back in. Dawnie took my arm and pulled me through the crowd to the bar, where she barked something and two pints of Guinness materialized in seconds.

"I ken tha bartender."

"You what?"

"I *know* the bartender."

That didn't surprise me in the least. Dawnie seemed to know everyone, and when the doormen started kicking us out at two, she rallied a group around her and barked instructions.

"Dougie, you ge' tha firewood, and don' forget tha paper and matches! Tom, you ge' tha beer! Pam, you grab tha bottle o whiskey at your flat. Me and John boy here will grab the fags. Meet at the Castle Sands in twenty."

With that she dragged me out into the night again, up the street to the Shell station to buy smokes. She lit two and passed one to me as we walked toward St. Andrew's Castle— the thousand-year-old fortress that lords it over a small beach known as the Castle Sands. We descended a dark, steep stone staircase to the empty beach, the crumbling turrets silhou- etted against the moon above us. It wasn't hard to imagine great fireballs and boiling oil and a hail of arrows raining down on an invading Viking fleet. But that night the sea was calm and the tide high; the water lapped gently against the soft sand. Within minutes the whole group arrived with all of the requested items, and in no time we were passing the whiskey bottle around the fire like a band of gypsies.

In the flickering light, I noticed a tattoo on Dawn's ankle that looked suspiciously like the Winged Foot Golf Club logo. "Is that the . . . ?"

"Aye. 'Tis."

"Fine golf course, lovely logo, too, but . . ."

"I lost a bet."

"You wagered a tattoo on a golf match?"

"Nae. No' a golf match. A drinking match! Some dobber from New York was braggin' 'bout how he'd tanned ten pints tha nigh' before, and I says, 'I bet I can drink you under the table.' Well, he took one look a' me and laughed and said, 'How much you want to bet?' So I says, 'If you fall on yer arse before I do, you get a tattoo of St. Andrew and the cross.' And he says, "If you fall on your arse before I do, you get the Winged Foot.' Turns out he was a fair swiller."

As if to prove the point, she threw back another shot

from the bottle and passed it to me. If that story was true (and it sounded like as good a reason as any to get a Winged Foot tattoo), that New York *dobber* must've been one *hell* of a swiller, because hours later, when Dawnie polished off the last splash of whiskey, the sky was turning gray and the water that had been such a gentle, reassuring presence the night before had disappeared, drained away to Norway or somewhere, exposing great fins of rock that looked like roots growing out from the foot of the castle. That was meant to be my first morning in the caddie yard, but after I stumbled back to my room, I slept clear through till the afternoon and limped down to the caddie shack around one, thinking, *Great way to make a first impression!*

But once again, timing proved to be everything. When I arrived at the window, Rick was in the same jam as the day before—the yard was empty, and he was trying to rally the veterans to *turn and burn*. He was very happy to see me. "Ready to go?"

I was walking down the first fairway in minutes, and when I got back in, around five, I was sent straight to the tee again by the afternoon caddie master, Robert. This became my routine—I drank at night with the boys (and Dawnie), slept till noon, caught an early afternoon loop when Rick was struggling to cover them and an evening loop that *no one* wanted, not even the cash-hungry youngsters, because it would carry well into the gloaming, that long Scottish twilight that seemed to last till midnight. Several times I got off the course at ten p.m. with light to spare.

My dad wasn't very enthusiastic about my Scotland trip to begin with. When I told him about it, he said, "You're going to lug bags around until you're fifty and your back gives out, and then what?" And he would've rolled his eyes clear around his head if he'd seen this daily routine, because once again, caddying was contradicting everything he'd tried to instill in me: show up early, fresh-faced and ready to work, and you will be rewarded. I didn't show up early or fresh-faced once at St. Andrews, but I still went thirty-six almost every day for weeks on end, and the hundred-pound bills multiplied in my wallet until the seams nearly burst.

I posted a note in the caddie shack asking for a room to rent, and a St. Andrews University student named Grant, who was caddying for the summer, offered to sublet me one in his place for a couple of months. He lived with his girlfriend in an old stone cottage on Bridge Street, just a short stumble from Aikman's and the Shell station. The room I rented was upstairs; it had dormered ceilings and windows, an old creaky radiator, and a wooden desk where, when I wasn't out drinking with the caddies, I would write late into the night—working on my now extensive caddie/travel journal. There was a washing machine in the kitchen, but no dryer, so we hung our laundry on a line in the small, walled-in yard or, on rainy days, above the radiator in the living room. It was, like most dwellings in St. Andrews, the picture of romance.

Grant charged me £400 a month, which was probably only a fraction of what they paid during the school year, but it still seemed like a lot to me, because the pound was worth almost double the dollar, so it worked out to nearly $800. The overvalued pound was quite a shock at first, but once I started caddying and was on the *receiving* end, it didn't seem so bad. At St. Andrews, we carried singles, but most players paid me at least £60 ($110), a lot of them paid me £80 ($150), and a surprising number, say one out of ten, paid me

£100 or more. Whenever the Scottish caddies complained about the "stupid, loud-mouthed" Americans (which seemed to give them endless pleasure), I was quick to remind them that I hadn't been paid more than £60 by any other nationality, not even the Brits. And I was sure the British R and A members at least would buck up on occasion, because they played in the States a lot and counted Americans among their fellow members, but they never paid me well, and I even had a few who were cheaper than the notorious French *frogs*.

The R and A had a block of tee times reserved every day after lunch, and the members would emerge, just as I'd seen them that first day, from their great stone clubhouse behind the tee, their cheeks rosy and bellies full, feeling rightfully proud of their status. Like the four Yorkshiremen I caddied for one day who were up from Alwoodley or Ganton or somewhere. Now, I don't want to suggest that all R and A members are quite as self-satisfied as that group, because in my limited British experience, Yorkshiremen seemed the very embodiment of pride and chumminess. Their eyes shone a little brighter than those of their fellow Brits, gleamed with tears of nostalgia and patriotism as if some great foreign battle had just been won and they were a superlative away from bursting into song.

For these four Yorkshiremen, the object of their passion that day was the *unparalleled* Royal and Ancient lunch. They were still rubbing their bellies and licking their lips, sighing in carnal delight three hours after we teed off. I've no doubt it was a feast to be remembered, but I'd heard enough about beef and potatoes and pudding by the back nine, and when he had a short birdie putt to close out the match on sixteen,

I was eager to get it in the hole, because a storm was about to blow in off the North Sea and they'd promised to quit as soon as the match was decided.

The rain was already hitting the East Sands when I got my man all sorted out with the line, speed, wind direction, dew point, barometric pressure. I think he even checked to make sure his socks were pulled up before settling down over the ball with shoulders scrunched, ass out, and kneecaps in. He gave it his trademark nervous waggle and head cock and seemed ready to roll it in and save us from the rain, when all of sudden he stood up and said, "How about that lunch!"

I couldn't believe it! I heard the other caddies groan from clear across the green and expected at least one of his playing partners to say, "Knock the bloody thing in already!" But no, they just nodded and grunted in affirmation as if those were the sagest words ever spoken and then chimed wholeheartedly, "Yes, *outstanding* lunch!"

And then, as if to punish us all for their gluttony, the heavens opened up and unleashed a torrent of icy rain, which caused my player, of course, to miss the damned putt. But even that couldn't dampen his spirits. He cheered: "The match goes on!" When we reached eighteen a good thirty minutes later (because the group in front of us stopped to take the mandatory photos of the Old Course Hotel, Road Hole Bunker, and Swilcan Bridge despite the fact that you could barely see any of them in the rain), my player ruffled my soaked hair, peeled a fifty from his billfold, and said, "Fine job, John, my boy!"

Then he turned to his fellow Yorkshiremen. "Tea time, gentlemen! I saw the crumpets coming out of the kitchen this morning and they looked absolutely *scrumptious!*"

I turned to the Scottish caddies and said, "And you complain about the Americans?"

•   •   •

I loved every minute I spent on the Old, rain or shine, work or play, but my absolute favorite time to be out there was in the evenings when I didn't pick up a second loop and headed out to practice and play instead. I never teed off the first hole because it was always very busy and the starters were incredibly strict about requiring a local Links Pass to play for free—and that could only be obtained with proof of residency. I asked a couple of times, but they didn't look any more sympathetically upon my interloper status than the veteran caddies did. I probably could have gotten them to grant me an exception through Rick or Robert, but honestly I didn't really care, because the starters on the New Course let me play whenever I wanted, so I just teed off over there, played the front nine out to the estuary, and then cut over to the Old after the final groups had gone through. I took my time coming in. I hit chip shots and putts from dozens of different angles as the sun set over the Eden Estuary and lit up those greens like chiseled gold, every crease and fold highlighted in sharp, shadowy contrast. At that hour, the Old Course was like a map drawn in invisible ink—its true wrinkled face revealed in just the right light.

Being a caddie, I'd always appreciated the art of green reading, but never more so than at St. Andrews. And it wasn't just the size of the greens, which truly were unlike anything I'd seen before—St. Andrews has seven double greens that serve both the outgoing and incoming holes (two and six-

teen, three and fifteen, four and fourteen, etc.), so a badly
hit approach shot can easily result in a fifty-*yard* putt. And
it wasn't just the severity of the contours, either, although
some were taller than me. The most impressive thing was
their variety. Some of the greens were actually quite simple
and flat, like the ninth, which I always found the hardest to
read because the break was so subtle, no more than a couple
of inches on a forty-footer. Some of the greens were elevated
and incredibly fast, like the par three eleventh, where you
could easily putt into a bunker if you weren't careful. Some
were narrow terraces that deflected the ball, like the twelfth,
or great bowls that collected it, like the left pin on thirteen.
And most of them were a topsy-turvy combination of all
these elements. I often spent hours playing just three or four
holes, hitting hundreds of shots from every angle, and I loved
it when I was out caddying and my player ended up with one
of the shots I'd practiced, especially if it was a really tricky
one where the play wasn't obvious at all, because if he trusted
me and pulled it off, I looked like a hero. And if he asked
how I was so familiar with links golf, having caddied here for
only such a short time, I told him I'd spent three seasons at
Bandon Dunes. And if he'd been to Bandon, he immediately
understood.

My favorite green in all of St. Andrews wasn't even on
the Old. It wasn't on any course. It was a huge practice green
called the Himalayas, located near the New Course clubhouse. The massive, heaving Himalayas (worthy of its name-
sake) was set up as an eighteen-hole putting course, but there
weren't any lines or wooden planks or anything remotely near
the hideous American equivalent "putt putt" with windmills
and waterfalls and God knows what. The routing of the

course, different every day, was marked only by numbered flags. But the contours of the green were so wonderful that if you had half a speck of imagination, you could see great battlements, bridges, funnels, and moats everywhere. The kids loved it, and so did their parents. I realized that half of those mothers and fathers I'd often seen crossing the first fairway in front of the Royal and Ancient with kids tugging excitedly at their sleeves weren't going to the beach, as I'd assumed, but were coming here. They rented putters and balls from a little shack beside the green and putted happily alongside groups of teens and young couples on dates and older married couples on date nights—like the four octogenarians I saw one evening, the ladies in their stockings and bonnets and the gents in their tam-o'-shanters and tweed, battling it out like the final round of the Open Championship, heckling each other with glee and not conceding a single putt. If there was one scene that encapsulated the Utopian Social-Democratic Republic of St. Andrews more than any other, this was it.

When September arrived and my wallet was sufficiently stuffed with hundred-pound notes, I decided it was time to get out and see some more of Scotland, play some golf, and pay Carlo a visit up in Dornoch. He'd spent the summer after our memorable round at Shinnecock and National caddying at Dornoch and had fallen so in love with the famous course and a local girl named Kay that he'd never left. I rented a car and drove up the East Coast. I played golf in Carnoustie, Aberdeen, Boat of Garten, Nairn, and of course, Dornoch, where Carlo welcomed me on the doorstep of the restaurant that he and Kay owned on one of the tiny village's two main streets. He looked like a natural born Scotsman in his tam and tweed and, with his easy charm, made a fine front man for the restaurant, but the real secret to its success was Kay's unbelievable cooking. (I smiled at the thought of a poor Dornoch caddie getting stuck with those four Yorkshiremen after they'd eaten lunch here!) She prepared for us a heaping plate of langoustines (Scottish crayfish) caught in the Dornoch Firth that morning, and Carlo poured us his finest bottle of pinot grigio. We sat out on the small terrace on the street and reminisced about all our shared golf memories—psychedelic night golf at the Olympic Club, playing the Double Helix at National and Shinnecock, designing a wedge course around our college campus in Boulder, etc. It was amazing how far caddying had carried us, and here we were, reunited on the "big loop" once again, halfway around the world.

I couldn't wait to tee it with Carlo on the links of Dornoch, but he was too busy at the restaurant that first night, so he said, "Go on without me. There's no one out there now. Just turn right past the cathedral and left at the bowling pitch. You can't miss it."

As I walked to the course, the first fingers of fog began to waft into town—what the Scottish call the haar. Soon it was so dense, it looked like the creamy head on a pint of Guinness filtering down into the dark beer. Wispy arms swirled around the lampposts and benches, tendrils slid along the rooftops and dropped down the walls like ghostly strands of ivy. The town became an apparition—the muffled clapping of my footfalls and rattling of my irons the only sounds. It reminded me of a quiet New England town in a snowstorm, only with flakes the size of dust motes—billions of little pinpricks of moisture hitting my face and hair.

The first tee was right where Carlo had said it would be, between the clubhouse and the practice green, and I could see a bunker up the left side of the fairway, materializing and dematerializing every few seconds. I aimed about ten yards right of it and launched a drive into the curtain of fog. I found my ball lying dead center just short of the 150 plate and could just make out the flag floating and flapping in the air ahead, like a bird of prey hovering over a mouse in the grass.

The next hole was a par three. A narrow plateau of a green surrounded by bunkers—a shadowy hulk like the prow of a sunken battleship. I hit a solid seven iron and listened. I heard the distinct, hollow thump of a ball landing on the deck.

And so it went. I followed my well-honed golf instincts and used the barely discernible but familiar features of the landscape to guide me—the great bank of gorse on the left side going out, the bunkers, mounds, and plateaus that defined the fairways and greens. After six holes, I was even par, and I hadn't even missed a green.

Carlo had told me that after six the course climbs to the top of a ridge, and this is a good place to cut over to the back nine—to the par-five twelfth—and start playing in. I was contemplating the path up through the gorse when a thin shadow emerged from the whiteout and called, "Well, hallo! I didn't think thar was anyone ulse crazy enough to play in this blasted soup! How goes it?"

"I'm even par."

"Are ye? Wull done!"

As he drew near, the tall, thin man looked barely more than a wisp of mist himself. He wore the ubiquitous tam on his head and carried a bag as thin as he was, what I call an arrow sling. It couldn't have held more than seven clubs. If there was a ghost of the Dornoch Links, this is exactly what

I'd imagine him looking like. But specter or not, he seemed friendly enough, and besides, I figured there was no one better to ask about the course than the person haunting it. "Do you know where the twelfth tee is? I was going to cut over from six."

"Have ye nuver played the course?"

"Never."

He tipped his cap and chuckled. "Even par in the haar? Now that is umpressive!"

He led me over to twelve and stood by the tee as I drove. He nodded approvingly. "Aye. Unother good one."

He wished me luck and disappeared up the hill, heading either home or back to the spirit realm.

I hit a three wood on the second shot and almost reached the green. I pitched it to a foot and tapped in for birdie. I yelled into the fog, "I made birdie!"

I listened for a response. Thought I heard a distant cheer. But it could've been a gull's cry out over the sea.

I came back to earth a little on the next five. Bogeyed the long fourteenth and the uphill sixteenth. I arrived at the eighteenth tee one over.

Darkness had fallen completely now. The gray deepened to charcoal. The lights of the clubhouse were little halos in the distance. It was like swinging with my eyes closed. There was no point looking up for the flight of the ball, so I kept my focus completely internal, like a diver visualizing his body rotating in the air. I could feel my hips and shoulders turn, my weight shift, and my wrists hinge. I knew exactly where the clubhead was throughout the swing and could tell the shape of the ball flight by the sensation of impact. All those rounds of night golf as a kid came flooding back to me. I was like a blindfolded archer repeatedly striking the bull's-eye. And sure enough, I hit another solid drive and found my ball, a little gleaming white orb, just past the 200 marker.

I figured the green had to be in front of the clubhouse, so I aimed a four iron at the lights and let it fly. It was too great a distance to hear it land, but I held my finish and listened anyway, savoring my last full shot. I was completely surprised when a voice with a distinct New York accent shouted, "Holy shit! I just almost got killed by a fucking golf ball!"

And another. "Bullshit! There's no way anyone's playing in this."

I started jogging toward the voices.

"Don't pick up my ball!"

"Did you guys here that? There's someone out there!"

The voice yelled, "What kind of ball is it?"

"A black Titleist 3!"

A moment of silence.

"Holy shit! It *is* a black Titleist 3!"

There were four of them—New Yorkers on a golf trip staying at the hotel next to the course. They'd just arrived, put down a few scotches, and decided to check out the course in the dark. They were very excited to have stumbled upon some real golf action. They hovered over my ball the way spectators gather around an errant tee shot at a tour event. I'd completely misjudged the location of the green, missed it thirty yards right. And I'd short-sided myself, too—from this angle, the pin was tucked just over the top of a bunker.

I told them it was an important shot, that I was one over par. They backed up a little, made room for me and stood respectfully silent and still. I opened the face on my 60-degree wedge, almost wide enough to balance a drink on it, and took a full swing. The ball lofted up over the bunker and thumped safely on the green. We all ran to see where it had stopped. It was ten feet above the hole!

The guys now gathered around the pin. One of them tended it because it was so dark I couldn't see the cup even from that short distance. I slowly walked the line, feeling the contours beneath my feet.

"I think it's just outside the left edge."

They bent down, peered through the darkness. We decided on a ball out left.

I rolled the putt gently, started it right on line. They cheered it toward the hole, and it really had no chance of missing with all of that psychic goodwill. It dropped into the center of the cup.

The guys went nuts. They slapped me on the back and ruffled my hair. They danced around the green and waved the pin and gave each other and me high fives all around. They were so excited I thought they were going to hoist me up on their shoulders and carry me off the green.

I've shot better scores than one over par (and it was only thirteen holes), but that round in the haar felt like the best round of golf I'd ever played. It was certainly the most memorable. And I know those guys are still talking about the crazy bastard who came walking out of the fog on their first night in Dornoch and got up and down for par on the eighteenth.

Carlo and I drank a bottle of scotch to celebrate, and late the next morning we moseyed down to the links to play with our mutual friend Colin—the one who'd published my very first golf story. He was spending the summer in Inverness, helping to build a new course down there, and had driven up that morning. It was an unseasonably warm day, 85 degrees and not a breath of wind. It felt more like summer in Connecticut than northern Scotland. In fact, it felt like an entirely different place in broad daylight, and my round in the haar now seemed like a dream. Having teed off so late, we were stuck behind a lot of tourist groups, too, so, uncharacteristically for Scottish golf, we waited on nearly every hole. And when we reached the par-three fourteenth, it was so backed up, there were two groups on the tee.

To pass the time, we dropped our bags and walked up over the dunes to the beach. The sea looked so cool and inviting, we decided to go for a swim. The sun had warmed the water in the shallows, and I was having such a grand time splashing about that I stayed in long after Colin and Carlo headed back to the course. When I finally climbed over the dunes about fifteen minutes after them, soaking wet in my boxer shorts, my clothes in hand, they were already up on the green and there was a group of local ladies standing on the tee. They took one look at me and started giggling. One of them nodded at my boxer shorts plastered against my legs and asked, "Is the water cold?"

And this set them off giggling even harder. I turned beet red and mumbled apologies. I hopped around on one foot and almost fell over trying to pull my pants on. I didn't even bother with my shoes, just hit my tee shot barefoot and nearly shanked it. I hurried off toward the green, calling over my shoulder, "Thank you, ladies! Sorry!" I was certainly doing my best to make an impression on everyone in Dornoch— the New Yorkers, the ghost, and now these ladies.

When we reached the eighteenth, the first tee was bustling with afternoon groups. Caddies scrambling to turn and burn, collect their cash, and get a second loop. As we were lining up our putts, we heard a distant thumping noise that grew louder and louder. We looked to the sky and saw a huge helicopter banking in over the North Sea. It was headed right toward the green. When it was over our heads, the thrumming blades were so loud that the ground was shaking, and grass blowing wildly in every direction. Every dog, cat, and mouse in Dornoch must've fled for its life. Even I had to resist the urge to run, because it looked as though it was going to land right on top of us. And it practically did—it touched down just yards behind the green.

The doors slid open, and eight Americans piled out, decked out in so much logoed golf gear, they looked as though they were sponsored by Scottish Golf Tourism. They tromped confidently to the first tee, cigars in mouths and chests puffed out, clearly riding the wave of their dramatic entrance and the grandiosity of their whole Masters of the Universe golf tour. I turned and looked out to sea, wondering if the yacht that surely accompanied this chopper was anchored out there somewhere. But I figured it was probably over in the Irish Sea and these guys had played somewhere like Royal County Down that morning—arriving over there with the same SWAT team swagger.

Ironically, I was now the one appalled by the gaudy Americans, and the Scottish caddies were salivating and stumbling over each other to get to the chopper and grab the golf bags stacked in the back. How quickly American excess is forgiven when it comes in the form of tips in excess of the standard caddie fee!

I spent a week in Dornoch and golfed every day—up at Brora, where the greens are surrounded by electric fences to keep the sheep off, down at Tain, where you put the greens fee in a wooden honor box, and of course, every evening at Dornoch with Carlo, our bags loaded with scotch and cigars and water bottles filled with red wine that we sipped on the bench at the top of the hill on seven overlooking the entire course and surrounding North Sea coast. I went antique shopping with Kay one morning down in the picture-book town of Cromarty on the eastern tip of the Black Isle, and on our way home, we motored back across the firth aboard a tiny two-car ferry. The other mornings, I strolled Dornoch's cobblestone streets, stopped in at the bakery to buy pasties—pastries stuffed with meat and spices—and sat and ate them on the bench in front of the cathedral while reading up on the football and cricket scores in the local paper. I could totally see how Carlo had fallen in love with this simple way of life. After just one week, I found it very hard to leave, myself.

But the journey back to St. Andrews was incredible, too. I drove down along the shores of Loch Ness and Loch Linnhe, where boats sailed in from the sea and moored next to islands with castles on them. I traversed mountainous Glencoe and the purple, heather-covered Trossachs, which are so surprisingly majestic, they inspired Washington Irving to call the Scottish Highlands "a humble Switzerland." I continued westward down the entire length of the Mull of Kintyre to play the amazing rough-and-tumble Machrihanish Links and an adorable nine-hole course next to it on the tip of the peninsula overlooking the Irish Sea. I crossed back over to Glasgow by ferry, with a stop for lunch on the Isle of Arran, and made it to my friend Jonny's house in Prestwick for dinner. I'd met Jonny years earlier when he spent a summer caddying in the Hamptons at Atlantic. He was a mem-

ber of Prestwick, so we played there several times. As hard as
it was to pick a single favorite Scottish course, Prestwick was
right up there in my top five with Dornoch, the Old, Cruden
Bay, and Turnberry, where I played the final day of my tour
before driving back across the middle of the country to St.
Andrews.

I'd been gone for more than three weeks, and St. Andrews had changed so much, I hardly recognized it. The
university students were back in town, so every restaurant
and bar was overflowing with handsome young people flush
with anticipation of a new school year. And the Old Course
was undergoing preparations for the annual Dunhill Links
Championship, so the grounds crew was buzzing around frantically watering, mowing, and trimming while a construction
crew raised grandstands and tents and strung ropes around
the fairways and greens.

The girl whose room I'd rented had returned, too, so I
started hotel-hopping. I even stayed a couple of nights at
the Old Course Hotel overlooking the course and the caddie shack. I would wake up in the morning, order room ser-
vice, throw open the shades, and watch the caddies go off
four by four until the yard thinned out and I suited up and
jogged across the seventeenth fairway to the first hole. The
Old Course Hotel was owned by Herb Kohler, who'd made
his fortune in water fixtures, so it's not surprising they had
an amazing Thousand Waters Spa with nozzles and jets and
giant disk-shaped shower heads that hissed and bubbled and
sprayed in every direction. I came out of there every morning
looking like a baby who'd just been bathed, powdered, and
swaddled by Swedish nannies. The Scottish caddies, who

were used to seeing me look and smell a bit more *rugged*, sniffed the fragrant air around me suspiciously and said, "Aren't we dapper this morning!"

But I couldn't afford to hotel-hop for long, and because I didn't have a loop in the Dunhill Championship, sadly my days in St. Andrews were numbered. I began to say my farewells over many tearful rounds of scotch and then, in the second week of October, I boarded the bus and retraced the very route I'd come in on three months earlier—back out through the old mill town of Guardbridge, through the farm fields and rolling hills to the station in Leuchars where in a moment of fitting symmetry an RAF jet blasted overhead just as I was boarding the train back to Edinburgh to catch my flight home to the States.

11

MASTERS

On my way back to Bandon from Scotland, I stopped over in New York to spend a week with my family in Connecticut. When I called to give my mom my flight information, she said, "You're going to be shocked when you see your father."

"Why? What's wrong with him?"

"We're not sure yet. He's just really skinny."

Dad was waiting at the back door when I pulled in the driveway. My mom wasn't kidding. He looked like a skeleton. He seemed to have aged twenty years since I'd last seen him, on my way to Scotland just three months earlier. I was so rattled, I blurted out, "Dad, you look terrible!"

"Thanks, son. Nice to see you, too."

He wasn't the hugging type, but I hugged him anyway. He crumpled like a bundle of twigs in my arms. There was something seriously wrong with him and being around him for a week it was impossible to ignore. It was an odd feeling being concerned about my father. He'd always been so functional and self-sufficient that in the past I'd usually been on the defensive around him—often feeling that the focus was on me because of his constant simmering disapproval of my rootless life. But now the focus was clearly on his poor health, and no amount of small talk or routine behavior could obscure that. Even his usual attempts to be stern with me on the subject of my "future" had lost their bite, and when I found out how long he'd been losing weight and not feeling well I was the one who chided him for not telling Mom earlier or going to see a doctor.

When I headed back to Bandon, we still didn't know what was wrong with him, and it was another month before the definitive tests came back, but just the thought of his being seriously ill cast a shadow over the brightness of the past summer and the plans I was making for the winter. There'd been several Augusta National caddies working with me in St. Andrews, and they'd gotten me excited about the prospect of following my season at the Old Course with a season at Augusta. My dad's condition didn't negate these plans; I had to work somewhere for the winter, but it did make the excitement I'd been feeling about them seem selfish and trivial.

And then sometime in early December, our worst fears were confirmed. He was diagnosed with pancreatic cancer. I'd never heard of pancreatic cancer before, but it didn't take long to figure out it was one of the worst kinds of cancer to get—the recovery rate is almost zero and the most optimistic life expectancy about two years. Now it didn't matter how stubbornly either of us tried to suppress our emotions—I could feel a multifronted emotional storm rising inside of me, and I can't even begin to imagine how he felt.

I'd gotten the job at Augusta for the spring season, so I was planning to drive across the country in the new year anyway, but now I headed home to Connecticut for Christmas because my dad was scheduled to undergo surgery in January to remove the tumor from his pancreas. This was not a simple procedure. It basically required rewiring his entire stomach, and there was no guarantee he was going to survive the operation. It goes without saying that it was not a joyful Christmas. But it wasn't a tearful and sad one, either, because that would've required us to let our guards down, and we kept them up as strongly as ever. My dad tried to act normal and put on a brave face. He was as practical as they come. He'd built everything around him with discipline and hard work, and now he was using that same discipline to try not to be overwhelmed by the one thing that was beyond his control. And I, who'd never struggled to come up with words in my life, suddenly couldn't think of anything to say. Everything that came out of my mouth sounded stupid and inconsequential, either too sensitive or too insensitive. My mom tried her best to draw the attention away from the elephant in the room by focusing on the comfort of Christmas rituals like cooking a Christmas roast, decorating the tree, playing carols in the living room. And that might've worked if the few days surrounding Christmas existed in a vacuum, but they were followed by many tense weeks leading up to the operation.

When the day arrived, I finally found myself in an

external physical environment that mirrored the way I felt on the inside: the ICU waiting room. Families huddled together in nervous silence, biting their fingernails, tapping their feet, and pacing the room. I stood up, sat down, stood up again. Neither seemed comfortable. I kept staring at the clock. The second hand took forever to circle the dial, and sometimes I couldn't tell the difference between its ticking and the pounding of my heart. Every so often, a nurse would arrive and say a name, and a family would rise. There would be a hushed conference, and they'd either scream and burst into tears or hug each other in relief. Thankfully, when my dad's name was called, the news was good. The operation had been a success. He was conscious but groggy, but when I saw him lying on the gurney in his thin cotton robe with his hair disheveled, his eyes closed, and his mouth agape under the clear plastic oxygen mask, he didn't look conscious at all. I froze at the end of the bed and stared at him.

It was as though the curtain had just been pulled back on the Wizard of Oz. The man who'd pulled all the levers and run the kingdom my whole life was revealed to be a fragile human being. It's impossible to describe exactly how I felt seeing him like that, but I know I experienced a mixture of love and sadness and guilt. Above all else, I realized what a terrible job we'd done communicating with each other over the years, and that now seemed like such a shame. Looking back now, I know that the barrier between us had already begun to crumble, but in that moment it felt as insurmountable as ever. If I'd been stumped for words before his operation, I was absolutely dumbfounded standing there after it.

The nurse noticed my hesitation. "He's conscious. I can wake him and tell him you're here."

"No, no," I said. "I don't want to disturb him."

I handed her a card I'd bought at the gift shop and asked her to give it to him when he woke up. Then I reached out, touched his leg, and left. I drove straight to Augusta.

Over the next three months, I would try to sort out everything I was feeling on the inside, while, on the outside, I put on a game face and focused on the one thing that was second nature to me—caddying. Augusta provided the ultimate distraction, because every feature of that golf course was the scene of some heroic shot or tragic mistake, and like everyone else who'd watched the Masters on TV for the last twenty years, I could remember almost every one of them and exactly where I'd been when they happened. The membership roster and daily tee sheet were a who's who of the business and sports worlds, especially the golf world, because everyone competing in the Masters Tournament came to play practice rounds leading up to the tournament, and many of the past champions who weren't competing, like Jack and Arnie, came to play on the fairways they'd helped make famous. And then, of course, there was the annual tournament itself, which was a whirlwind weeklong spectacle. I could not have picked a better place to distract me from what was happening at home.

For the first week, I rented a room in a motel on that commercial strip outside the club, the one that had been as crazy as a Grateful Dead show parking lot when Timmy and I went to the tournament eight years earlier. Now, in the absence of all that action, it felt empty. It had the vapid, soulless feel of so many commercial strips in America today— the ones on the outskirts of towns that are lined with chain stores that suck the business away from the historic centers.

Not surprisingly, the old industrial heart of Augusta—the factories, warehouses, and wharves down on the banks of the Savannah River—had long suffered a dark period of broken glass, boarded windows, and spray paint. But now there were signs of postindustrial, bohemian life—neon microbrewed beer and fair-trade coffee signs glowing in repaired windows, café tables on the sidewalk, creative murals painted over the graffiti.

Historic Augusta was preserved in residential pockets, too—quiet, leafy neighborhoods with white-columned ante-bellum homes overlooking dogwood-shaded streets. I rented a cottage behind one of these homes near the Forest Hills Golf Club, where Bobby Jones won the Southern Amateur in 1930 during his famous Grand Slam summer. Forest Hills was now just an inexpensive daily-fee course that had fallen into great disrepair, but the course's beautiful bone structure remained, and its poor conditioning had one very positive benefit—it was nearly always empty, so I could walk eighteen in just over two hours, which I did almost every evening after caddying.

Once I settled into a routine, caddying at Augusta felt more like the small, quiet East Coast yards I'd grown up in than the thrilling bustle of the last few years in Bandon and St. Andrews. I guess this shouldn't surprise me, because it is an old, traditional club and there are only eighteen holes, so there were never more than fifty or sixty caddies working on a given day. Plus, even though the membership and guest list is as high-profile as it gets, most of these "celebrities" were golfers and businessmen, not Hollywood stars, so the bling factor tended toward expensive cuff links and silk handker-chiefs. Last, but perhaps most important, guests who visited the National for more than a single day stayed in the cabins on the property, and the hosting members stayed with them even if they lived locally. Augusta was like a sealed oasis, and our interaction with the guests took place exclusively on the golf course. When we drove out through the gates at night, it was like leaving a bubble. The rarefied world of Augusta National did not spill over into the town of Augusta at all as far as I could tell.

But as low-key as my life in Augusta turned out to be, the hiring process had been anything but. For some reason, the club had recently outsourced the caddie program to a for-profit *corporate caddie management firm* that hired and trained the caddies, covered our liability, wrote us our paychecks, submitted our tax forms, etc. If you are shaking your head and wondering what a corporate caddie management firm is, you are not alone. I'd only heard rumors of their existence, but I suppose, after all my years of looping, I shouldn't have been surprised that someone finally decided to make some money off our ragtag circuit, especially now that the popularity of the "walking game" was sweeping the country and caddies were no longer confined primarily to the suburbs of major cities like New York and Chicago. Why Augusta felt it needed a corporate caddie firm when their yard had survived a half century without one is beyond me, but that was hardly my business, and my desire to work at Augusta far outweighed my desire to take a political stance on behalf of caddies' rights. So I sucked it up and called the "human resources" phone number that had been provided to me by the Augusta caddie shack to take a telephone interview.

OK, I thought. *No problem. I'm good at interviews.*

I dialed the number and was greeted by an automated

voice that informed me I would be taking a multiple choice test. I would be asked a question and then given four possible answers. I was to press 1 for the first answer, 2 for the second, and so on.

My mind started racing. *Oh shit! What exactly is a slope rating? How does grain work? How do you convert meters to yards? Is it ten percent?*

I'd been caddying for twenty years, and I was still nervous.

The voice delivered the first question: "If you saw a twenty-dollar bill on your boss's desk and no one was around, would you (1) definitely take it; (2) take it only if you needed it; (3) think about taking it; (4) definitely not take it?"

What?

I pressed 4.

Second question: "If a coworker took twenty dollars from your boss's desk and offered you half would you (1) . . . ?"

This question was rephrased about thirty times in various twisted forms. They even switched the answers around so that (1) became Definitely Not and (4) Definitely Yes— apparently trying to trick me into contradicting myself.

And the permutations of the question became increasingly absurd, to the point where I swear they asked me, "If you found a twenty-dollar bill up your ass, would you . . . ?" and I was so rattled by that point that I said I'd (4) definitely return that one, too.

When the test ended, a woman's voice came on the line. I breathed a sigh of relief.

She said, "I am not going to respond emotionally to your answers so as not to give you the impression that you have answered the questions correctly or incorrectly."

Could this get any weirder?

"Why do you want to caddie at Augusta National?"

I passionately described how Nicklaus's charge on the final nine in '86 was a life-changing event. How when he nearly holed out on sixteen I leaped from my seat and how I felt guilty for celebrating when Seve's approach at fifteen found the water and Norman's at eighteen found the bleachers. I told her it was such a superhuman feat to hole so many putts in a row that it confirmed my belief in God or, at the very least, the supernatural. And even though Nicklaus was a little overweight and a little nearsighted at the time, he was basically a modern-day ninja.

Dead silence.

"Hello? Are you still there? Is that what you were looking for?"

"I will not respond emotionally. Next question."

I was completely rattled by the end of the interview. I had no sense of how I'd done. She told me Augusta would call soon to inform me of my employment status. Then she hung up.

Days passed. A week passed. Still no word.

I checked my voice mail obsessively. I checked my e-mail, too (even my junk mail), despite the fact that I wasn't sure whether I'd given them my e-mail or not.

Maybe I should've said Larry Mize's chip-in against Norman in '87. After all, he was the hometown hero! Shit!

Finally, I broke down and called the caddie shack. "Hi, I took the caddie test a couple of weeks ago . . ."

"Oh yeah, hey, John. Looking forward to working with you. That test is ridiculous, huh?"

I wanted to say, *Geez, were you guys ever going to call me back?* But I just said, "It wasn't so bad."

As much as I like to rip on the stupid caddie corporation, I benefited from it in one major way. Traditional yards (like the way Augusta used to be) are tough nuts to crack. They tend to lean heavily toward seniority, the best loops locked up by veterans and doled out at the caddie master's discretion (usually influenceable for a price). I would've had to ride a lot of pine and buy the boss a lot of whiskey to get any good loops in the old Augusta yard. But the new corporate caddie masters broke up the cartel and democratized the system. They assigned loops by lottery. Now a new guy like me had an equal shot at the best jobs. This was especially beneficial at Augusta where there was a bigger difference between the good and bad loops than anywhere else on Earth.

We carried single bags, so the minimum pay with tip was a paltry $88.50, and there was a healthy contingent of old codgers who apparently had this number tattooed on the inside of their eyelids and many more who thought paying $100 or $110 was being generous. To make matters worse, there was a no-tipping policy for guests and, unlike other clubs where guests generally disregard such policies, golfers were very careful not to be seen breaking any rules at Augusta for fear of jeopardizing their coveted invitation to play there. This led to some very creative tipping—hundreds palmed in handshakes, folded into scorecards, tucked into empty cigar containers.

Fortunately there were also a number of members who paid $150 or more and looked the other way when the guests pulled out their wallets. There was even the rare guest, like Phil Mickelson, who showered the caddies with hundreds right in front of a blushing, protesting member. You can do that when you're a past champion.

The trick to the lottery was knowing who paid and who didn't. This is where seniority still had its advantages. The old guys kept close tabs on the financial habits of everyone who played there.

The lottery worked like this: Every caddie was assigned a numbered chip. This number was yours for as long you worked at Augusta. Mine was 136. Each day all of the available loops were written on a dry-erase board with little hooks on it. In the morning the caddies who weren't already assigned a job put their chips in a hat. The hat was shaken and the chips drawn one by one. When yours was pulled, you walked up and hung it next to the name of the player you wanted to caddie for.

There were always a number of celebrity names on the board—Arnold Palmer, Sean Connery, Warren Buffett, President or Prince So and So—and these were often selected first. But the majority of names were unknown or, I should say, unknown to me.

As a rookie, you could try to ask a veteran before the lottery, "Who should I pick?" And he might say, "I'd take that third spot next to Mr. Smith." And that might be good advice or it might be bad advice, because veterans were also known to lie to rookies, get them to put their chip on a crappy loop and leave the good ones for their friends still in the hat.

In the beginning, when the board was wide open, loaded with great loops, you could hear the caddies praying, willing their chips from the hat: *136, 136, 136, please God, 136.*

And then as the good loops slowly disappeared and the board became increasingly less attractive (toward the end downright ugly), the caddies hid their heads in their hands and prayed for their chips to sink to the bottom of the hat, because the chips left over at the end of the lottery were drawn first the following day.

One morning, there was a single loop left on the board—a five-day job with the cheapest, most excruciatingly boring member in the club, a guy who played nine holes, stopped for a two-hour lunch, and then played nine more in the afternoon . . . all for the bare minimum of $88.50.

My chip was still in the hat along with ten or so others.

Grey, the caddie master, held the hat out in front of him with sadistic glee and gave it a nice long shake. The caddies hissed and jeered. Those who'd already gotten loops hung around just to see the blood. Being drawn for this loop was the caddie equivalent of being sent to the guillotine.

I buried my head in my hands and prayed.

And then I heard it.

136!

The caddies roared! They yelled my nickname: "Sunshine!"

They clapped me on the back. I almost fell to my knees. *Noooooooooo!*

But it wasn't the end of the world. Like all loops, good and bad, that one would eventually come to an end. The old, shriveled guy with his bucket hat and zinc-oxide-lathered nose would leave town, taking with him his two-hour lunches, his $88.50 tickets, and his litany of clichéd golf expressions. "That's a Monica Lewinsky—all lip, no hole." "That's a blondie—a fair stripe down the middle." "That's a Madonna—goes both ways." And so on and so forth. Soon he'd be gone, and then I'd be back in the hat with another shot at glory. In the end, it all evened out.

And at Augusta, it wasn't always about the payday. There

were so many amazing people playing there on a daily basis—famous coaches, politicians, professional golfers, and pioneers of business and technology—that you were often faced with a chance of a lifetime, a chance to spend a day or several days side by side with, say, Bill Gates, whom I chose on a wide-open board with plenty of big-ticket loops left on it, even though he was known to be a light tipper.

Rumor has it that he'd paid the caddies huge when he first joined and then got scolded by the chairman for it, so now, afraid to ruffle feathers, paid just over the minimum. He was not alone in being afraid to ruffle feathers at Augusta. I've never seen so many powerful men walk on eggshells—their Augusta privileges rank right up there in importance with their jobs and their wives. I'm sure this is due in part to the fact that it is the club of all clubs, the campus shared by all the BMOCs, where past US presidents and titans of society and industry have shared secrets and struck deals. But I've noticed that no matter how powerful these businessmen are, how comfortable or confident in the boardroom, the one thing that reduces them to nervous little children is the presence of great golfers. Perhaps this is because golf is the one game in which it is possible to actually "take the field" and play a game with one's heroes—playing a best-ball with Jack or Arnie being akin to, say, catching a pass from Joe Namath. Augusta is that field—it is the place where golf greats, past and present, and business and political greats, past and present, come to play together. It is the cross-section of these two worlds. And as intimidating as this could be for anyone on either side, I think Mr. Gates may have felt a touch more pressure than most, because he was not only new to Augusta National, he was also relatively new to the game of golf. He'd clearly worked very hard on his game in anticipation of (and perhaps even to precipitate) his acceptance into the club, and he could scrape it around in a hundred or so and keep a decent pace of play. But golf definitely didn't come naturally to him, and he still relied heavily on his caddie to get around the course as competently and gracefully as possible. And for seventy-two holes over two days, that caddie happened to be me.

It was quite the power loop. He was there with his close friend Warren Buffett (also a member) and his CEO, Steve Ballmer. Mr. Buffett was just as I'd imagined he'd be—the benevolent grandfather, a heartwarming chuckle and a twinkle in the eye. Short and wizened with fluffy white eyebrows and leathered old hands that melted around yours like old broken-in baseball mitts. The only other person I've met with hands like that was Stephen Stills. They had the relaxed softness of supreme confidence. It was a pleasure to watch him and Bill share their whiz-kid banter on the driving range and before and after each round. Unfortunately, Mr. Gates and Mr. Buffett couldn't play together, because they were the only members among two foursomes, and Augusta requires there to be a member in each group. Because they were separated though, I think Bill paid far more attention to me than he otherwise would have.

I have a lot of experience dealing with beginning golfers and pride myself in being a source of stability and confidence on the course. I play the role of humble mentor well. So it didn't really surprise me when he quickly came to trust and rely on me—on club and shot selection and the line and speed of his putts—but I was surprised when he opened up about his professional and personal life. It's not that this was unusual; players confided in me all the time, but this was, well, *Bill Gates*. He told me all about the Microsoft antitrust lawsuit (articulately and convincingly defended his position), his friendship with Bono and work to fight AIDS in Africa, and (perhaps his favorite subject) his nationwide charter-school program. When we were out forecaddying on the ninth hole, a veteran caddie in our group turned to me with raised eyebrows and said, "I've been out with Mr. Gates several times, and I've never heard him talk so much."

I was flattered and honored. Honestly, I can't even imagine what a business-school student would have given to spend eighteen straight hours side by side with Bill Gates discussing everything under the sun. It was like a private seminar.

But the fact that I wasn't a business-school student and didn't want anything from him (not even a big tip, because I knew ahead of time that I wasn't going to get one) was probably why he felt so comfortable with me in the first place. It was probably refreshing for him to have someone by his side who wasn't kissing his ass or trying to get something from him. In fact, the opposite was true. I was providing for him, helping him play well and feel at ease among his golfing friends. And that's all he cared about for those two days.

By the end of the first day, we were fast friends.

The second morning, he greeted me warmly. We started on the tenth tee, a long downhill par four with a treacherous bunker in front of the green. Ten is one of several deadly holes at Augusta that can quickly get away from a golfer and lead to disaster and embarrassment (even among the pros). Bill visibly tightened up on these holes, and I could see it happening that morning on the tenth tee. He gripped the club a little tighter, swung a little more woodenly, lifted his head a little sooner, and as a result, he thinned his drive about 180 down the right side. It rolled into the light rough. On the way to his ball, I told him I'd given some thought to his charter-school program. He immediately lit up. He enthusiastically answered my follow-up questions and delved into the finer points. He completely forgot about his poor tee shot and the trouble that lurked ahead, that giant bunker in the middle of the fairway. I smiled to myself and very nonchalantly handed him a club that would keep him short of the sand, and he hit it like it was nothing and resumed the conversation. I did the same thing on the third shot, and when his ball came to rest on the back fringe some forty feet above the hole, he smiled ear to ear as though he was amazed to discover that he was the one who'd just hit it there. Ah, the power of the caddie mind trick.

We'd switched around the foursomes that morning, so there was a new caddie in our group, whom I'd never been on the course with before—not one of the old-school veterans who emanate wisdom and patience, but a bossy younger guy who'd been there only a few years and had some territorial issues with the new guys and assumed that just because we were new to Augusta, we'd been born yesterday. When we got up onto the green and it was Bill's turn to putt, this caddie stepped up to tend the pin. But instead of just tending it silently, he began barking instructions to Bill.

"Right out here, Mr. Gates. Big break here. It's downhill, but not as fast as it looks. Give it a solid stroke."

Bill and I had already gone through our quiet routine and settled on a line. The caddie's sudden intrusion came as a shock, and all of the tension that I'd worked so hard to dispel came flooding back. Bill turned to me. His eyes asked, *Stick to the plan or listen to this guy?*

I was between a rock and a hard place. I didn't want to contradict the other caddie. You never want to contradict another caddie on the course; it's bad form. But he couldn't have committed a more egregious act than reading my putt for me. That is the number-one no-no in the caddie etiquette book. I should've stepped up and reassured Bill, but it was early in the morning, and my split-second decision making wasn't up to speed yet. I nodded and shrugged and hoped for the best.

I saw Bill adjust his aim a little farther left and take his putter back a little farther—the words *not as fast as it looks* clearly echoing in his head. He hit it so hard, it raced down the hill, rolled right through break, and disappeared off the front of the green. The front of the tenth green is so steep, his ball ended up thirty yards down the fairway. The silence was deafening. Technically Bill was still away.

Finally one of the other players cleared his throat and said, "I'll go ahead and putt, Bill."

Bill was lobster red and not just from embarrassment. He was steaming mad. He gave me a look that I'm sure many Microsoft employees and competitors have seen over the years. Gone was the demure, submissive, beginning golfer.

Through clenched teeth he hissed, "Go pick up my ball and tell that caddie to keep his opinions to himself."

• • •

I've often been asked what my most memorable loop at Augusta was. This is a really tough question to answer. The rounds with Bill Gates were certainly up there, as were those when I caddied in Arnold Palmer's group for two days and a Master's practice round for Shingo Katayama. There were many. But the one that always comes to mind, the one that left the most indelible impression, didn't involve anyone famous at all. It took place the Monday after the Masters, and the course was the celebrity.

That morning all of the members of the media and the tournament volunteers got their chance to play—the last chaotic gasp of Masters weekend. And then in the early afternoon, everyone was gone. The circus had officially left town. And that's exactly what it looked like—paper plates and cups and napkins littered everywhere, the grass trampled, the grandstands and concession stands and ropes still standing, silent and empty. The scoreboards were still hung with the leaders' names and final scores and, most amazing of all, the pins were still in the Sunday positions, fluttering with the official yellow Masters flags.

There were just four of us on the course—a Royal and Ancient member and his son and me and another caddie. We were walking the very greens that the Tour pros had stalked the day before. Reading the exact putts that won and lost the tournament. Not another person in sight.

This was the peak moment of what had been a slow, incredible transformation of the course. For most of the year, the greens ran at nine or ten—very smooth, downright slippery in some places, but none of the breaks were beyond anything I'd seen before. Ten feet here and there, halfway to the hole on downhill putts.

Then as the tournament neared, the greens crew slowly began to shave them down, and the breaks increased. The ten-footers became twelve, then fifteen, then twenty. The downhill forty-footers became sideways tappers that you had to play off the toe. It was like watching a sleeping dragon awaken.

During one of the practice rounds, Gary Player putted from the back of eighteen to the front right pin, some sixty or seventy feet away. He tapped it one foot dead sideways, almost backward, and walked nonchalantly down to the hole. The ball crept ever so slowly sideways. Began its imperceptible turn to the right and slowly gained speed. Gary reached the hole while the ball was still creeping, stood behind the hole, and leaned on his putter. I think he even checked his nails to see if they needed filing. The ball snaked down the green, turned right and then left and then right again. It arrived a seeming eternity after he'd hit it and nearly went in. The crowd groaned and cheered. Gary bowed.

And just days later, there we were—the four of us alone on the fairways under the grandstands and scoreboards, the roars of the gallery still fresh in our minds. Even though I wasn't playing myself, I felt like a little kid living out that Masters fantasy that I'd imagined so many times over the years on those clamshell-littered greens in springtime Connecticut. After we'd putted out on the fourteenth green and the father and son had started walking back to the fifteenth tee with their drivers in hand and the other caddie had started up the fifteenth fairway to forecaddie, I allowed myself a precious, private moment. I dropped a ball on the top of the green—way, way above the hole—in the one place you do not want to end up on Sunday in the Masters, but a place I'd seen many players marooned over the years. I whispered, "Nicklaus with a putt to take the lead" and I rolled that ball with my player's putter, stroked it ever so softly, and followed it to the hole with my putter raised in classic Nicklaus fashion. I'd read it perfectly and it almost went in. When it burned the edge, I did my best Ben Wright impersonation and yelled, "The Bear has come out of hibernation!" Then I picked up the ball and my player's clubs and ran out to forecaddie.

The next day the greens were a little slower. And a little slower the day after that. The greens crew raised the blades on the hand mowers, let the grass grow back to a sane height. The dragon slumbered once again.

• • •

There has been much written about the Augusta caddies—the old veterans who caddied in the Masters before 1983, when Tour players began to be required to use local loopers—especially Carl Jackson, who was the last one to win, with Ben Crenshaw in 1995. That was an emotional victory for Crenshaw because his mentor, the famous teacher Harvey Penick, died just before the tournament. Crenshaw was a pallbearer at his funeral. No one will forget Crenshaw's tears on the eighteenth as he putted out for his unlikely late-career win.

But the victory was also emotional for the Augusta caddie yard. The pride in having one of their own in the winner's circle again and most likely for the last time, because all of the current Tour players have their regular, full-time guys now and wouldn't think of playing a Major Championship without them. So it's really only the amateur invitees—the US Amateur and British Amateur finalists, for example—who still use local caddies in the Masters. And a lot of them offer the job to friends and family to share in the experience, so even the amateur loops aren't always available. It is slim pickins to get a bag in the Masters these days, and that made Carl Jackson's win even more special.

My friend Walker, an Augusta native whom I'd met playing one day at a public course in town, caddied in the same group with Carl Jackson and Ben Crenshaw in a practice round for the '94 Masters, just one year before their victory. He told me how terrified he'd been walking up that first fairway side by side with all those Tour pros and their loopers, Johnny's huge Tour bag banging against his ankles and the eyes of thousands of spectators on him. Walker was a good golfer, but had no caddie experience, and here he was in the game's tensest arena trying not to totally mess up a million little details—like where to stand when he was tending the pin for Johnny. He'd heard something about a "through line" (the line that extends from a player's ball "through the hole" to roughly three feet behind it) and the importance of not stepping on one. But it was like fractal geometry trying to figure out where his feet were in relation to all three players' lines and through lines and he could never be sure if he was standing on one or not. Carl could see the poor kid was in over his head and sweating bullets. When they were walking down the second fairway, he laid a gentle hand on Walker's shoulder and said, "Just follow my lead, son, and you'll be fine." From that point on, if Walker had any questions, he just looked to Carl and the veteran caddie steered him through the round. And it's not as though Carl didn't have other things to do. Hell, he and Ben won the tournament the very next year!

I love that story, because the same thing was true during my first rounds out at Augusta. Granted, they weren't in the pressure cooker of the Masters, but I still found those remaining few old-veteran Augusta caddies to be humble, gracious, and kind to the new guys like me. These were the guys whose pictures graced the caddie-shack walls, along with a plaque listing all of their best Masters finishes year by year, with the players they'd caddied for. They'd seen it all and had nothing to prove, like Carl's friend Johnny, a seventy-something-year-old caddie I got paired with my first week at Augusta. The National was nowhere near as difficult to figure out as the Old Course, but it had its little secrets, like the devilish wind on the par-three twelfth that is so famous for blowing one way on the tee and another up on the green, which was exactly what it was doing the day I was out there with Johnny. I threw up a pinch of grass and watched it sail left while the flag was flapping hard to the right, and then everything changed and the grass went the other way and the flag fell dead. I obviously looked perplexed, because Johnny walked over, patted me on the back, and said, "Don't look down here. Look up there."

He pointed to the tallest trees on the hill behind the thirteenth tee. They were clearly blowing straight back at us. I put the eight iron I'd been considering back in the bag and pulled seven.

When my player's ball landed pin high on the narrow green, he beamed at me. "Great club!"

Johnny winked and smiled.

The surreal thing about Augusta is not only how much history has taken place there. I've worked at several courses that have hosted Major Championships and have famous histories of their own: St. Andrews, Shinnecock, Olympic. Augusta is unique because history is ever present, continually in the making. You can caddie side by side with Carl Jackson and ask him personally what that victory in '95 was like. You can caddie for a past champion and ask him about his most famous shots as you stand right where he hit them. And you never know, every time you go out with a Tour player or an up-and-coming amateur, you might be caddying for a future champion; you might find yourself rooting for him years later, remembering the amazing shots you saw him hit and wondering, *Did I see it coming?*

I had one of those moments caddying in a group with Arnold Palmer. He was playing a recreational round with friends and was being every bit as generous a host and magnanimous a gentleman as he was reputed to be. We'd already played for the better part of two days and were on our final nine holes. We got to that same twelfth tee, and one of his buddies asked him about a moment from his Masters career that had happened in that very spot. I think it was the controversial ruling in '58, the year he won his first green jacket, one of the most famous stories in all of Augusta history. I can't be sure, because I didn't hear the original question, and once Arnie began speaking, I was immediately spellbound by his tone and body language, so I don't remember the exact words he said.

As he patiently began his answer and then grew slowly more passionate as the story unfolded, I looked around at the faces of the other men in the group, wondering if they were as awestruck as I was to be standing there listening to Arnie recount one of his Masters memories in the very spot where it had happened fifty years ago. And clearly they were. It didn't matter how long they'd known Arnie or how many rounds they'd played with him. Their eyes grew wider and their jaws dropped slowly lower with every sentence he spoke, with every furrow of his brow and tilt of the head. And when he flashed one of his famous smiles and pointed to the green to emphasize an important detail of the story, our heads swung in unison and looked to the green as if we could see the very scene he was describing right there in front of us. And because that scene had taken place before I was born, I imagined it all in black and white—Arnie wearing his classic button-down sweater and shiny wingtip shoes, a cigarette dangling from his mouth and a stray strand of hair curling down over his forehead. He was crouched in his classic knock-kneed stance staring down the hole as though trying to melt it with X-ray vision. And then when he gave it his wristy stroke and the putt bounced along the line on its way into the hole, he danced after it and gave one of his patented leg kicks that brought the adoring crowd to their feet.

At some point, Arnie had stopped talking and stepped up to the tee. I came to my senses, because I was standing right behind him, almost in his backswing. I moved quickly out of the way. If he was bothered by me, he didn't show it. He drove his peg into the ground and stood up tall. He waggled his club and stared down the hole with a purpose I had not seen in the prior sixty-five holes. It was as though telling that story had brought him back to his glory days just as vividly as it had us. I looked around again at the other players' faces. They'd backed up to give Arnie room and were watching just as intently as I was, their jaws still hanging from the story, as though they didn't dare shut them lest they break the spell. Arnie took his classic, trademark swing, and I was sure that ball was going to come off his club like a rifle shot and track down the pin, but Arnie's old joints didn't cooperate. The club came down a little behind the ball and emitted the telltale thud of a fat shot. The ball ballooned softly into the middle of the creek.

"Goddamn it!" Palmer hollered. He slammed his club into the turf.

No one peeped. But everyone's eyes were shining. Smiling inwardly. He may not have executed the shot, but the young Palmer had indeed emerged, allowed us a glimpse of the competitive fire that stoked so many of his legendary charges.

That's what it was like inside the gates of Augusta National. But when I walked off those fairways at the end of the day and drove out those gates and over to Forest Hills for my solo evening rounds of golf, I was suddenly a world away from the National. And it was alone on those fairways on warm, spring evenings, the air redolent with pine and Bermuda grass and blossoming cherry (and the occasional Marlboro), that I thought of what was happening at home, reflected on my relationship with my father and the long road I'd traveled—how disappointed I was that golf, which was such a huge part of my life and has been such a uniting force for so many fathers and sons, was something we never shared. I was reminded of that every time I caddied for a father and son. Every time I witnessed their competitive banter and their classic body language, like a father leaning in to offer unsolicited advice and his son shrugging him off. And even more poignantly, the moments when I trailed behind a father and son as they walked side by side in silence, not paying each other any attention, simply enjoying being together.

And that was the thing that golf did more than anything else: it provided the time and the space, the practiced rhythms and rituals of interaction that allowed relationships to unfold over time—not in a single round or even a weeklong trip, but over years of rounds and decades of trips. Golf helped build memories. And of course I'd experienced this with friends, but some of my greatest memories were of being alone on the golf course. I could feel how the game had changed me, helped me grow. I felt wiser. I felt the miles I'd walked. But I couldn't share *any* of that with my dad. He didn't even speak the same language.

That is what I thought, playing alone on the fairways of Forest Hills. And I remember one moment when I was battling back and forth about canceling my caddie plans for the upcoming summer and heading home instead, and that stirred up a whole stew of emotions, and I was surprised how much anger was inside of me, too. I was on the fourteenth hole, on the far side of the property where the back nine turns and starts heading in, and it all just poured out of me. I yelled, "If you wanted to spend time with me so badly or really get to know me you could have called or visited anytime over the past ten years. You could have taken an interest in my life!"

And I repeated those words over the phone that night to my oldest friend, George, whom I'd called to vent, because he'd known my dad all the way back to his earliest childhood, for as long as he could remember, and if anyone understood my frustration, it was him.

He listened patiently, and when I calmed down, he said, "John, you're not going home for your dad. You're going home for you. Closure is for the living. When your dad dies, he will be at peace one way or another. You will be the one still here dealing with your emotions, resolved or unresolved."

I immediately recognized the wisdom in those words. They were the tipping point. When George spoke them, my anger and my resistance broke, and I knew that I had to go home. A few short weeks later, when the Augusta season ended and the course closed for the summer—when they pitched the air-conditioned tents over the greens right after "caddie day," our ten-hour, forty-five-hole season-ending golf-beer-barbecue fest—I packed up my van and headed north to Connecticut and to my father.

12

HOME

The Stanwich Club,
Greenwich, CT,
2007–2009

The months following my dad's surgery had been very difficult for him as he struggled through a long, rocky recovery. When I returned five months later, he still looked very frail, and I could see the wear on my mom's face from the stress and anxiety—the many late nights and sudden trips to the hospital because of complications and infections. But thankfully, the worst of it seemed to be behind him now, and he was finally, slowly returning to relative health. He'd regained a couple of pounds and some color to his face, and was beginning to move around again—work in his woodshop in the garage, do some light yard work, and even drive his car into town to pick up his prescriptions and a copy of the *New York Post* at the drugstore. He tired easily now, so a day bed was put in the sunroom, where he would nap in the afternoon in front of the TV. But ever stubborn in his refusal to play the invalid, my father dressed very properly every morning, even on days he didn't leave the house—his shirts neatly pressed and tucked in, his belt cinched up around his waist, the leather laces of his docksiders double knotted.

And he was as stern and meticulous as ever. He lined up written notes and to-do lists on the table beside his bed and, in the surest sign that he was on the mend, wasted little time before raising his favorite subject with me: my "plans and direction." Normally I found this subject tiresome and annoying, but now his words sounded a little kinder and less pessimistic. And I don't think it was just a change in my attitude or sympathies; I sensed that his tone had changed, too, had lost its edge. Even if my father didn't want to admit that the odds of beating pancreatic cancer were stacked heavily against him, he must have subconsciously acknowledged that our time together was limited, because he didn't dismiss my decisions and life path as categorically as he had in the past.

I wouldn't go so far as to say he embraced me, though. We'd spent so many years at odds with each other that the barriers between us, our wariness and defensiveness, were ingrained. I was under no illusions that our ten-year standoff was suddenly going to be an overt lovefest, but I did allow myself a little macabre humor that the one positive outcome of his illness was that he couldn't just get up and walk away from our conversations as he used to. Once he was reclined in his bed, I pretty much had him cornered. We'd exchange the typical short pleasantries that normally comprised the entirety of our conversations, something along the lines of:

"This is some heat wave we're experiencing!"

"I hear it's supposed to break on Tuesday, high-pressure system coming."

"Sure hope so."

Then he'd expect me to play by the old rules and get up and leave. But now I just sat there in the chair opposite his bed, smiling, taking in the fine atmosphere of the sunroom as if I was just noticing for the first time what a nice room it was, and when he realized I wasn't showing any signs of leaving, he prodded. "Boy! Look at the time. I don't want to keep you any longer" or "Sorry to interrupt, but Jim Lehrer's about to start."

But I wasn't budging. I had him right where I wanted him. I just smiled and said, "Goody! I love Jim Lehrer!"

I could actually see him squirm. But if I waited him out, he had no choice but to let me stay. And eventually he started talking to me again, because the only thing more unnerving than my constant presence was my constant *silent* presence. It was no *Tuesdays with Morrie*, but as we sat together over the summer months, we slowly broke the ice. I remember vividly the first time we shared a heartfelt laugh. It was something silly, just a casual observation that we both found hilarious. But we weren't accustomed to enjoying genuine belly laughs together, so as trivial as the source of the laugh had been, it still caught us both by surprise.

Afterward my dad said, with his trademark dorky sincerity, "I really enjoyed our conversation."

And then the next time we spoke, I mentioned a place we'd both visited separately (Vancouver Island, British Columbia) and, unbeknownst to each other, loved equally. We talked about how similar the rocky, pine-forested coastline was to that of Maine. He commented on how beautiful it was to see the snowcapped peaks rising right out of the water—the Olympics, the Coast Range, and the volcanic cone of

Mount Baker lording it over the San Juan Islands. And when I mentioned how I hoped to take the ferry up the inland passage to Alaska someday, he was reminded of a summer he'd spent in Labrador as a boy. We were both so excited to pipe in and share our memories and impressions that we kept interrupting each other and then apologizing.

"Sorry, you go ahead."

"No. My fault, you go ahead."

Before we knew it, two hours had passed.

This time I was the one who said, "I really enjoyed our conversation."

I even mentioned it to my mother, who was cooking in the kitchen. "Dad and I had a really nice conversation!"

And then at the dinner table, Dad said, "John and I had a really nice conversation."

My mom looked at the two of us with raised eyebrows, probably not sure how to react to two grown men getting excited about talking to each other.

Our talk of British Columbia led to talk of Bandon Dunes, because my dad had never been to the Oregon coast and was curious about it. I told him about seeing whales breach from the fairways, which naturally led to a further discussion of caddying—a subject we had, amazingly, never really delved into because it had always been a source of contention, as if caddying were a friend my dad didn't approve of, someone he thought was a bad influence on me. But as I told him more about caddying, he began to find it quite interesting and perhaps not so bad after all. He especially loved my story about Bill Gates, because it had never occurred to him that a golfer would divulge so much of his personal and professional life to his caddie, especially when that golfer was someone as important and well respected as the founder of Microsoft. I'm not quite sure what he'd visualized a caddie's role to be— perhaps something like a bellhop or a waiter. I got a really good laugh out of him when I said we were more like hair stylists and that these big-deal businessmen poured their hearts out to us on the golf course just as their wives did at the salon.

In turn he told me about his business trips when he was younger to visit prospective clients in places he'd never been before, like Atlanta and Milwaukee, being wined and dined and completely immersed in their worlds, all while trying to remain professional and sell himself—the nerdy New York City slicker with his horn-rim glasses, bow tie, and bashful smile. He said he'd felt like a fish out of water and commented that at least when I was dealing with hotshots on the golf course, I was on my turf—in an environment I knew intimately and where they deferred to me. This was a very keen observation. He was beginning to understand and appreciate me and was actually very eloquent and funny in the process. It's amazing that I'd gone thirty-five years thinking he was a boring mute.

It was an unexpectedly warm, if bittersweet, homecoming. The time passed far too quickly, and before we knew it, fall arrived and my dad asked, "What are your plans for the winter?"

I couldn't help smiling at that familiar old line. Once again it was a rhetorical question. We both knew I didn't have any plans. But this time he said it a little differently. It wasn't loaded with disapproval as it had been in the past. I know he appreciated the fact that I'd come home, but I also know that my sudden constant presence after all these years was a reminder that he was sick. Having me there must have felt a little like a deathbed vigil. I took the hint and made plans to head back out to California, where I could find some winter caddie work and finally start making plans for a real future—a future beyond the golf course.

I chose Los Angeles because I knew my writing, which had steadily improved thanks to years of contributing to magazines, could be put to good use there. This was not some quick, knee-jerk decision. It was a big deal for me, because before my father had fallen ill I'd planned to keep riding the caddie train to the next amazing destination. I'd even had several very exciting possibilities in mind—Cypress Point on the Monterey Peninsula was right on the top of my list, as was a new private course on the Big Island of Hawaii called Nanea, where a fellow caddie from Bandon had a spent a winter and completely sold me with tales of perfect waves and beautiful women, otherworldly lava flows and black sand beaches. A lot of the Bandon caddies had spent winters in New Zealand, too, at the stunning oceanfront courses Kauri Cliffs and Cape Kidnappers. So it was no small matter to forgo all of those options for the Hollywood rat race, a scene that I was all too familiar with, thanks to my year at Sherwood Country Club.

I realize now that my decision was driven largely by my desire to please my father. Perhaps it was my way of returning the favor of his recent acceptance and appreciation of my years of caddying and the fact that he no longer dismissed them as just an escapist frivolity. I was finally granting him his long-held wish for me to get a *real job*. When I got out to California, he called me on the phone to check in and see how things were going, not just once but at least once a month. This may sound like a perfectly normal, unremarkable thing to do, but he literally hadn't called me in *years*.

The only time I'd ever really spoken to him on the phone was when I'd call home to check in with my mom and she would force us to speak. "It's your son on the phone. He'd like to say hi"—even though I'd said no such thing. And those conversations were always brief and awkward at best. Now he called every month. We'd speak for ten or twenty minutes and he'd tell me about his improving health, how he felt so much better, and that he and Mom were planning a trip overseas. When I returned for Christmas a few months later, he almost looked his old self. In fact, people who hadn't known him before his illness didn't even realize he was sick at all. He'd always looked young for his age, so now he just looked like a normal seventy-six-year-old. I know I was probably seeing things through a rosy, hopeful lens (as I'm sure he was, too), but when I left for California again after Christmas, I honestly felt somewhat optimistic.

Spring arrived in Los Angeles, and I'd gotten a caddie job at Riviera to supplement the still very small writing income I was receiving from various projects, including a travel writing assignment up to British Columbia, which I'd pitched to my editor at *Travel + Leisure Golf*. At the time, my choice of topic seemed innocent enough. It was a little known but surprisingly good golf destination settled by the British, who'd built two classic, centuries-old courses in the capital city of Victoria. But once I got up there and revisited all of those places my father and I had reminisced so fondly about, it occurred to me that my choice of this particular place was perhaps not so coincidental after all. In fact, when I called him after a day of skiing at Mount Washington and excitedly described the mountain's rocky chutes and wooded glades and the view of the sea and Coast Range from the peak and heard the genuine longing in his voice to go there and experience it himself, I was overwhelmed with emotion. I was very sad that we were just now becoming friends after all these years when, all rosiness and hope aside, doing these things together was most likely no longer a possibility. The hard truth about pancreatic cancer was that his improved health was just a temporary reprieve before the inevitable and final return of the illness. I couldn't stop my mind from revisiting the very uncomfortable memory of seeing him lying on that gurney in the ICU after his operation, and I realized I never wanted to see him like that again. Or at least I didn't want the *next* time I saw him to be like that.

But those sentiments didn't offer any real, practical solution to the dilemma I was facing. I knew I couldn't just go home and sit by his bedside as I'd done over the summer, because my dad was genuinely happy to see me finally focused on my "future," and the last thing he wanted was for me to put my life on hold for him. In fact, that would have made him very unhappy. It was a true catch-22.

Then one morning in May, after I'd returned to Los Angeles, I woke from an incredibly vivid dream. I sat up straight, eyes wide open, my friend Tucker's voice still echoing in my head from the dream. "You should hitchhike the Top 100!"

I remember when Tucker, who was a caddie in Bandon, had said those words in real life. It was several years earlier when we were out together on a particularly long, arduous loop on Bandon Dunes. We both had aspirations beyond caddying and were throwing ideas back and forth about what else we could do with our lives. I'd told him about my caddie memoirs and how I'd wanted to write a book ever since that hitchhiking adventure from Aspen to San Fran ten years earlier. Tim loved the hitchhiking idea, the whole vagabond spirit of it, and thought I should combine it with golf. He said, "Why don't you hitchhike to the Top 100 courses in the US? Sneak or talk your way onto all of them. If anyone can do it, it's you!"

As romantic and wonderful as that idea sounded, it seemed to me at the time like a logistical nightmare—a gigantic, expensive years-long adventure that would be next to impossible to pull off. Yet there I was sitting up straight in bed with those very words reverberating in my mind like a prophecy. I reconsidered the concept. I knew I could easily pull off the hitchhiking part, and it wouldn't be a problem to play golf along the way. God knows I'd played enough golf across every inch of the country on courses both great and small, real and imagined. It was only the Top 100 that presented any real obstacle. If I jettisoned that part, it was completely doable.

I jumped out of bed and called my mom. I breathlessly told her what I was thinking, even as the plan was still forming in my mind. The words tumbled out of my mouth—I was going to hit a parting golf shot off the beach in Santa Monica, thumb a ride right there on the Pacific Coast Highway, and hitchhike clear across the country with my golf clubs strapped to the side of my pack. I would play as many courses along the way as possible and play through the backcountry, too—through the Southwest desert, Rocky Mountains, Great Plains, Great Lakes, and New England. I was going to create a website and blog about the whole thing and raise money to fight pancreatic cancer. And I was going to call it Golf My Way Home.

The silence on the other end of the line was deafening. I

clenched my teeth, crossed my fingers, and waited for her response. The entire thing was basically a brilliantly disguised and elaborate excuse to head home and be with Dad, to share with him in real time that same adventurous spirit we'd recently shared through conversation and recollection. If we couldn't do it together, this was the next best thing—I would do it solo, dedicate the trip to him, and document it. It would give me something meaningful to devote my energies to in the present and, I hoped, bring us even closer together.

I'm not sure what I would have done if my mom had hated the idea. I know it must've sounded crazy to her, but she knew me better than anyone, and it probably didn't sound all that different from what I'd been doing for the last ten years anyway. My dad was, as expected, skeptical. His reaction reminded me of that classic line from the movie *The Graduate* when Dustin Hoffman character's dad said to him, "Ben, this whole idea sounds pretty half-baked!" He didn't see how any of it was relevant or related—golf, hitchhiking, pancreatic cancer—or even possible, starting with the basics of the website, the logistics and dangers of hitchhiking, the challenges of fund-raising. But beyond all of that, I think he really just didn't want any attention focused on him.

But my mom held considerable sway over my father. She convinced him to pretend to like the idea for my sake, and in the end, after I pulled the whole damn thing off— hitchhiked 6,200 miles from Santa Monica to Connecticut, caught 127 rides, played thirty-seven golf courses, and raised over $20,000 for pancreatic cancer research—if he didn't exactly *love* it, he at least admired my guts and determination. And it gave us a hell of a lot to talk about once I got home.

The trip lasted a hundred days, from the middle of June

to the beginning of October. I probably could've hitchhiked in a straight shot across the middle of the country in as little as ten days, but that wasn't the point. It wasn't a race. It was about the people and places and experiences along the way. It was about the adventure. And on the fifth day, when a couple hang-glided my lost BlackBerry to me in Sedona, Arizona—literally landed next to the golf course I was playing and brought it to me—I knew the journey was going to surpass even my wildest expectations.

As I'd suspected, the people I met along the way were extremely kind and generous. They gave me rides far beyond their own destinations to put me in position for the next ride. They invited me to stay in their homes and to play golf at their clubs. They donated money, followed the blog I created for the trip, and most important, they provided all of the wonderful stories and memories that became the content for the blog. What Golf My Way Home accomplished more than anything was the simple act of bringing my father and me closer together. I will never forget the look on his face the night I walked into some fancy restaurant to meet my parents at the end of my journey with my giant dirty backpack, my shaggy three-month mullet, and frayed, flea-bitten clothing. My dad, who would normally be mortified by such unkempt personal appearance, jumped out of his chair, smiled ear to ear, and said, "You bugger!"

The expression "You bugger!" was right up there with "Darn tootin'!" at the top of my dad's praise chain. He might as well have hugged me and hoisted me up on his shoulders and spun me around for all the world to see.

I remember that night so vividly because he was his old self. He ordered a second bottle of wine, asked me a million questions, and listened intently to everything I said. He smiled and laughed and told a few funny stories of his own. I remember dinners like that when I was a boy, usually on family vacations, when both my parents were in top form— my mom by far the more eloquent and loquacious of the two but my dad rising to the occasion and playing the perfect foil—adding a well-timed comment or two, made all the more surprising and funny because he normally said so little. That was one of his great tricks: don't say much, because then when you do speak, people will really listen.

I'd come home in such brazen fashion and talked so enthusiastically about continuing to work on the project that, for the first time, he didn't even bother asking me what I was planning to do next. He just accepted my presence at home. The next few months were very much like the months we'd spent together the summer before, but even better, because the ice between us was long broken, so now it was just assumed that I would sit with him for hours and talk. He actually looked forward to our conversations. If he was in the middle of reading a book, he'd clap it shut and ask me how my day was going. I wouldn't have traded that time together for the world, but it did make me wonder why the hell we'd wasted all those years being pissed at each other when we could've been this close all along. But I guess you live and learn and life unfolds on its own time. And I was lucky it turned out the way it did in the end, because if I'd let the anger I felt on that fairway down at Forest Hills in Augusta get the better of me, I might never have come home at all.

We had five good months together before the cancer spread and the pain overwhelmed him, before he moved into hospice for good to be permanently attached to a morphine drip. Once the morphine kicked in full-time, the dad I knew was no longer.

It was April then, and I'd started caddying at Stanwich again. I hadn't been there in ten years. There was a new caddie master, named Henry, a hotheaded Italian who expressed his love for you by losing his temper. By this measure, Henry must have really loved me. All kidding aside, Henry was incredibly respectful of me that spring. If it was slow in the morning, he let me go visit my dad at the hospice, behind Stamford Hospital and only twenty minutes from the golf course. Henry would call me if he had a loop for me in the afternoon. He bent over backward to make my life as easy as possible.

Amazingly, a lot of my old caddie friends were still in the Stanwich caddie yard—Buzz, Buddha, Robo, and Jason, who was now a schoolteacher up in Trumbull but still came down on the weekends to caddie for guys he'd been looping for for twenty years now. Big Kent was there, too, but I barely recognized him, because he'd trimmed down from 300 to about 220 and looked downright spritely. I teased him about the days when he used to fall asleep everywhere—on the bench in the caddie yard, in carts in the cart barn, even *tending the pin*!

"I have sleep apnea," he said.

"Sleep what?" I asked.

"Sleep *everywhere*!" Buzz yelled from across the yard.

It was as though nothing had changed.

I've always appreciated the beauty of Stanwich, but that spring its fairways were such a complete contrast to the hospital's sterile white halls that it had a particularly ethereal quality. It was an escape from my increasingly dark reality, especially on Monday afternoons, when I played alone for hours, often thirty-six holes, right up till dark.

I have one specific memory of a tree behind the sixteenth green. It was a little tree covered in white flowers. It was late in the afternoon, and the sun was angling down through the taller trees to the west. The little tree was glowing in a pollen-filled beam, the wind scattering its white flowers like snowflakes. They blanketed the grass all around it.

At that point, it was painful for my dad to even sit up, much too painful to move him from his bed to his wheelchair, so we'd stopped taking him out to the garden. We still opened his doors to let the sun in, and there was a rhododendron bush on the terrace that he could see from his bed, but as I stood under that white flowering tree, I suddenly felt this overwhelming desire to share it with him. I wanted him to be there, to be able to stand and walk and enjoy a beautiful spring moment like that again. I had this really sad feeling that we hadn't shared enough while we had the time.

I was with my father the last night he was alive. He was in and out. I don't know how else to describe it other than to say he was "in between worlds." He was conscious, but he would only focus on me half of the time. The other half, he was looking over my shoulder, reaching his arms up toward something beyond me.

When he did focus on me, he smiled really brightly, as though he'd just returned from somewhere and suddenly recognized me. He asked if he could borrow some money (which just goes to show, even at the end you haven't seen it all). When I asked him what he needed it for, he said dead seriously, "I'm going somewhere."

I promised him I'd leave it with the nurse. He seemed satisfied with this.

Sometime in the early morning, he drifted off to sleep,

and I left him. As I drove home, I knew that was the last time I was going to see him.

That day I was caddying in the member-member tournament at Stanwich. I was forecaddying on the fifteenth hole when my phone buzzed. It was a text from my mom.

Your father passed away this morning.

All my life I'd been in a rush to finish my loops. I'd counted the holes until I could grab my own clubs and play, counted the rounds till the end of the season, when I could pack my bags and explore a new part of the world. I wasn't immune to the hypnotic, therapeutic feel of all of the rituals and the rhythms of caddying—the art of shining and handing off a club properly, making perfect yard-long paces, eyeballing distances, and intuiting wind strength. I wasn't immune to the beauty of my surroundings nor the comfort of camaraderie, nor even the unique pleasure of anonymity, of starting fresh in a new place free from preconceptions and past baggage. But caddying had always been a means to an end for me, never a refuge in itself. But in that moment, for the first time, that's exactly what it was.

I didn't tell my players what had happened, I didn't let out any of the profound pain and sadness I was feeling inside. I smiled more brightly. Studied the putts harder. Paced off the yardages more crisply and precisely. I'd never been so happy to just go through the motions. It was the first time I'd ever counted the holes and dreaded the end of the round. I wanted that loop to last forever.

Acknowledgments

I used to scoff when actors and actresses gushingly thanked their agents at awards shows, but now that I have one I fully understand. So (tearfully, with the first edition clutched to my chest) I'd like to thank my agent Farley Chase for acting as both editor and agent during the proposal process and for so deftly navigating the increasingly rocky waters of the publishing world. You made it seem easy. Thank you to my editor, Jenna Ciongoli, for treating a first-time author like an old pro (even when I sent you the tenth e-mail in a single day). Thank you to Domenica Alioto for seamlessly taking over while Jenna tended to more important things (motherhood). I have been very lucky to have had great editors all along, going way, way back to my now embarrassing first published stories that Colin Sheehan somehow snuck into *The Golfer* magazine when the publisher wasn't looking. And more important, Colin, thanks for being a lifelong best friend (and seeing Max Creek shows at Lupos every Wednesday). And Tom Dunne at *Travel + Leisure Golf*, a great writer who taught me how to sharpen my gratuitous ramblings into coherent 1,500-word articles—a skill that helped me keep sight of the overall narrative of this story when I was (happily) drowning in the details. And my cousin Amy, my unofficial (unpaid) editor, who read every draft along the way—I now swear you to silence as to how bad those first versions were!

Thanks to all of my bosses (caddie masters) along the way: Skip, Rick, Joe, Lenny, Greg, Billy, Jeff, Brendan, Gary, Ken, Rick, Robert, Gray, and Henry for hiring me and not firing me even when I often deserved it. OK, I did get fired once, but I know if it was your decision you *wouldn't have* done it, Jeff! Special thanks to Ken Brooke at Bandon Dunes for being a great friend and supporter far above and beyond the duties of caddie master and to Henry at Stanwich for somehow, amazingly, keeping your (in)famous Italian temper in check and treating me with great compassion during my dad's illness and passing.

Thanks to all of my friends on and off the links who shared in these adventures, too many to name here. Chris Surmonte, my soul brother, who shares the love of life and golf—the imagination to play cross-country golf and hitchhike to Pebble Beach and design courses around the University of Colorado campus (the Seve stick!). DeWitt and Jenny Cannon for adopting me into their West Coast family and making me feel like a blood brother. Georgia Welch, who convinced Boo Boo Bear, Prissy, and the ghost of Mother Superior that I was a worthy addition to Maycroft (even though I accidentally peed on Mother Superior's grave one night). Tomas Hannell, coconspirator of the Miller tees, snakebite, Sony Sportsfoot, and seeing Jesus at the Merry Manor. Migs and Kaetlyn for opening the doors to Rivendell to me (and the greatest private par three in the world!). Sarah Barton for renting me the suite at the "Holiday Inn" and paying the hot tub bills when I injured my foot. Steve Weidel for reading and supporting *Loopers* in its infancy and sharing many Marlboros on the fairways of Forest Hills. Natalie Speidel for being my favorite bartender who "just wants to meet a Mets fan!" Helena "LaLa" LaValla for nurturing me through the true beginning of my writing career when Yellow, Beary, and I pondered endless story lines in the sandbox and floor hockey arena and crafted such classics as "Godzilla Invades Connecticut."

Lastly and most important to my mom (aka: MomBoss/MomSoft—depending on the moment), who never thought I was crazy, even when I was solo hiking across the Canyonlands or hitchhiking across North America or living in a van on top of a mountain. For forever believing that I would eventually make something of those fleeting glimmers of promise and actually sit down at a *desk* in a *house* and someday write about all the adventures that you unfailingly followed over the years via telephone and e-mail (and the ones we dreamed about on starry nights at Ben Barra).

ABOUT THE AUTHOR

John Dunn is a writer whose work has appeared in a number of magazines, including *The Golfer* and *Travel + Leisure Golf*. For twenty years he worked as a caddie at golf courses around the world. His research for this book was collected over the years on courses and beaches and in bars all across the country and abroad.